HENRY HIGHLAND GARNET

A voice of
black radicalism
in the
nineteenth century

JOEL SCHOR

CONTRIBUTIONS IN AMERICAN HISTORY, NUMBER 54

 GREENWOOD PRESS

Westport, Connecticut • London, England

Library of Congress Cataloging in Publication Data

Schor, Joel.
    Henry Highland Garnet.

    (Contributions in American history ; no. 54)
    Bibliography: p.
    Includes index.
    1. Slavery in the United States—Anti-slavery
movements. 2. Slavery in the United States—
Emancipation. 3. Garnet, Henry Highland, 1815-1882.
4. Abolitionists—United States—Biography.
I. Title.
E449.S294   322.4'4'0924 [B]   76-8746
ISBN 0-8371-8937-3

Library of Congress Catalog Card Number: 76-8746
ISBN: 0-8371-8937-3   322.44092

First published in 1977   G235

Greenwood Press, Inc.
51 Riverside Avenue, Westport, Connecticut 06880

Printed in the United States of America

*To the Schors
and the Sheers,
to Dotty, Mary Rebecca, and Michael Arthur*

Contents

Acknowledgments

Without the inspiration, guidance, and instruction of Drs. Martha Putney, Elsie Lewis, Rayford W. Logan, and Howard Bell, this work would have been much impoverished. The student can hardly repay such individuals for their assistance. The same can be said of Dr. Lorraine A. Williams and Dean Carroll L. Miller who provided the financial support indispensable for completion of the manuscript. I also thank the members of my committee whose suggestions have improved the text. My special thanks are given to Mrs. Dorothy Porter, formerly of the Moorland Foundation, to Dr. Carleton Mabee of the State University of New York, and to Dr. Geoffrey Johnston of the United Theological College, Jamaica, West Indies. I thank Miss Henrietta Edmonds, who first suggested that I look into the life of her famous great grandfather. It was exceedingly generous of my wife, Dotty, to assist in the typing, which took many hours.

Introduction

Heretofore, historians have tended to treat black abolitionists as either a homogeneous group of contributors to the single goals (which they were) or as intellectuals divided into "optimistic" integrationists at one extreme and the "pessimists" who favored emigration and a black nationality on the other.[1] The difficulty with the first approach is that it creates an impression that blacks were united in both their means and their ends. As the following pages will reveal, the reverse was true, and conflicts were bitter, sometimes lasting until death. It is true that black abolitionists made contributions of enormous proportions, but some had more impact than others. That is why it is necessary to probe their points of conflict and to evaluate them. When placed in historical context and examined in terms of the interaction with his peers, Henry Highland Garnet emerges as their mentor.

The second view of black abolitionists as pessimists or optimists likewise leads to distortion. "Although the noted abolitionist, recently turned emigrationist, Reverend Mr. Henry Highland Garnet, regarded continuing discrimination and prejudice as an argument for colonization abroad, and even declared that Negroes were a separate nationality in the United States," writes August Meier, "the optimistic majority were prepared to stake all on their American nationality."[2] While this statement is partially correct, it is simplistic; it attaches values to these individuals which are not wholly deserved. Just as man is largely a product of his environment, so the historical circumstances in which he thought and acted must be taken into account in making any such judgment. That inquiry has also been undertaken in the pages which follow. The effort has been made to examine Garnet's actual accomplishments and ideas, his rationale (insofar as is possible), and his overall importance in the years preceding and including the American Civil War.

Although his activism continued after 1865, some of his goals had been translated into law by that date.[3] The period of Garnet's greatest activity and accomplishment runs from 1840 to 1865.

When the historian George Washington Williams heard Garnet speak, he glowingly proclaimed Garnet to be the "equal in ability to Frederick Douglass especially excelling in logic and terse statement."[4] Not only was Garnet the equal of Douglass, but he was also an intellectual catalyst for Douglass. In the view of a former editor of the *Journal of Negro History*, "Garnet created the idea which Frederick Douglass tempered and presented to the world in a more palliative and acceptable form."[5] These ideas included political abolition and the use of limited violence to free the slave in the 1840s, emigration in the 1850s, and the endorsement of the Republican party in the 1860s. In his time, Garnet's views were thought to be radical, if not always original. He was one of the most militant men of his generation. It is for these reasons that Garnet's role in the abolitionist and civil rights movements deserves more attention than it has thus far received.

NOTES

1. Benjamin Quarles, *Black Abolitionists* (New York: Oxford University Press, 1969). Although I have made heavy use of Quarles' excellent works, his writings on black abolitionists do not reveal the divisive conflicts that played so large a role in their decisive impact.

2. August Meier, *Negro Thought in America, 1880-1915* (Ann Arbor, Michigan: University of Michigan Press, 1966), p. 5. This work remains a valuable synthesis, regardless of minor simplifications.

3. Since the material to be discussed ends in 1865, brief mention should be made of Garnet's later activities. Garnet championed the equal rights movement for Negroes after the Civil War and the cause of Cuban independence and maintained his interest in African culture. Grateful Republicans offered him the diplomatic post of minister resident and consul general to Liberia. He accepted the position against the advice of close friends and died of tropical fever shortly after his arrival in Monrovia in 1882.

4. George Washington Williams, *History of the Negro Race in America, 1619-1880* (Reprint; New York: Arno Press, 1969), p. 579.

5. William Brewer, "Henry Highland Garnet," *Journal of Negro History* 13 (January 1928): 36-52. Brewer believes that Garnet's influence on Douglass, Remond, and other Negro leaders was considerable, but the exact amount will never be known.

HENRY HIGHLAND GARNET

1

The Radicalization of Henry Highland Garnet

By 1840, the Jacksonian period had come to an end; yet, with the many democratic advances of the era, the status of the black man remained relatively the same. Both the Whigs and the Democrats virtually ignored the slavery issue in the South. At the same time, the free Negro in almost every Northern State encountered a variety of discriminatory legal, economic, and social barriers which at worst resulted in complete proscription. In New York, the constitution freely gave white men the suffrage while insisting on a property qualification for blacks. The presidential election in that year resulted in the victory of General William Henry Harrison, the former Indian fighter, and of his running mate, John Tyler, a slaveowner. In general, the Whig party to which they belonged favored the industrial and agrarian interests of established wealth, although their support was widespread. Their triumph, then, meant a successful continuation of conservative rule throughout the country.[1]

Hence, for those Americans committed to freedom and equality the year 1840 began ruefully. The white antislavery forces were divided permanently, and in the spring they had split into two camps: one headed by the redoubtable William Lloyd Garrison, now well into his second decade of agitation, and the other made up of a newer antislavery faction gathering strength from areas west of New England. The Tappan brothers, James G. Birney, Gerrit Smith, Judge William Jay,

Henry B. Stanton, and Joshua Leavitt were among its outstanding
spokesmen. Black abolitionists were likewise divided, but the split was
mitigated by the challenge of newly emerging leaders—educated fugitives. These men had escaped by their wits and had learned to tell hard
new truths about slavery and discrimination; they would now propose
original solutions for destroying the decadent institution. So appeared
Henry Highland Garnet.[2]

Garnet was born on 23 December 1815 into a slave family living on
the estate of a Colonel William Spencer near New Market in Kent
County, Maryland. It is said that Garnet's grandfather was a captured
Mandingo chieftain; this ancestry may have been the source of the im-
perial manner, defiance, and tenacity in debate which was to character-
ize the grandson in manhood.

Garnet knew slavery for only the first nine years of his life.[3]

In 1824, his parents fled with their children and other relatives
through the woodlands and tidal swamps of Maryland to Wilmington,
Delaware. Sleeping during the daylight hours, they journeyed throughout the night. The young Henry kept pace with the adults as long as he
could and then was carried upon their backs. After several days, the
little group arrived in Wilmington, thoroughly exhausted, but free.[4]

The Quaker and underground railway sponsor Thomas Garrett provided them with shelter, food, and clothing. Losing little time, the
family journeyed on to New Hope, Pennsylvania, in Bucks County.
There they rested a few months, when they decided that life would be
more secure for them in New York. "There was something more glad-
dening in the State [of New York] in which freedom was newly enter-
ing, than in the other State [Pennsylvania] whose so-called free border
was in poisoned contact with the direful institution of slavery."[5]

The family arrived in New York City and underwent its own meta-
morphosis, shedding the old reminders of subordination as a prelude to
a new life. The father, in a simple ceremony conducted at home, proclaimed his family free, gave thanks to God, and renamed every member. "Wife, they used to call you·Henny (Henrietta), but in the future
your name is Elizabeth." His daughter he renamed Eliza, his son Henry,
and himself George.[6]

The exact origin of the name *Garnet* is unknown; it frequently
appears misspelled *Garnett*. The name may have been taken from
Thomas Garrett, who helped them escape, and modified slightly; this

practice was not uncommon among fugitives.[7] Henry remembered Garrett; years later, he visited Wilmington and in a public address thanked him.[8]

From Crummell we have a few lines describing Garnet's parents in their New York home on Leonard Street. George Garnet, according to Crummell, was a tall man like his son with beautifully moulded limbs and fine, delicate features. Unlike his son, he was grave and sober in his demeanor and spoke infrequently but was solid and weighty in his words. With his quiet strength and dignity and his deep religiosity, his character was much like the Quaker's. Of the father, Crummell said: "I remember well the self-restraint his appearance always evoked among my playmates, and a certain sense of awe which his majestic presence always impressed us with."[9]

Garnet's mother, Crummell continues, was comely, beautiful, and tall, with a bright, intellectual face and lustrous, laughing eyes, which were "the very soul of fun, wit, frolic and laughter." Garnet had these same eyes. From both parents Garnet derived his humor, intellectual fire, steadiness of character, and strong native thought. Crummell stated that "from such a stock, with both physical and mental greatness in both lines of his ancestry, Henry inherited that fine physique, that burning vitality, that large intellectual power, that fiery flame of liberty, and those high moral and spiritual instincts, which are generally characteristics of the great."[10]

Garnet's early years in New York from 1826 until 1828 were one of the happiest periods in his life. Although he had attended school for a brief period in New Hope, his formal education did not begin in earnest until 1826 when he enrolled in the New York African Free School on Mulberry Street. Here he joined the company of students who, like himself, were to become internationally known: Ira Aldridge, the Shakespearian actor; Samuel Ringgold Ward, a brilliant antislavery intellectual and also Garnet's second cousin; Dr. James McCune Smith, perhaps the greatest nineteenth-century Negro scholar; and the eloquent Reverend Alexander Crummell who tried to Christianize and introduce Western ideas among Africans. Garnet quickly became the leader among them; he was instrumental in forming a small club of schoolmates who at the ages of thirteen to sixteen resolved not to celebrate July the Fourth as long as slavery existed. His radicalism was manifest in his early teens. About this group, Crummell wrote:

For years, our society met on that day [July the Fourth], and the
time was devoted to planning schemes for the freeing and upbuild-
ing of our race. The other resolve which was made was, that when
we had educated ourselves we would go South, start an insurrection and free our brethren in bondage. Garnet was a leader in these
rash but noble resolves; and they indicate the early set and bias of
his soul to that quality of magnanimity which Aristotle says "exposes one to great dangers and makes a man unsparing of his life;"
thinking that life is not worth having on some terms.[11]

Henry's mentor in the schoolroom was Charles C. Andrews, a strict
disciplinarian and convert to the monitorial system of education advocated by the school founders, the New York Society for the Manumission of Slaves. The state of New York had already accomplished the
primary goal of the society—the abolition of slavery. It then became
Andrews' task to implement the second and third goals—the protection
of liberated slaves from reenslavement and the education of Negro children "of all classes." The fact that Andrews was under both private and
public scrutiny made his position as an educator of blacks a sensitive
one; therefore, he went to great lengths to encourage his students'
studies. He employed the renowned Reverend Samuel E. Cornish to
visit the homes of his students and discuss with parents the importance
of punctual school attendance. Once students had been admitted to the
school, the parents were presented with printed regulations and were
advised on how to facilitate the youngsters' education.[12]

Classes began early in the morning and lasted until 5:00 P.M., with
some time free for lunch. Students went to school six days each week
with Wednesday and Saturday afternoons off, and they received instru-
tion in reading, grammar, arithmetic, writing, moral instruction, geog-
raphy, and lessons from Scriptures. Andrews introduced courses in
navigation and astronomy for advanced students; he built up the school
library and brought into the institution a museum of natural history.
His students were motivated by the school fairs and the special classes
which Andrews formed for the better students.[13] Garnet and his peers
then studying under the auspices of the African Free Schools received
an excellent grammar school education.

Garnet was one of three hundred who attended the grammar school
on a daily basis. Thirteen hundred colored children received no formal

education during the same period in New York City. While the common explanation was the lack of appreciation of education in the Negro home, there were deeper reasons. After graduation, the Negro found "every avenue closed to him, which is open to the white boy, for honorable and respectable rank in society." He was "doomed to encounter as much prejudice and contempt, as if he were not only destitute of that education which distinguished the civilized from the savage, but as if he were *incapable* [author's italics] of receiving it."[14]

In reviewing the fate of his students, Andrews found that a few obtained employment as sailmakers, shoemakers, tin workers, tailors, carpenters, and blacksmiths, but in almost every instance racial prejudice barred them from gaining a thorough knowledge of their trade. "Many of our best lads [in view of these difficulties] go to sea as stewards, cooks, sailors, &c. Those who cannot procure trades, and do not like to go to sea, become waiters, coachmen, barbers, servants, laborers, &c."[15]

The parents' recognition that education was of limited utility under the circumstances was realistic. This knowledge, coupled with the fact that many Negroes were unable to clothe adequately their children, produced a reluctance to involve them in the schools. As the years passed, this feeling was encouraged by the transfer of the African Free Schools to the city school system and by the disorders and riots of 1834. Parents were afraid to send youngsters over long distances to school.[16]

When the American Convention for Promoting Abolition was held in Baltimore in 1828, some of Garnet's peers contributed poems and essays for the occasion. The sentiments and themes expressed were similar—praise of freedom, denunciation of slavery, and appreciation for teachers and friends. Speaking for his classmates, George Moore offered his thanks to the convention for its interest in the freedom and education of Negro children.[17]

Perhaps because of the difficulties in obtaining suitable employment in New York City, Garnet took a job as cabin boy in 1828 and made two voyages to Cuba. Little is known of him during the time he was sailing. When he returned to New York in 1829, he found profound tragedy awaiting him.

Neither the manumission societies of New York, their schools and agents, nor the legal machinery of local government could guarantee the fugitive his freedom from capture. Garnet had been spared these fears

while at sea. Now, upon his arrival on the wharf, he learned that slavehunters had found and invaded the family home.[18] Crummell provides
an eyewitness account:

> One evening, in the month of July or August, a white man, a
> kinsman of the late Colonel Spencer, the old master, walked up
> to Mr. Garnet's hired rooms, on the second floor of the dwelling.
> He knocked at the door, and Mr. Garnet himself opened it. "Does
> a man by the name of George Garnet live here?" was the question
> put. "Yes," was Mr. Garnet's reply; and immediately, as in a flash,
> though years had passed away, he recognized one of his old mas-
> ter's relatives. The slave-hunter, however, did not recognize George
> Garnet. "Is he at home?" was the next question, to which with
> quiet self-possession, Mr. Garnet replied: "I will go and see."
> Leaving the open door Mr. Garnet, without saying a word to
> his wife, daughter, and a friend in the room, passed into a side
> bed-room. The opened window was about twenty feet from the
> ground; between the two houses was an alley at least four feet
> wide; the only way of escape was to leap from the side window
> of the bed-room into my father's yard. How Mr. Garnet made
> this fearful leap, how he escaped breaking both neck and legs, is
> a mystery to me to this day; but he make the leap and escaped.
> In my father's yard was a large ill-tempered dog, the terror of
> the neighborhood. The dog, by a wondrous providence, re-
> mained quiet in his early evening slumbers. After jumping sev-
> eral fences Mr. Garnet escaped through Orange Street, and the
> slave-hunter's game was thus effectually spoiled.[19]

While George Garnet escaped, his daughter was arrested and was
tried as a "fugitive from labor" before Richard Riker, recorder of the
city of New York. She was set free by proving an "alibi," which in this
case meant that she proved a residence in New York City at the very
time when the witnesses for the prosecution swore that she was in
Maryland and a slave. Garnet's mother barely managed to elude the
slavehunters; she was taken in by neighbors who operated a grocery
store across the street from the Garnet home. All of the household
furniture was destroyed or stolen; the family was left with nothing
when it began its life once again.[20]

The news brought Garnet to the brink of madness. With his earnings from the voyage, he purchased a large claspknife, openly carried it in his hand, and marched up Broadway, waiting to assault the slavehunters. His friends took Garnet away from the city to Long Island, to the home of Thomas Willis, a Quaker minister. Eventually, Garnet went to Smithtown, Long Island, to the home of Captain Epenetus Smith, who indentured him for two years.[21]

Captain Smith was a disciple of George Fox and was in full sympathy with the Society of Friends which opposed human bondage as a cardinal principle. From his son, Samuel Smith, comes the first description of Garnet: "The appearance of the boy was prepossessing; his eyes were bright and unclouded, and above them was a massive forehead and a finely shaped head, which might have been chosen as a model for an artist. His preceptions were quick, and the ingenuousness of his nature soon won the hearts of the entire family."[22]

At the time he first met Garnet, Samuel Smith was ten years his senior. Smith was a conscientious scholar and became Garnet's tutor for about three years until Garnet was about eighteen years of age. From the pupil-teacher relationship sprang a lifelong friendship. This phase of his education ended when, while playing in an athletic sport, Garnet injured his knee. The knee became swollen and so inflamed that he could no longer walk on that leg. He was to hobble on a crutch for thirteen years thereafter until the limb was finally amputated at the hip. Garnet was probably altered emotionally for life;[23] the useless appendage became his personal thorn, challenging and goading him onward into relentless attack upon the twin monsters of his people, subordination and slavery. Shortly after the accident, he returned to his family in New York City, which had only recently been reunited.

That the fragmentation of his family in 1829, coupled with his injury, proved a crucial turn in Garnet's development is confirmed by Crummell:

> So the anguish of this family calamity gave birth to a giant soul! From this terrible ordeal Henry Garnet came forth like gold thoroughly refined from fire! The soberness which comes from trial, the seriousness which is the fruit of affliction, the melancholy and the reflection which spring from pain and suffering, for he was not a cripple, soon brought Garnet to the foot of the Cross.[24]

Sources disagree as to the exact date of Garnet's baptism into the Christian faith. Crummell, writing in 1865, gives the year 1833, when Garnet became attached to the Sunday school of the First Colored Presbyterian Church of New York City. In 1830, the youth returned to the New York Free School for a year during which the colonization views of his old mentor, Charles Andrews, led to the teacher's dismissal. Garnet continued his education in 1831 in a newly organized high school for Negro youth where he began the study of Latin and Greek. While pursuing these classical studies, he became associated with Reverend Theodore S. Wright's church. His conversion and his relationship with Wright, which was to continue for many years, opened new vistas to Garnet.[25]

The new high school for Negroes in New York City was generally considered revolutionary insofar as the prevailing notion of the times was that blacks were unsuited for advancement beyond the grammar school level. Only a few schools of higher learning in New York State admitted blacks until the Civil War. Reverend Wright was one of a few energetic black fighters against this kind of educational proscription. To Wright belongs the credit for bringing Garnet into the Presbyterian ministry, deepening his commitment to abolition, and furthering his education.[26]

Wright was born of free parents and was the first Negro to receive a degree from Princeton's theological seminary. He was active, as his father had been before him, in the early Negro convention movements. Wright was strongly opposed to colonization, belonged to the underground railway, and pressed members of the synod to open the schools to Negroes to demonstrate their faith in the equality of man. He also belonged to the Executive Committee of the American Anti-Slavery Society during the 1830s and was very outspoken, particularly on the prejudice he encountered among his white abolitionist co-workers. Influenced by Wright, Garnet was to become involved in many of the same organizations and to hold similar views, at least for a decade.[27]

While Negroes from New York often began their resistance from direct personal experience, antislavery whites in New York joined the movement largely as a result of a dynamic, religiously oriented ferment which was sweeping the state and affecting other areas to the west, south, and north. This ferment resulted from the revivalism of Charles

Grandison Finney who had come under the influence of George W. Gale, a Presbyterian minister who later founded Oneida Institute and Knox College.[28]

Among Finney's converts (and they were to become the bedrock of western abolitionism), the new gospel interpretation produced an enormous impetus toward social reform. Finney's "Holy Band" soon included Theodore Dwight Weld, who also was to champion women's rights, the poet John Greenleaf Whittier and Captain Charles Stuart, the Jamaica-born reformer. Weld, who by 1830 was the most powerful advocate of temperance in the West, was invited by wealthy New Yorkers, notably the Tappans, to evangelize their city in 1831. With tens of thousands flocking to his standard, Finney swept into New York City.[29]

Finney made many converts, but, more important than numbers, he won over members of the governing board of the large benevolent societies, the so-called "Great Eight." These influential people included Thomas Smith Grimke, Gerrit Smith, Anson Phelps Stokes, William Jay and the Tappan brothers. Arthur Tappan, imbued with the spirit of secular brotherhood, found others to aid him in channeling reformist energy into providing secondary education for Negroes, a new and revolutionary endeavor. Such a project, if successful, would not only disprove the notion that the Negro was unfit for higher education, but it would also provide a viable alternative to the American Colonization Society's program of deporting the newly freed blacks from the United States. Garnet became intimate with all of these individuals as well as with the idealistic home missionary to Negroes, Simon S. Jocelyn.[30] The others overlapped at times and were to include a large personal following among Negroes within and outside of the state and national Negro convention movement.

Perhaps at the instigation of Wright, who was prominent in relief and uplift organizations for Negroes in the city, a group of younger men, which included Garnet, established the Garrison Literary and Benevolent Association in honor of the New Englander in April 1834. It was a youth club, including those aged four to twenty, for the "diffusion of knowledge, mental assistance, moral and intellectual improvement." While Garnet was the secretary of the associaton, resolutions were passed against intemperance and "profane swearing"; and original addresses, compositions, and recitations were submitted on a variety of

subjects by the membership which met in a special room in a public
school. One of the school trustees, distressed by the name of the club,[31]
insisted that it be changed or else the society would not be allowed to
hold meetings in the school room. Upon receiving the news, the
students, led by Garnet, decided to resist. "If there is a trustee of our
school, so full of corruption as to deprive us of meeting in this room to
improve ourselves on account of the name of our *Society*, let him do so.
The name of Garrison shall ever be our motto." The group passed by a
unanimous vote resolutions declaring the action of the trustee an "un-
called for usurpation of authority"; it declared the name permanent and
instructed the Executive Committee to find another place for the meetings.[32]

In the fall of 1834, there appeared in Garrison's *Liberator* a notice
that an academy formed by abolitionists in Canaan, New Hampshire,
called Noyes Academy after the man who donated the land, was going
to admit "colored youth of good character on equal terms with whites
of like character." In the summer of 1835, Garnet, with Wright's recommendations was sent to this new high school along with two friends
from New York, Crummell and Thomas Sidney. The journey of these
three youths from New York to Canaan reveals the persecution inherent
for Negroes traveling from one northern state to another. In the 1830s,
the journey from New York City to Canaan required a number of days
and two means of transportion: a steamboat took the travelers as far as
Providence; from that city through Boston to Canaan, coaches were
necessary since there were no railroads in that area. Because Negroes
were not permitted cabin passage on the steamboat, the three com-
panions, all stately dressed, were exposed to the elements, without bed
and without food. Nor were they allowed to ride inside the coaches.
From Providence to Canaan, a distance of some four hundred miles, the
disabled Garnet rode night and day on the top. Rarely were there inns
or hotels to give the trio food; nowhere was shelter given.[33] Crummell
was deeply moved by Garnet's ordeal:

> I can never forget his sufferings—sufferings from pain, sufferings
> from cold and exposure, sufferings from thirst and hunger, suf-
> ferings from taunt and insult at every village and town, and oft
> times at every farm-house, as we rode mounted upon the top of
> the coach, through all this long journey.

It seems hardly conceivable that Christian people could thus treat
human beings traveling through a land of ministers and churches!
The sight of three black youths, in gentlemanly garb, traveling
through New England was, *in those days, a most unusual sight*
[author's italics]; started not only surprise, but brought out universal sneers and ridicule.[34]

For Garnet as for many others of his color, travel would mean racial
persecution for many years to come. Yet, he continued to brush aside
the humiliation. Frequently, he asserted his citizen rights in public
accommodations, regardless of any risk and suffering.[35] The asthma
from which he suffered and which was later to contribute to his death
in Africa was exacerbated by the exposure and lack of food during his
travel experiences.

As indicated earlier, the notion of higher education for Negroes was
considered a radical innovation throughout New York and New
England. Finney's linking of revivalism and abolition reached its peak
about 1836 and then began to decline. While he made many converts,
reformers constituted a small, if influential, minority lacking in political
power. Among this minority of social experimenters and reformers,
abolitionists were merely a remnant. Prejudice had defeated Tappan
and Jocelyn in New Haven and in Canterbury, Connecticut, where the
philanthropist financed the fight to save Prudence Crandall and her ill-
fated school for black children. For many farmers of New Hampshire—
sustained by state and local politicians—the pyschological threat of the
Canaan Academy with its open admissions policy proved unbearable.[36]

The travelers were cordially received at Canaan by about forty white
students and began their studies. On 4 July 1835, a short time after
their arrival, they attended an antislavery rally in Plymouth, New Hampshire. Garnet was described on that occasion by one of his teachers,
Nathanial P. Rogers:

Garnet, 19, of full, unmitigated, unalleviated, and unpardonable
blackness, quite "incompatible with freedom"—crippled of severe
lameness, which was much aggravated by the exposures and oppressions of a recent *stage ride in New England* [author's italics] —a
humble Christian and member of the Presbyterian Church; nine
years ago a slave in *Maryland of this Republic* [author's italics],

ransomed from a republican tyrant, by the labours of an exhausted father, who had first to ransom then support amid the
frowns and hindrances of a Christian community, himself, his
wife and his children; an enlightened and refined scholar—a writer
and speaker of touching beauty.[37]

The youths were called upon to address the gathering; Garnet spoke
first, followed by Crummell and Sidney. Garnet described his own feelings rather than making the expected formal statements. He ended with
the resolution that it be the "duty of every Patriot and Christian to
adopt the principles of the immediate abolitionists, for the safe and
speedy overthrow of Slavery, that every man who walked the American
soil, might tread it unmolested and free." When questioned by Rogers
about colonization in Liberia before their speeches were given, Crummell and Garnet both expressed strong opposition and hoped that those
people already sent to Africa would be returned to this country. Although Garnet would cooperate with the New York State Colonization
Society during the 1850s until well into the Civil War, he remained consistently opposed to the principle of involuntary emigration as a condition of emancipation. In 1881, he became a vice-president of the American Colonization Society from New York.[38]

While the young men were speaking in Plymouth, a group of farmers
gathered in Canaan and "resolved to remove the academy as a public
nuisance!" The meeting was organized by those who had opposed the
school since its beginning in 1834. While they were decidedly a small
minority of the citizenry (more than two-thirds of the local people were
willing to "live" with the academy), they were a determined group.
Evoking fears of amalgamation, they planned the destruction of the
school. Hundreds assembled, and about sixty or seventy of them
approached the academy building armed with missiles and clubs. A
magistrate appeared, addressed the crowd, and began taking names,
whereupon the crowd withdrew. The matter might have ended at this
point if some Southern slaveowners who happened to be in the vicinity
had not roused the crowd with talk that abolitionists were responsible
for their anxieties. At this time, the local opponents of the school decided to hold another town meeting to vest their violent resolves with
authority.[39]

A town meeting was held on 31 July, and the result of votes was given to the public through the newspapers. Armed with weapons, the crowd gathered on 10 August and with ninety yoke of oxen carried the school building from its foundation into a swamp about half a mile from the original site. After threatening the lives of the black students if they were still in the area in one month, some of the mob returned to the boarding house the same evening for the Negroes.[40] Crummell wrote:

> Meanwhile, under Garnet, as our leader, the boys in our boarding-house were moulding bullets, expecting an attack upon our dwelling. About eleven o'clock at night the tramp of horses was heard approaching, and as one rapid rider passed the house and fired at it, Garnet quickly replied by a discharge from a double-barrelled shotgun which blazed away through the window. At once the hills, for many a mile around, reverberated with the sound. Lights were seen in scores of houses on every side, and the towns and villages far and near were in a state of great excitement. But that musket shot by Garnet doubtless saved our lives. The cowardly ruffians dared not to attack us. Notice, however, was sent us to quit the State within a fortnight. When we left Canaan the mob assembled on the outskirts of the village and fired a field piece, charged with powder, at our wagon.[41]

Before the destruction of the academy, Garnet had become acquainted with a former pupil of Prudence Crandall, Julia Williams, who later became his wife. Of Julia Williams, he confided to Crummell in 1837: "Oh what lively being she is! Modest, susceptible, and chaste, a good Christian and a scholar. Did I think myself worthy I know not but I should venture my bark upon the stream. I don't want you to think that I am in love, yet I do not know that I shall keep a correspondence with her."[42]

The return trip to New York City was probably as difficult as the initial one, even though the youths took an overland route. At Troy, New York, which was to become his first ministry, Garnet became so ill that Crummell and Sidney had misgivings for his life. On the river boat down the Hudson River, they made a bed for him of their coats

and provided shade with their umbrellas; he was too ill to sit erect. Upon
Garnet's arrival in the city, he was confined to bed for nearly two
months.[43]

After the youths had been home for several months, they learned
that Oneida Institute at Whitesboro, New York, was opening its doors
to blacks. After 1830, Oneida became the favorite of Arthur Tappan's
educational philanthropy in the West. It was organized on a manual
labor plan, a scheme similar to that of recent-day reformatories. During
the school term, from spring to fall, the students worked a part of each
day on a farm, thereby earning the larger portion of their board, and in
the long winter vacation most of them taught school to earn their tui-
tion. Geroge W. Gale, its founder, was a zealous and practical farmer.
Prices for his products were good, and the plan worked. In this kind
of arrangement, Tappan saw the possibility of higher education for
the plain people, so he plunged into it vigorously. The Reverend Beriah
Green, a scholarly convert to abolition through the efforts of Theodore
Dwight Weld, was president of Oneida and was listed in the catalog as
professor of intellectual and moral philosophy.[44]

Green, the author of two books, thirty-five pamphlets—many of
which were devoted to antislavery—and a great variety of periodical
articles, was a pious and prolific exponent of reform. Following Finney's example, he began to apply his Calvinist beliefs to everyday life.
"He was especially eager that the benefits of the Gospel," his son
wrote, "should inure to 'the oppressed and forlorn,' to use his [Green's]
favorite words." Green reasoned that if Christian ethics were not
applied in the secular sphere and if Christians refused to help their fellow men in need of help such as ("the drunkard, the slave, the respecter
of persons, the dupe and the victim of popular prejudice"), then the
Christians were false to the faith.[45]

In 1836, the year of Garnet's arrival at Oneida Institute, Green delivered a sermon in the local Presbyterian church entitled "Things for
Northern Men to Do." In the sermon, he urged the congregation to
resist slavery by thoroughly examining and freely discussing the institution, by learning to regard the enslaved as the children of a common
Father, by recognizing the benefits of emancipation in general, by
petitioning the Congress to end slavery in the District of Columbia,
and by disassociating from churches which continued to admit slave-

holders.[46] This position was not unique for the times; it was close to that of Green's colleague at Oneida, Nathaniel P. Rogers, and to that of the Garrisonians.

During his senior year, if not much earlier, Garnet was exposed to these views in a course on intellectual philosophy. The nonviolent, moral suasionist views made an impression upon him and it was only with reluctance that Garnet was later to abandon them. He also learned Greek, New Testament, Hebrew poetry, logic and rhetoric, political economy and the sciences of government, courses which were later to be useful to him in the pulpit and on the speaker's platform.[47]

As an elementary school pupil attending the New York African Free School, Garnet had been one of the brightest students. After his leg became useless during his fifteenth year and caused him chronic pain, wrote Crummell, "his education was constantly interfered with by long spells of sickness until 1841, when his leg was amputated. How, under these circumstances, he did study, how he took the place he did among his schoolmates is a marvel." Professor Rogers said that Garnet was "an enlightened and refined scholar, a writer and speaker of touching beauty."[48]

In Crummell's view, Garnet's illness interfered with the systematic training of his intellect; he was never the laborious student. His mind was more the product of intuition than of scholarship. "I use the word *intuition* here to indicate that special faculty of my friend," wrote Crummell, "by which, without any labored processes of reasoning, and free from all metaphysical verbiage, he invariably reached, as by a straight and sudden dash, the clearest conception of his argument."[49] To paraphrase Crummell, Garnet was always able to bring that conception to the mind of even the simplest of his hearers. Instead of methodical preparation and force of logical analysis, Garnet possessed a "feminine instinct," a higher penetrative quality, as much moral as intellectual which leads the mind in flashes of insight to the very center of its subject.[50]

Associated with his intuition was a brilliantly original and creative imagination. Crummell's earliest remembrance of Garnet's intellectual gifts was of his schoolboy poems. "The skill, the tenderness, the exquisite beauty of those boyish productions charm me," he recalled, "even as a remembrance, to the present." However, the orator in

Garnet spoiled the poet. As he grew older, the strong rhetorical element eclipsed his poetic instincts. His imaginative faculty enhanced his eloquence in his speeches and gave them a unique splendor and polish which attracted the learned and the scholarly.[51]

Humor, satire, and sarcasm characterized the youthful Garnet. Crummell provides two examples:

> "Would you have," was the query of a disgusted and indignant white gentlemen—"Would you have me marry a dirty, stinking, greasy, black negro wench?" "No," said Garnet, with the greatest simplicity and politeness; "but would you have *me* [author's italics] marry a dirty, stinking, greasy, white wench?"

Another example of Garnet's satire occurred when he was delivering a class oration in 1836 before a large audience at Oneida. In the midst of his speech, a heckler startled the whole church by throwing a large squash upon the stage. In the tumult that resulted, Garnet quietly hobbled forward on his crutch, and looking gravely on some of the smashed pieces, said, "My good friends, do not be alarmed, it is only a soft pumpkin; some gentleman has thrown away his head, and lo! his brains are dashed out!" From that day on, the young heckler was called "Pumpkin-head Cills."[52]

Superimposed over these qualities was a gigantic strength of intellect and body. Crummell felt that "after the amputation of his leg he [Garnet] developed into a new life of vigor and mightiness."[53] An Oneida education required substantial emotional stability, not only because of the rigorous demands of the curriculum, but also because the institution was under attack in 1836 from the New York State Senate. Having been defeated the year before at Canaan, New York abolitionists mustered forces in May 1836 at Utica and passed a number of resolutions charging the Senate and press with trying to undermine and subvert their school. At that meeting, they resolved "that the recent attempt in our legislature to diminish the pecuniary resources, and to tarnish the character of Oneida Institute, on the ground that its officers and students vote as they please, and embrace a religion which pronounces slavery to be a sin, is not only a dangerous infringement of our political compact, but a daring and wicked evasion of God's moral government.[54]

This time the counterattack proved successful, the school remained open, and Garnet was graduated in 1839.

During holidays and vacations, Garnet devoted himself to the abolitionist cause. He spoke before the Phoenix Literary Society in New York City on several occasions. The Phoenix (later Phoenixian) Literary Society was composed of young literary-minded Negroes and met throughout the mid-1830s; it was a forum and testing ground for future orators and creative writers. On 9 February 1837, Sidney read Garnet's poem "Alonzo" before the society.[55] While the poem has been lost, it was probably inspired by a poem of the same name written in 1830 by Matthew G. Lewis, a popular romantic writer. It had the well-worn theme of a courageous knight who was going to fight in a foreign land and was leaving his love behind.[56] Alonzo the warrior of "gigantic height," with "armour sable to view," was perhaps young Garnet's image of himself as a Mandingo warrior in a hostile land rescuing his people from bondage. Although he remained a loyal citizen until passage of the Fugitive Slave Law in 1850—which all but obliterated his civil liberties—Garnet probably felt from an early age a strong kinship with the ancestral home, the Africa of his cultural memories. It was no mere coincidence, therefore, that his most bitter opponent among Negro abolitionists was not Frederick Douglass, William Wells Brown, or William C. Nell (though these men disagreed repeatedly with him), but George T. Downing, the affluent, practical-minded businessman. When Garnet, "the warrior," grew old and dejected, he "returned" to Liberia to die.[57]

The rights' struggle frequently involved Garnet in trying to defend his personal friends against attack. In the 1830s, New Haven was a veritable hell for abolitionists. On 31 December 1836, a mob in that city prevented Jocelyn from speaking, followed him home, and did extensive damage to his residence. George Moore, Garnet's old school friend and an agent in New Haven for *The Colored American*, met a worse fate: he was thrown in jail in January 1837 on a rape charge. Upon hearing the news, Garnet wrote to Crummell that he and Sidney intended to protest the arrest through public speechmaking. It is not known whether they were able to obtain Moore's release.[58]

Garnet addressed the Phoenix Society on 4 July 1837. Unfortunately, his address and an original poem entitled "The Captive's Dream

of Liberty" have been lost or may never have been published.[59] During
the summer, another organization which was to be composed of
"Colored Young Men" throughout the state was being formed under
the auspices of Philip Bell, proprietor of *The Colored American*. Its purpose was to flood the state legislature with petitions asking that black
citizens be granted rights in common with other citizens.[60]

On 21 August 1837, the Colored Young Men's organization held its
first regular meeting at Philomathean Hall in New York City; Garnet
along with Charles Reason were appointed vice-presidents. Garnet was
also appointed as one of the Committee of Ten to draw up and circulate
for signature petitions requesting the franchise. His motion "that the
laws which deprive free American citizens of the right to choose their
rules, are wholly unjust and antirepublican, and therefore ought to be
immediately repealed" carried unanimously by the group.[61] The Committee of Ten prepared the petition for a state constitutional amendment removing all color discrimination from voting. In view of Garnet's
later ideological developments, one particular paragraph stands out:

> Whatever lawful measures we may take, their efforts cannot
> politically degrade us more than we now are. But if anything
> can produce a favourable change, it will be a knowledge of our
> being seriously and earnestly engaged in endeavoring to effect
> our own elevation. Early indications on our part, of a determi-
> nation to seek our own elevation, will also have a beneficial
> influence upon many of our Law-Makers; and it will also turn
> their minds to the subject preparatory to the presentation of
> our petitions.[62]

These words reveal a willingness to experiment with new approaches as
yet undefined. If the minds of the lawmakers can be turned by good
example, he believed, fine and well. If not, then, "whatever lawful
measure we may take, their efforts cannot politically degrade us more
than we now are." One of Garnet's most significant contributions
throughout his tumultuous career was in the area of proposing new approaches to emancipation and civil equality, or reviving older ones,
regardless of considerations of popularity.

Garnet was not unique in calling for a new assertiveness among
Negroes in the late 1830s; he was one of a number of younger men

caught in a generational break with older leaders who espoused caution in the struggle for racial freedom. The younger group's direction away from the old Moral Reform Society and toward militancy and greater independence from white abolitionists was largely inspired by events in the West Indies, notably the manumission and enfranchisement of former slaves. On 1 August 1838, the day commemorating West Indian emancipation and political equality, abolitionists held celebrations throughout the Northern states. Garnet and Crummell spoke to a group of fellow citizens at Utica on that occasion. Only a few descriptive lines of their addresses were written down. As reported in *The Colored American*: "The gentlemen evidently felt the importance of the occasion, and their addresses were deeply interesting, and richly fraught with instruction; and we exceedingly regret that modesty of the gentlemen has prevented them from giving us their addresses for publication."[63]

Garnet spoke on the same occasion a year later in Troy, New York. Before delivering what has been described as an "eloquent address," Garnet was preceded on the platform by his father who had lately been minister in the Methodist Episcopal Church. George Garnet gave the benediction.[64] Only an extract remains of his son's earliest recorded oration.

Situated as I am, at this period of my life, had I appeared before you upon a less important occasion, I might justly be held up to censure. But however sweet the music of the streams that murmur through the academic groves, may seem to be, yet far sweeter are anthems of freedom. It is the distant voices of freeborn souls that have brought me hither—it is the shouts of the islanders of the sea, that come careening upon every wave that rolls westward. Bright, and glorious must be that event in the annals of time, which shall eclipse this triumph of righteous principles, over which we have this day met to rejoice. And if these blessings are not *immediately* ours, they are *remotely* [author's italics]. The light which the present epoch of English history shall display among "ocean's golden isles," shall reflect over all the dark places of the earth—the dungeons of cruelty—the prison houses of despair, and the tombs of buried rights, shall be illuminated by it. The bloody man-thief and heartless human robber may exhaust all their store of fiendish torture in order to hush the hosannas, but it is all in vain. Should they go down to the pit, and conjure up every fiend that suffers there to come to earth, and set up one hideous yell, still, from the shores of the Potomac to the banks of the Sabine, it will be made known, if it is not proclaimed aloud, it will be whispered in the breeze.

It is perhaps unnecessary to enter into the history of the abolition of slavery in the British colonies, therefore let it suffice to say, that after many years of the most arduous struggle, the philanthropists of Great Britain secured for their oppressed brethren the enjoyment of their rights. The first efficient act in regard to the subject, placed the death of slavery at 1840; and thus the friends of humanity subscribed to the doctrine of gradual emanicpation. But discovering their error in thus grossly violating principle, and being desirous to atone for the mistake, they cause the act to be rescinded, and terminated the existence of slavery immediately. Therefore, on the first of August, 1838, at twelve o'clock, at midnight, the hoary-headed monster died, at his late residence, in the British West Indies. He did not die of a long and painful illness of two years, as at first he would, but he died suddenly of that sin destroying complaint called immediatism. His death occasioned great joy and loud acclamations. His funeral was numerously attended, there being present no less than 800,000 persons. They buried him in the "deep sea," and long may the waves roll over him. Let there be no trace of the foot-prints left upon the soil which he once trod. Let no monument be erected to perpetuate his memory—let the evils of his long life be interred with him.

Garnet rejoiced that justice was being done by "glorious Britannica" in freeing her West Indian slaves. He then concluded that those Americans who had anticipated chaos and economic ruin as the end result of emancipation were "false prophets, and it is in vain, that they cry O Baal! O Baal!"[65]

This address, given in 1839 before he had graduated, already reflects the prose mastery and the religious intensity characteristic of Garnet's more mature public utterances. His unwillingness to compromise with the doctrine of "gradualism" is typically Garrisonian. Subsequently, he would disagree over the best means for effecting emancipation. Finally, the pro-British sentiments and the interest in Jamaican freedom which Garnet articulated in 1839 found fruition in his labors among the British and freed Jamaicans some ten years later.

The victory celebration over, Garnet returned to school and to graduation.

In mid-September, Garnet learned that Alexander Crummell was having difficulty being admitted to the General Theological Seminary of the Episcopal Church. Early in September Crummell was discouraged from applying to the seminary by his bishop, Benjamin T. Onderdonk, who was also prominent in the American Colonization Society. He told Crummell "that more evil than benefit would result, both to the Church and himself [Crummell], from a formal application in his behalf for admission into the Seminary." After some vacillation, Crummell persisted in his application before the school. The Board of Trustees met and denied the application, despite protests from dissenting members and the expressed willingness of the faculty to teach Crummell.[66] On 17 September 1839, Oneida students held a public meeting, and Garnet and two other students were chosen to transmit the group's views to Crummell. Garnet's statement, rich in indignation at what to him was obvious hypocrisy, appeared in *The Colored American* as a letter from the Oneida students to Crummell.

> Esteemed sir,—
>
> It is with deep regret that we learn by the last number of *The Colored American* of the proceedings of the above mentioned Seminary, in relation to yourself. And we take this early opportunity to express our feelings in regard to so glaring an outrage against humanity, religion, and the Almighty.
>
> We congratulate you for the manly and commendable stand which you have taken, in not consenting to bow and succumb to time nurtured, hoary-headed prejudice—and for thus showing to the world that moral principle disdains to yield to the influence of slavery either directly or indirectly.

Garnet told Crummell that God would stand with him no matter how painful the price that was asked. "Your heart may be pierced through

and through with the dagger of mean, and hard-hearted injustice, yes."
However, he added that God "will see to it, that the actions of those
by whom the offence has come shall be weighed in the balance." He
concluded that only race prejudice lay behind Crummell's rejection and
that his fellow students were with him wholeheartedly.[67]

So ended the youthful education of Henry Highland Garnet. Crummell left the diocese to gain his religious education while Garnet stayed
behind. In Troy, New York, at the Liberty Street Presbyterian Church,
Garnet prepared for the next move.

NOTES

1. Norman A. Graebner, Gilbert Fite, and Philip White, *A History of the
American People*, 1, (New York: McGraw-Hill Book Co., 1971), pp. 375-77; John
Hope Franklin, *From Slavery to Freedom: A History of Negro Americans* (7th
ed.; New York: Alfred A. Knopf, 1967), pp. 214-41; C. Vann Woodward, *The
Strange Career of Jim Crow* (2d rev. ed.; New York: Oxford University Press,
1966), pp. 17-21; August Meier and Elliott Rudwick (eds.), *The Making of Black
America*, 1 (New York: Atheneum, 1969), p. 232 (see article on New York by
Dixon Ryan Fox); Leon F. Litwack, *North of Slavery: The Negro in the Free
States, 1790-1860* (Chicago: University of Chicago Press, 1961), pp. 8, 75, 77,
80-84, 87-91.

2. Benjamin Quarles, *Black Abolitionists* (New York: Oxford University
Press, 1969), p. 68.

3. James McCune Smith, *A Memorial Discourse by Henry Highland
Garnet* (Philadelphia: Joseph M. Wilson, 1865), pp. 17-18; William Brewer,
"Henry Highland Garnet," *Journal of Negro History* 13 (January 1928): 37;
Carter G. Woodson, "Henry Highland Garnet," *DAB*, 7 (1931); 154.

4. Smith, p. 19; Brewer, p. 38.

5. Smith, p. 20.

6. Ibid.

7. William E. Farrison, *William Wells Brown* (Chicago: University of Chicago Press, 1969), p. 58.

8. Alexander Crummell, *The Eulogy of Henry Highland Garnet, D. D.
Presbyterian Minister, etc.* (Washington, D.C.: n.p., 1882), p. 8n.

9. Ibid., p. 8.

10. Ibid., pp. 8-9.

11. Ibid., pp. 25-26.

12. Charles C. Andrews, *The History of the New York African Free
Schools* (Reprint, New York: Negro Universities Press, 1969), pp. 10, 30-31,
69-70.

13. Ibid., pp. 74-87, 106-109.

14. Ibid., pp. 117-118.

15. Ibid., p. 122.

16. Leo H. Hirsch, Jr., "New York and the Negro, From 1783 to 1865," *Journal of Negro History* 16 (October 1931): 430-431.

17. Andrews, pp. 65-66.

18. Smith, p. 25.

19. Crummell, p. 10.

20. Smith, p. 25.

21. Ibid., pp. 25-26.

22. Samuel Smith, *Letter to the Signal* , 3 December 1883.

23. Ibid., p. 2.

24. Crummell, p. 11.

25. Ibid., pp. 11-12; James McCune Smtih, pp. 23, 27-29. Smith gives a different date for Garnet's baptism.

26. Hirsch, pp. 429-432; James McCune Smith, pp. 28-29.

27. Wilhelmena S. Robinson, *International Library of Negro Life and History* (New York: Publishers Co., Inc., 1968), p. 148; *The Liberator*, 20 June 1835, p. 98; Herbert Aptheker, *The Negro Peoples in the United States* (New York: The Citadel Press, 1951), pp. 169-173.

28. Finney "deplored the 'mouthing . . . lofty style of preaching' popular in his day, and talked in the pulpit `as the lawyer does when he wants to make a jury understand him perfectly . . . the language of common life.' " Finney stood the doctrine of Calvinism on its head; he reversed the common emphasis on salvation as being the end of desire spurred on through fears of hell. For him (and this notion was revolutionary), salvation became the beginning of religious experience instead of the end. As one writer put it: "The emotional impulse which Calvinism had concentrated upon a painful quest for a safe escape from life, Finney thus turned toward benevolent activity." In this view, converts did not escape life; they began a new life in God's Kingdom in which their aim was to be useful and helpful to their fellows. Gilbert H. Barnes, *The Antislavery Impulse, 1830-1844* (New York: D. Appleton-Century Co., 1933), pp. 9, 11-12.

29. Barnes, pp. 12-16.

30. Ibid., pp. 17-21, 27.

31. Evidently, the trustees found Garrison too controversial a figure to allow his name to be used for an organization which met on school property.

32. *The Liberator*, 19 April 1834, p. 63; Herbert Aptheker (ed)., *A Documentary History of the Negro People in the United States*, 1 (New York: The Citadel Press, 1967), pp. 151-152.

33. Garnet's leg was a constant source of discomfort to him throughout his youth (Crummell, p. 12).

34. Ibid., p. 12.

35. *The North Star,* 28 April 1843, p. 3. See also Chapter 5 below.

36. Lewis Tappan, *The Life of Arthur Tappan* (Reprint; New York: Arno Press, 1970), pp. 147-158. The decline in antislavery sentiment is mentioned in

Alice (Felt) Tyler, *Freedom's Ferment: Phases of American Social History to 1860* (Freeport, N.Y.: Books for Libraries Press, 1970), p. 497. In Crummell, p. 12, there is some discussion of the open admissions policy.

37. *Herald of Freedom*, 8 August 1835, p. 46.

38. Ibid. Consult the *African Repository and Colonial Journal* 8 (July 1882): 47, and 57, back cover, for the listing of Garnet as an executive.

39. *Herald of Freedom*, 22 August 1835, pp. 50-51; 5 September 1835, pp. 54-55. Essentially the same account is given in *The Liberator*, 5 September 1835, p. 141, and 3 October 1835, p. 158.

40. James McCune Smith, p. 30; Crummell, p. 12.

41. Crummell, p. 13.

42. *Letter*, Garnet to Crummell (Schomburg Collection), 18 May 1837, p. 1.

43. James McCune Smith, p. 31.

44. Barnes, pp. 38-39. See also the *Catalogue of the Officers and Students of Oneida Institute, 1836* (Whitesborough, N.Y.: Oneida Typographical Association, 1836), p. 1.

45. Samuel Green, *Beriah Green* (New York: No. 18 Jacob Street, 1875), pp. 4-7.

46. Beriah Green, *Things for Northern Men to Do: A Discourse* (New York: Published by Request, 1836), pp. 6-22.

47. *Catalogue of the Oneida Institute*, p. 8.

48. Crummell, p. 14.

49. Ibid.

50. Ibid., p. 15.

51. Ibid.

52. Ibid., p. 17; James McCune Smith, pp. 31-32.

53. Crummell, p. 17.

54. *The Emancipator*, 12 May 1836, p. 8. Also in the *Voice of Freedom*, May 1836, p. 2.

55. *The Colored American*, 18 February 1837, p. 3.

56. Matthew G. Lewis, *Ambrosio or The Monk*, 2 (New York: J. A. Chessman, 1830), p. 96.

57. Ibid., pp. 97-98. Also Crummell, p. 27, points to Garnet's positive feelings for the land of his ancestors. The antipathy between Downing and Garnet over the merits of the African Civilization Society occurred repeatedly and will be discussed in a later chapter.

58. *Herald of Freedom*, 31 December 1836, p. 173, discusses Joscelyn; *The Colored American*, 7 January 1837, p. 3, lists Moore as a New Haven agent. *Letter*, Garnet to Crummell, 18 May 1837, p. 2, mentions Garnet's intent to make a protest.

59. *The Colored American*, 8 July 1837, p. 2; 19 August 1837, p. 3. Although Crummell mentions a book of Garnet's poems, it was lost. Garnet's surviving family has very little information on it.

60. Ibid., 8 July 1837, p. 2, and 19 August 1837, p. 3.

61. Ibid., 2 September 1837, p. 3.

62. Ibid., 28 January 1838, p. 11.

63. Ibid., 25 August 1838, p. 106.

64. Ibid., 28 September 1839, p. 2. Notice of the ordination of George Garnet appeared in the 8 June 1839, issue, p. 3.

65. *Herald of Freedom*, 18 November 1839, p. 149.

66. *The Colored American*, 28 September 1839, p. 3. Also *The Emancipator*, 3 October 1839, pp. 90, 92.

67. *The Colored American*, 28 September 1839, p. 3.

2

Liberty Party Organizer and Suffrage Fighter to 1843

In the 1840s, while Garnet was a leader during a new phase of militancy (referred to by one writer as "Black Power—The Debate in 1840"), he was enlarging upon the efforts of those who had preceded him. The desire for self-elevation among the black community led directly to the formation of the Liberty Street Presbyterian Church of Troy, New York.[1]

Until 1839, Negroes worshipped in the meeting house of the First Presbyterian Church of Troy, a white New School Church led by Nathaniel S. S. Beman. They met during December of that year and decided to petition the Session or ruling body of the First Presbyterian Church for permission to form a new church for themselves. After receiving permission to do so, they organized their church on 17 January 1840. As pastor, they called the recently graduated Garnet, even though he was not as yet officially ordained or licensed to preach. Ordination for Garnet was still three years in the future.[2]

Beyond a few pages of *Session Minutes* and two short newspaper clippings, little is known of Garnet's work in the church. Under his stewardship, however, the church grew to ninety members, a 200 percent increase over the initial number. After he left Liberty Street in

1848, a series of disasters, most notably the Fugitive Slave Law of 1850, resulted in a diminution of the congregation, causing many to flee to Canada.[3]

While no clear statement of Garnet's Christian mission appears in print, it is not difficult to piece together his perception of that purpose. For him, as well as many other New School Presbyterians moral questions were not to be restricted solely to the religious sphere; they were also secularly rooted. Slavery was indeed a moral question, being a monstrous sin as distinguished from a social evil. It followed that the slaveholders, traders, and apologists who perpetuated it were sinful. Therefore, Christian worship which conferred grace upon the faithful should exclude these traffickers in human flesh until they freed the bondsmen. "In every man's mind the good seeds of liberty are planted," Garnet wrote in 1843, "and he who brings his fellow so low, as to make him contented with a condition of slavery, commits the highest crime against God and man." [4]

Theologically, this position has no clear sanction. Biblical references to slavery do not inevitably lead to such a conclusion; hence, the scriptural argument against slavery was liable to the charge of propaganda. The familiar accusation then current charged the minister with using his pulpit as a forum for abolitionist agitation. In truth, the pulpit was a forum—then as now—for whatever beliefs the minister wished to advance, whether pro- or antislavery. With equal truth the proslavery Christian church was just as guilty of the accusation as the abolitionist. For Garnet, secular and sacred realms were separate in such matters as the power over church property, the power of the Session over the Board of Trustees, and the use of the church for secular music; yet, these worlds were not mutually exclusive. Slavery, discrimination, and prejudice overlapped.[5]

It therefore followed that Garnet would vigorously support the American Missionary Association's goal of abolition whenever the opportunity arose. Garnet's acquaintance with Lewis Tappan, his public stance against slavery, and his black skin ideally suited him for the role of home missionary. As early as 1843, he served the association as a lecturer on emancipation as well as on temperance, which was a second principle of the association. For these efforts he received an annual salary supplement from the association of about $100.[6]

Garnet the minister and Garnet the home missionary was also Garnet
the organizer of black New Yorkers into politically active groups.
Throughout the 1840s, these groups would back Liberty party candidates. Garnet the organizer was also the editor and correspondent of his
ephemeral newspapers. Ironically, Garnet's chief ally in the white community of Troy, the Reverend Beman, had an adopted stepson, William
L. Yancey, without whose brilliant oratory and indefatigable labors, in
the opinion of Dr. Dwight Dumond, there would have been no secession, no Southern Confederacy.[7]

Garnet endorsed an organized antislavery political effort in 1840.
The annual meeting of the American Anti-Slavery Society in New York
City in that year served as a turning point in his abolitionist position. As
late as 6 May 1840, Garnet was a committee member of the Pittsburgh
and Alleghany Anti-Slavery societies which "heartily disapproved" of a
third political party. These societies voted to ignore the Liberty party
candidates and encouraged their members to refrain from active participation.[8]

If Garnet's convictions differed from those of the rest of the convention, there is no contrary information. In his address to the opening
session of the American Anti-Slavery convention, Garnet eloquently
asserted the right of all Negroes, slave and free, to full citizenship rights.
Throughout the address there was no hint of a shift in his strategy,
nothing to indicate that he was appealing to a particular faction among
the abolitionists assembled together at the Broadway Tabernacle. The
resolution on which his remarks were prefaced was carried unanimously;
it was entirely Garrisonian in tone.[9]

In the address, Garnet made two major points. First, while slavery
was wicked, the slave innocent, and the master a criminal, the slaveholder should be spared violent retribution:

> Avenge thy plundered poor, oh Lord!
> But not with fire, but not with sword;
> Avenge our wrongs, our chains, our sighs,
> The misery in our children's eyes!
>   But not with sword—no, not with fire,
> Chastise our country's locustry;
>   Nor let them feel thine heavier ire;

Chastise them not in poverty;
  Though cold in soul as coffined dust,
Their hearts as tearless dead, and dry
  Let them in outraged mercy trust
And find that mercy they deny.[10]

The second element in the speech was Garnet's sense of mission, which was connected with his feelings of attachment to his ancestral home:

I speak in the behalf of my enslaved brethren and the nominally free. There is, Mr. President, a higher sort of freedom which no mortal can touch. That freedom thanks be unto the Most High, is mine. Yet I am not, nay cannot be entirely free. I feel for my brethren as a man—I am bound with them as a brother. Nothing but emancipating my brethren can set me at liberty. If that greatest of all earthly blessings, "prized above all price," cannot be found in my own native land, then I must be a stranger to it during my pilgrimage here below. For although I were dwelling beneath the bright skies of Asia, or listening to the harp-like strains of the gentle winds that whisper of freedom among the groves of Africa—though my habitation were fixed in the freest part of Victoria's dominions, yet it were vain, and worse than vain for me to indulge the thought of being free, while three millions of my countrymen are wailing in the dark prison-house of oppression.[11]

Garnet was to prove faithful to his original purpose, giving a lifetime of service to his enslaved and oppressed brothers wherever he journeyed—America, the Three Kingdoms, Germany, Jamaica, and Africa. Garnet's willingness to "turn the other cheek" must have appealed to the Garrisonian desire to prevent through emancipation the possible bloody vengeance of God.

When Garnet addressed the convention on 12 May 1840, divisiveness had not yet come out into the open. Three days later, the American and Foreign Anti-Slavery Society came into existence. The society was formed during the convention and consisted of those who had become disenchanted with Garrison's leadership.[12]

The immediate causes of the split within the American Anti-Slavery convention were the issues of women's rights and separate political action; also, some members had developed a personal contempt for Garrison. The most important issue was probably separate political action. Article III of the new faction's constitution was worded carefully so as not to preclude political action by abolitionists. Although it was not stated that the new organization would support the Liberty party, Article III left members a margin of individual choice.[13] It is also true that many new members were not political abolitionists; however, the leaders were more open-minded toward a third party attempt. Some were already Liberty party men.

As a result of the division among white abolitionists, blacks were obliged to choose sides, although submerged tensions of some duration had existed among Negro abolitionists. As with the white abolitionists, the issue of women's rights alone was not the divisive one. When it was raised during the state convention of the Massachusetts Anti-Slavery Society in 1839, Negro abolitionists threw their unanimous support to Garrison. Moreover, when the rival Massachusetts Abolition Society was formed by the dissenters, it was condemned by Negroes from New England and Philadelphia.[14] The great majority of black abolitionists from New England refused to join the American and Foreign Anti-Slavery Society when it was formed in New York. Garnet, Theodore Wright, and Samuel Cornish were three of the five Negro Presbyterians to join the new society. So it was that Negroes of New York, led by their clergymen, struck out in a new direction.

The splits between white abolitionists of New England and New York and between black abolitionists of New England, Philadelphia, and New York were in part the result of ideological differences over the same goals. The ideological divergence was in turn a reflection of differences in the origin of antislavery forces. The Garrisonians, initially followers of Benjamin Lundy, championed moral suasion and propaganda by word and by personal example to achieve emancipation. Garrison's personal emergence as the leader of American antislavery meant the acceptance of his views and of his personality, which by the 1840s had increasingly alienated both Negro and white supporters.

On the other hand, those Negro leaders who had been trained in abolitionism by Garrison began to accept his views; in many instances it took them years of reassessment to abandon these views. That is why men such as Garnet, Cornish, Wright, and Charles B. Ray were to become the vanguard of black abolitionism, ahead of the more moderate Frederick Douglass, William C. Nell, Robert Purvis, William Wells Brown, Charles Remond, and William Whipper. According to Dumond, "after 1840 the anti-slavery movement was political; the hustings were the forums; every candidate for office in an anti-slavery community was an anti-slavery lecturer; and the halls of Congress were the battle ground. Further along in his work, Dumond states, "when Garrison gained control of the American Anti-Slavery Society in 1840, it had outlived its usefulness and was little but a name."[15] Litwack is even more emphatic as to the weakness of the Garrisonian ideological and tactical position. "Nonresistance," he wrote, "the rejection of political action, disunion, and a proslavery interpretation of the Constitution did not strike many abolitionists in the 1840s and 1850s as being either suitable or realistic weapons with which to abolish southern bondage or northern proscription. Indeed the final triumph of Garrisonian objectives resulted almost entirely from the employment of strictly non-Garrisonian methods—political agitation and armed force."[16]

"I was the first colored man," Garnet wrote in his famous rebuttal to the Garrisonians, "that ever attached his name to that party [the Liberty party], and you may rely upon my word, when I tell you I mean 'to stand.' "[17] If not the very first of his race to join, Garnet was probably one of the first. The records of both state and national movements among Negroes reveal that Garnet hammered relentlessly away for a Liberty party endorsement. He remained a loyal political abolitionist and party organizer until 1860 when, after many party splits and realignments, one of their candidates was elected president of the United States.[18]

Garrison immediately felt the effects of the division among Negro abolitionists. At a meeting honoring him in Theodore Wright's church in New York City, before his departure for England, a motion of support for Garrison and his colleagues was laid before those assembled. It was introduced by one of his supporters, Thomas Van Rensselaer, a member of the American Anti-Slavery Society. Immediately, sharp opposition developed from Garnet and others on the ground that delegates from the newly formed American and Foreign Anti-Slavery Society were not represented on the committee to go overseas.[19] To the dissenters, Garrison no longer represented their thinking. As a result, the Garrisonian contingent left the United States without any endorsement.[20]

In joining the rival antislavery society, withholding support of Garrison in Wright's church, and sponsoring a convention of black New Yorkers in favor of the suffrage, Garnet alienated many of Garrison's white and black abolitionist supporters by the middle of 1840. Nonetheless, within the entire circle of abolitionists, Garnet was a recognized leader whose prestige and influence were in the ascendancy. While the Garrisonians did not object to the calling of a suffrage convention of black New Yorkers, they did protest its exclusive character, as did many Negroes.[21] Garrison, Robert Purvis, and William C. Nell, to name three, believed that such an approach would strengthen the walls of proscription. They believed that a black organization would advance segregation in America instead of reducing it. Charles B. Ray, Ward, and Garnet, on the other hand, took the position that in certain areas where white abolitionists disagreed on the propriety of Negro suffrage, particularly in voting, separate action was necessary.[22]

The franchise fight in New York State in which Garnet was to have a prominent part placed other Negro leaders in a quandary. Dr. James McCune Smith, for example, considered the movement a "caste convention to abolish caste"; on the other hand, he volunteered to cooperate with James G. Birney and Garnet if they so requested.[23] A brief examination of the premises of the Garrison school will help elucidate both the conflicts which ignited in the early 1840s among black abolitionists and the differences which erupted between Garnet and Garrisonians in particular.

As previously stated, the Garrisonians advocated nonviolent means for the emancipation of slaves and the elevation of free Negroes to full citizenship status. These means entailed propaganda through newspapers, lectures, fairs, boycotts of slave-made goods, and support of abolitionists throughout the world. Because Garrison believed the American Constitution to be a proslavery document and most religious institutions to be favorable to slavery, he denounced both. Garrison favored leaving the Union as Yancey was to twenty years later. Free Negroes in Garrison's view would best serve the interests of their enslaved brothers by remaining in close proximity with them; hence, he denounced attempts to colonize free blacks and opposed their emigration from this country.[24]

Recent scholarship has revealed that Garrison was motivated by a pervasive phobia—he feared that an armed slave insurrection would devour the nation should his efforts fail.[25] He wrote that "if we would not see our land deluged in blood, we must instantly burst the shackles of the slaves." He reiterated that "Immediate Emancipation can alone save [the South] from the vengeance of Heaven and cancel the debt of ages."[26]

According to Robert Abzug, Garrison espoused immediate emancipation because, he believed, time was running out on the nation in its bout with slavery. Walker's *Appeal* (1829) and Nat Turner's uprising (1831) had heightened these fears. For the New Englander, slavery caused the Turner insurrection, yet the responsibility was national. Only federal force had protected the South from rebellion.[27] While these fears abated somewhat in the late 1830s, Garrison continued to fear revolution when slaveholders refused to benefit from the example of West Indian emancipation. The proslavery press, he doubtlessly observed, continued to report emancipation as a failure. If slaveholders, then, were to abandon the "safe way" to emancipation in his view, what alternative remained?[28]

Finally, women's rights—that is, giving women an equal place in antislavery circles—was a cardinal principle for Garrison. Dumond deems the issue to be of only minor importance in the splitting of the American Anti-Slavery Society in 1840 (and the American and Foreign Anti-Slavery Society was not hostile to the aspirations of women). Garrison, however, used the issue to flay the upstart Massachusetts Abolition Society which had broken from him in 1839, although, in all probability, the real issue was political abolition.[29]

By the time Garnet went to Boston in May 1841 to address the Massachusetts Abolition Society, he had already become identified with political abolition. The convention framed three resolutions: the delegates declared it their duty to fight slavery through organized political action; they voted to withdraw Christian religious support from the Northern churches which upheld the slaveholders; and they strongly condemned the colonization of Negroes.[30] Although carefully avoiding the essential issue of political action, Garrison retaliated through *The Liberator*. Garnet was by now sufficiently known and powerful to incur criticism in *The Liberator*:

> The speech of our colored brother Garnett [*sic*] is spoken of as
> very eloquent; but we marvel that belonging as he does to a
> people meted out and trodden under foot, he should be willing
> to countenance an organization which put a padlock upon the
> lips of one half of the slave's best friends, rather than have every
> soul free to speak for the suffering and the dumb as God shall
> give it utterance. But this is owing to his *cloth* [author's italics], and
> not to his complexion.[31]

The word *cloth* is a subtle wordplay. In the literal sense, it alludes to
Garnet's ministerial background, but in another sense, it implies—for the
Garrisonian faithful—a political abolitionist, one at odds with Garrison.

Garrison was antagonistic to the Constitution and the Liberty party.
All the same, he was not averse to petition drives for civil rights on the
state and national levels, even though his endorsement of such activities
was a concession to principle. Had he remained in the country during
the summer of 1840, he probably would have supported the Garnet
faction in the suffrage fight in New York, provided the suffrage convention admitted whites.[32] Garnet played a leading role in the suffrage
efforts of the early 1840s.

As early as May 1840, a call for a convention of the "Colored Inhabitants of New York State" began to appear on the pages of *The Colored
American* and was repeated in many subsequent issues. Garnet's name
appeared on the call as a signatory from Troy. A member of the Committee of Correspondence was George Baltimore who was one of Garnet's congregants at the Liberty Street Church. In May, *The Colored
American* also reported that a large meeting had been held in Troy at
Liberty Street where numerous resolutions were passed: one stressed
the importance of a state convention of colored citizens; another endorsed *The Colored American* as the organ of Negro Americans;
another called blacks to action to remove all disabilities under which
they labored; and finally, one led to the appointment of a committee
of five to prepare an address to the citizens of New York.[33] This committee inspired by Garnet, produced a document of some five hundred
words, an eloquent rallying cry, written in the Aristotelian rhetorical
style of Garnet:[34]

The time has come, when to remain inactive in the midst of the ruinous forms of oppression with which we are surrounded, is to confirm the gainsaying of our foes, and to convince mankind that we are indifferent as to the recovery of our birthright privileges . . .

In America the face of things appertaining to the rights of many are fast changing. A portion of the citizens of the United States are ardently putting forth their untiring efforts to establish equal liberty. Some portions of the confederacy are aiming to remodel the frame-work of their legislative actions, that they may build upon the pure principles of unbiased liberty. In this work the Empire State is second to none. The right of trial by jury has been given to those claimed as fugitive slaves. This act is but the precursor of a wider, and a more extensive reform.

The crisis has come—the soil is ready for tilling, and will if cultivated yield abundantly. Then let us drive the plow shear, even to the very beam.

Fellow citizens of New York, awake, and put on your strength! Shame on the man that will sleep in the midst of his own shame and degradation—up, we beseech you. Your wives, children, and relatives are looking up to you imploringly. Awake, brethren! look around you, and be ye worthy exemplaries; let there be a convention of the colored citizens of New York, held in Albany on the first day of August 1840. Let the object of that convention be to concentrate our efforts in order that we may obtain the rights of American citizens. Let us come together, heart to heart and hand in hand, from every part of the State. Let Long Island send up a phalanx of her determined sons, that shall be as resistless, as the waves of the sea that beat upon her green shores. Let the city of New York, with her thirty thousand colored inhabitants, muster a mighty host. Let her intelligent young men have for a while the carriage-box of the aristocrat, and the table of the nabob, that they may be enabled to put into the hands of their children the tools of the thrifty mechanic. And let the other four cities that shine along the banks

of the Hudson send up an army of tried and zealous men, and
as they come let the cry be "To the rescue, to the rescue."

We know the farmers of the West will be in the council to
assist with their deliberations, even if they have to leave the
axe by the side of the oak, and the sickle in the grain. And
no less sure are we that those who dwell on the shores of
Champlain will meet to mingle their voices with our brethren
from Erie and Ontario.[35]

To arouse his fellows to action, Garnet first evoked a feeling of guilt in
his readers and then he appealed to the noble side of their natures. The
passages quoted above reveal his strong determination to build a powerful organized constituency that would in time compel the legislative
assembly to grant Negroes the suffrage.

As a result of the division that had already occurred among white
abolitionists and of the determination of some black New Yorkers to
hold a Negro citizens' convention, a lively debate arose among the
white followers of Garrison and those favoring independent action on
the one hand and among Negroes themselves on the other. From the
early summer of 1840 through the following spring, articles appeared in
The Colored American and *The National Anti-Slavery Standard* discussing the merits of a separate approach to problems affecting blacks only.[36]
Eventually, the convention movement among Negroes continued to
grow, although the debate was to remain undecided throughout the
antebellum period.[37] Garnet himself provided much of the aggressive-
ness and direction of the state convention movement in the 1840s.

After the Troy meeting, Garnet and others signed the call for a
"Convention of Colored Citizens" to be held in Albany, New York, on
19 August 1840. It was probably no coincidence that they chose that
locale as the convention city, since the Liberty party had held a large
meeting there the previous April. Albany, then, became a major forum
for the New York Negroes. Since most of the delegates who came were
of a like mind, few details of procedure or resolutions evoked any
spirited conflicts.[38] Theodore Wright called the convention to order;
Charles B. Ray was appointed chairman pro tem; and Charles L. Reason
and Garnet were named as two of the secretaries. Even Reverend George

Garnet attended as a delegate from Troy. During the proceedings, Garnet was made chairman of the Central Committee whose duty it was to gather and present the suffrage petition to the state legislature. Garnet was also charged with the responsibility for preparing an address to the Negroes of New York along with Wright and Ray.[39]

The resulting eighteen-hundred-word document began with a scriptural proverb which after 1840 was to become the motto of many newly forming antislavery societies: "Hereditary bondsmen, know ye not, Who would be free, themselves must strike the blow?"[40] By 1843, such a "blow" would contain more than a call for political abolition among blacks; it would actually urge the slave to resistance. However, in Garnet's 1840 address it simply signified the use of nonviolent pressure tactics through the petition.

"Improvement and elevation," Garnet wrote, "is the universal sentiment among us." He asserted that man's nature or destiny was ever progressive and that the time had come for an end to political injustice. He felt that the denial of voting rights on the same basis as whites had been the fundamental cause of oppression among free Negroes.[41] He called for united action:

> Brethren from this [denial of equal franchise rights] has
> proceeded our degradation. This has been the source of our
> suffering and oppression. And in all this, is there not enough
> to rouse the soul, and awaken the latent energies of every man
> of us? But a redeeming spirit is abroad, and new purposes have
> been decided upon among ourselves.
>
> Brethren, by united, vigorous, and judicious and manly effort,
> we can redeem ourselves. But we must put forth our own exer-
> tions. We must exert our powers. Our political enfranchisement
> cometh *not* [author's italics] from afar.[42]

Garnet underscored this second point—taking independent action on voting—because he believed no other way would bring success:

> Where rights have been wrested from a people, the restoration of
> them by those in power, as a matter of favor, can never be

expected. They are not to be bought or cajoled. They are to be obtained only by the continual presentation of the great truths pertaining to their specific wrongs, accompanied by corresponding energy and activity on the part of the aggrieved.[43]

The rest of the address was largely an appeal to rally every black person to the petition drive. In particular, he called for the clergy's active participation because "the clergy of the power-holding body are generally against us." The document ended with a triumphant affirmation of Garnet's faith in human progress, of which the Negroes' drive for political rights was merely a single part.[44]

When he addressed his people, Garnet spoke to their anguish and indignation. Moral outrage as expressed by a practicing minister helped galvanize a movement and in turn popularized the cause of liberty. Even before 1843, Garnet's leadership among blacks in New York State was marked enough to be disputed by other Negroes and by white Garrisonians.[45] His influence may have been greater among whites than among blacks.

Garnet's stately appearance on the speaker's platform before whites refuted the charge of mental inferiority that was being lodged against abolitionists, black and white. Truly black in color, intellectual, witty, eloquent, condemning, forgiving, and above all Christian, he created an overpowering impression. Weld and Tappan instinctively recognized the importance of black abolitionists as lecturers.[46] Larry Gara has written of them: "Except for a few of the abolitionists, no other reformers dealt as effectively with the issues of race prejudice. They were 'graduates' of the peculiar institution, said one antislavery worker, with their 'diplomas' written on their backs, and they had a vital role to fill, and they filled it well."[47]

Garnet's antislavery and civil rights address before the American Anti-Slavery convention in May 1840 was a complex argument, original in parts and a product of careful reflection. It contained many of the same arguments he would advance at the Judiciary Committee hearings of the state legislature in 1841 when he presented petitions that had been sent to him as the committee chairman. In this address, he advanced the claim of full citizenship for free Negroes on the basis of historical, religious, and economic considerations. Garnet began with the early settlers' dream of liberty which motivated them "to break asunder the ties that bound them to kindred and country, and to fix their dwellings, and to throw their destinies in the midst of a trackless wilderness." He then proceeded to the American Revolution, finding in the Declaration of Independence a prose elaboration of the same libertarian spirit. As regards the nation's founders and colonists before them, Garnet had no complaint.

> But, we complain, in the most unqualified terms, of the base conduct of their degenerate sons. If, when taking into consideration the circumstances with which the revolutionists were surrounded, and the weakness of human nature, we can possibly pardon them for neglecting our brethren's rights—if, in the first dawning of the day of liberty, every part of the patriot's duty did not appear plain, now that we have reached them midday of our national career—now that there are ten thousand suns flashing light upon our pathway, this nation is guilty of the basest hypocrisy in withholding the rights due to millions of American citizens.[48]

In the historical context, the hypocritical denial of citizenship rights to blacks, Garnet continued, was unjust. Quoting Andrew Jackson, Garnet pointed to the contribution of Negro troops in both the Revolutionary War and the War of 1812. He then alluded with subtle irony to Jackson the slaveholder:

> Such is the language of slaveholders when they would have colored men stand in the front of battle.—If they are forgotten by history—if they are not mentioned in the halls of Congress— if prejudice denies them a place in the grateful recollections of Americans in general, I trust they will at least be remembered amid the cloister of the Hermitage.[49]

In addition to serving the nation, the sections, and the people, Negroes in his view had made a religious contribution to America. Religion was to Garnet "the basis of civil society." He continued: "The greatest blessings which we have received as a nation have been given unto us on account of the little piety that has been found among us."[50] Then Garnet began speaking in a metaphorical vein:

It [religion] is the mighty pillar which holds up the well begun
structure of this government, which I trust it will ultimately
finish. Colored men have been with you in this labor. We are
with you still, and will be with you forever. We even hope to
worship in the earthly temples of our Lord. If they finally fall
as did the churches of Asia, on account of their sins, without
being guilty of contributing to their destruction, let us be
buried beneath their ruins. We do not wish to survive their
overthrow.[51]

This passage may represent Garnet's hope that religious values would
eventually control the actions of civil institutions and that good works
would become universal among mankind. Yet, in the South, he continued, the slaveholder's victim was being denied his spiritual immortal-
ity, and thus far the Lord of Hosts had refrained from just vengeance.[52]

Garnet's third argument for full citizenship was economically based.
"From the Chesapeake Bay to the Sabine River there is not a foot of
cultivated ground that has not smiled beneath the hard hand of the dark
American." Not only was the slave the blood and sinew of the Southern
economy, but also the domestic functionary, accumulating the capital
for the slave master on which his children received college educations.[53]
He concluded:

In submitting the resolution, sir, I would again call upon Americans to remember, that but a few years ago their fathers crossed
the ocean in search of the freedom now denied to us. I would
beseech them to remember that the great day of God's final
reckoning is just before us, remember his eternal justice, and
then remember the outcast bondsman, and let him go forth free
in the presence of God, in whose image he was created.[54]

The Negroes' birthright, patriotism, military service, and economic
input into the society, then, were some of the reasons Garnet was to
give when the state legislature called upon him to justify the granting of
black civil rights. From 20 August 1840 when the Albany gathering
adjourned until his appearance before the legislature on 18 February
1841 (except for a few weeks in December when Garnet's leg was amputated), he collected petitions for presentation to the Judiciary Com-

mittee of the state legislature, personally lobbied among the legislators, and sent enthusiastic progress reports for publication in *The Colored American*.[55]

Although the form of the petition was printed in the Albany convention minutes, at least four varieties of the same document were in evidence, the longest no more than five hundred words. The essential point in all of them was the request that the legislature amend the state constitution so that the elective franchise be extended to blacks on the same terms as enjoyed by other citizens.[56]

By 2 February 1841, Garnet had personally presented seventeen petitions, fifteen of which came from Negro citizens alone. New York City provided 1,700 names of a total of 2,806 for the entire state. Garnet was pleased by the drive and optimistic as to its outcome. On the evening of 18 February, he appeared before the Judiciary Committee to defend the claim of black New Yorkers to the vote. He presented the legislators with other arguments besides those already mentioned. He exposed the fallacy of the rationale used to disfranchise blacks when the act was first passed in 1821; and he alluded to the "deleterious" social consequences that the arrangement had had in producing "discouragement, pauperism and crime." He also pointed out "the unsoundness of the policy that oppresses and degrades any of the citizens of the commonwealth." He mentioned the willingness of blacks to share in everything which would enrich and honor "our common country" and he told them that "the public mind was prepared to do justice to us."[57] After his appearance, Garnet glowingly predicted affirmative action and succeeded in getting the issue before the electorate.

One final antislavery activity which Garnet undertook during the 1840s and continued until abolition was the harboring and assistance of fugitive slaves. Since Troy was located on the Hudson River, it was a natural way station of the eastern route of the underground railroad. While Garnet's statement made in 1859 that he had personally sheltered a hundred and fifty fugitives in a single year is probably an exaggeration, there is evidence of his direct involvement.[58] It is puzzling, however, that the large works on the railway exclude his name altogether.[59]

It may be concluded that before 1843 Garnet advocated and promoted political abolition, encouraged a predominantly Negro convention movement, favored nonviolent tactics and, had established himself among both black and white abolitionists as a new forward-looking intellectual. In these efforts, he brought many blacks into the abolition movement and held onto his dominance in New York until the Negro national convention of 1843 when his control was disputed by Frederick Douglass. As for a quantification of Garnet's impact, it may be said that he was important enough to the Garrisonians to be repudiated, that he had confused the scholarly James McCune Smith, and that he had facilitated the shift toward a third party effort by many Negroes. His value was quickly recognized by Louis Tappan who welcomed and partly subsidized his talents. Garnet's small church along with its Sunday School prospered. This church became a nexus for state and national meetings among blacks and a necessary stop on the underground railway.

In practical results, political abolition had only a feeble impact in 1840; only about seventy-one hundred votes were cast for the Liberty candidate Birney. "But the change in method was startlingly significant," wrote Albert Bushnell Hart; "it gave a new impulse to the flagging spirits of the abolitionists; it formed a new centre for the open discussion of slavery; it was one method of organizing opposition to the annexation of Texas; above all, in the next two national elections the political abolitionists proved to have the balance of power in decisive states, and thus gained an importance and consideration vastly greater than their scanty numbers would warrant." Their goal was to convince the Whigs and Democrats that unless concessions were to be made to antislavery feelings, they would face defeat at the polls. In that sense, the defeat of Henry Clay in 1844 and of Lewis Cass in 1848 was not spurious; it was a portent of growing political power among abolitionists.[60]

NOTES

1. Jane and William Pease, "Black Power—The Debate in 1840," *Phylon* 39 (Spring 1968): 19-26. Clarification will appear later in the chapter.

2. *Minutes of the Liberty Street Presbyterian Church* (Philadelphia: Archives of the Presbyterian Church).

3. Ibid.

4. Loren Katz (ed.), *Walker's Appeal and an Address to the Slaves of the United States of America* (Reprint; New York: Arno Press, 1969), p. 92.

5. *Session Minutes of the Shiloh Presbyterian Church* (Philadelphia: Archives of the Presbyterian Church).

6. Garnet was a member of the Albany Convention of Bible Missions which, in 1846, organized the American Missionary Association. In 1847, he was elected to the Executive Committee of the association and served for one year.

He was again elected to the Executive Committee in 1856 and was reelected in 1857, 1858, 1859, and 1860. On 8 January 1850, he was appointed a home missionary for a church in Geneva, New York. The amount of aid given him was $100 a year, which was about average for a home agent.

7. Samuel Rezneck, *Profiles Out of the Past of Troy, New York* (Troy, N.Y.: Chamber of Commerce, 1970), p. 76.

8. *The National Anti-Slavery Standard*, 11 June 1840, p. 1.

9. Ibid.

10. *The Emancipator*, 15 May 1840, pp. 10-11; *The National Anti-Slavery Standard*, May 1840, p. 1; *The Colored American*, 30 May 1840, p. 1.

11. Ibid.

12. Quarles, *Black Abolitionists*, pp. 45, 68. Also *The Emancipator*, 20 May 1840, p. 18.

13. *The Emancipator*, 22 May 1840, p. 14.

14. Quarles, pp. 43-44. See also *The Colored American*, 6 June 1840, p. 1, for a statement of support by Negro Garrisonians.

15. Dwight Dumond, *Antislavery Origins of the Civil War* (Ann Arbor: University of Michigan Press, 1959), p. 50.

16. Ibid., p. 87; Litwack, *North of Slavery*, pp. 243-244.

17. *The Liberator*, 8 December 1843, p. 193.

18. Dumond, pp. 107-111.

19. Dwight Dumond, *The Letters of James G. Birney: 1837-1857*, (Reprint; Glocester, Mass.: Peter Smith, 1966), p. 577.

20. Quarles, p. 45.

21. Jane and William Pease, pp. 21-26

22. Ibid.

23. Dumond, *Letters of James G. Birney*, pp. 624-625.

24. This information is common; a cursory reading of *The Liberator* for the year 1840 suffices. Also the biography by Russel B. Nye, *William Lloyd Garrison and the Humanitarian Reformers* (Boston: Little, Brown, 1955).

25. Robert Abzug, "The Influence of Garrisonian Abolitionists' Fears of Slave Violence on the Antislavery Argument, 1829-1840," *Journal of Negro History* 55 (January 1970): 15-26.

26. Nye, p. 54.

27. Abzug, p. 18.

28. Ibid., pp. 25-26.

29. Although Garrison had accumulated a number of abolitionist enemies for a variety of reasons, he vigorously opposed political abolitionists. He opposed Garnet and the members of the Massachusetts Abolition Society for the same reason. While Garrison may not have said so in so many words, his consistency renders such an inference a reasonable one.

30. *The Emancipator*, 17 June 1841, p. 26.

31. *The Liberator*, 4 June 1841, p. 91.

32. Garrison favored a joint effort to abolish the restriction on the franchise. As the suffrage campaign developed, whites did play a part. That is why the inference is so drawn.

33. *The Colored American*, 6 June 1840, p. 3.

34. Irene C. Edmonds, "An Aristotelian Interpretation of Garnet's Memorial Discourse," *Research Bulletin: Florida A & M College* 5 (September 1952): 20-28. The "epidectic and deliberative" rhetoric of the Memorial Discourse runs throughout Garnet's public statements, pp. 21-22.

35. *The Colored American*, 27 June 1840, p. 2.

36. Ibid. Also see ibid., 4 July 1840, p. 1; 15 August 1840, p. 3; 18 July 1840, p. 2; 19 December 1840, p. 2. *National Anti-Slavery Standard*, 18 June 1840, p. 6; 2 July 1840, p. 14; 30 July 1840, p. 31. *The Pennsylvania Freeman*, 17 March 1841, p. 2. This paper approved of the work of Albany.

37. Jane and William Pease, p. 26.

38. *Minutes of the State Convention of Colored Citizens* (New York: Piercy and Reed, 1840), p. 14. A heated debate arose only once, and it was over the wording of a resolution concerning the acquisition of property. Once agreement was reached, the matter ended.

39. Ibid., pp. 5-7, 10, 18-19.

40. Ibid., p. 20.

41. *Minutes*, pp. 20-21.

42. Ibid., p. 21.

43. Ibid.

44. Ibid., pp. 22-23. The direct quotation is on p. 22.

45. Carter G. Woodson, "Henry Highland Garnet," *DAB* 4 (1932): 154-155.

46. Dumond, *Letters of James G. Birney*, p. 330.

47. Larry Gara, "The Professional Fugitive in the Abolition Movement," *The Wisconsin Magazine of History* 48 (Spring 1965); 204.

48. *The Emancipator*, 15 May 1840, p. 10.

49. Ibid.

50. Ibid.

51. Ibid.

52. Ibid.

53. Ibid.

54. Ibid.

55. *Minutes of the State Convention of Colored Citizens*, pp. 18-19.

56. Ibid., p. 15; *The Colored American*, 2 January 1841, p. 2.

57. *The Colored American*, 13 February 1841, p. 1; 13 March 1841, p. 1

58. *The Weekly Anglo-African*, 17 September 1859; Quarles, p. 149. Ray's and Garnet's relationship is common knowledge; see also J. F. Johnston, *Proceedings of the General Anti-Slavery Convention, Called by the British & Foreign Anti-Slavery Society* (London: John Snow, 1843), p. 77.

59. William Still, *The Underground Railroad* (Reprint; New York: Arno Press, 1968); Levi Coffin, *The Reminiscences of Levi Coffin* (Reprint; New York: Arno Press, 1968); Wilbur H. Siebert, *The Underground Railroad* (Reprint; New York: Arno Press, 1968); Robert Smedley, *History of the Underground Railroad* (Reprint; New York: Arno Press, 1969); Larry Gara *The Liberty Line* (Lexington: University Press of Kentucky, 1961). Garnet is omitted.

60. Albert Bushnell Hart, *Slavery and Abolition* (Reprint; New York: Negro Universities Press, 1968), pp. 317-318.

3

Political Abolition, Full Suffrage and Slave Resistance

Having established a name for himself several years before 1843, Garnet did not suddenly win fame and notoriety because of his well-known *Address to the Slaves* as the short pieces written about him seem to indicate.[1] Although associated with the use of violence from 1843 onward, he made numerous addresses that year, one of which advocated slave resistance. Important as this speech was, his most influential address—at least in the view of his contemporaries James McCune Smith and Alexander Crummell—was delivered before the Liberty party convention which also met during 1843. Throughout 1841 and 1842, Garnet continued to promote the Liberty party and the petition fight of black New Yorkers for an unrestricted male suffrage.[2]

With the growth of the Liberty party in the early 1840s, Quarles has stated that it was inevitable that the equal suffrage issue would come before the constitutional convention of 1846 in New York. As Garnet had hoped, the legislature referred the question of Negro suffrage to the electorate. However, it was the white voters who disappointed him when they refused by a large majority to remove the property qualification. Aside from the obvious racial prejudice, the results were also attributed to the unwillingness of the state's Democratic majority to pass a measure which would add political power to either the Whig or Liberty party at the expense of their own.[3] It is difficult to determine which factor was the most significant in New York. If the experience of

Negroes in Philadelphia who were completely disfranchised because
they attempted to petition for full voting rights in Pennsylvania[4] is
representative of hostility to Negro rights within the Northern states,
then the conclusion must be that the Negro suffrage campaign neither
helped nor hindered the outcome. The property restriction remained
in New York during the entire antebellum period, no matter how fer-
vently Negroes petitioned and no matter how often the electorate had
the opportunity to vote the amendment down. Only with ratification
of the Fifteenth Amendment did the change occur. So far as the objective of the suffrage cámpaign was concerned, it was a failure. Yet, the
campaign, tied in as it was to the Negro convention movement, enhanced
the attainment of Liberty party goals, and Garnet deserves some credit
for this success. The same machinery assembled to promote the vote
could be used for other objectives, and a number of Liberty party supporters directed its operation.

Although the suffrage fight was lost, abolitionists did achieve a few
victories in New York before the Civil War. One success was repeal of
the "nine months law," which required a slave to remain in the state for
nine months with his master's knowledge before he could legally become free. Another was the cooperation of Governor William Seward in
refusing to deliver fugitives wanted in the South and his approval of an
act establishing trial by jury in runaway slave cases.[5]

In retrospect, the New York conventions of 1840 and 1841, while
not the first such state movements among blacks, were the first held
with chief emphasis on the suffrage. These were in all likelihood the
first state Negro conventions to send an appeal to the state legislature.
Finally, they were the first to go on record as being independent of
white domination. In that sense, they were the harbinger of a new age
in Negro thought and action.[6]

One final point about the suffrage convention of 1840 which may
or may not be attributed directly to Garnet was an expanding awareness of the ramifications of discrimination. In one of the resolutions
adopted by the convention, a connection was made between legal proscription of a minority and its effects upon the society as a whole. It
read:

Resolved, that whenever in the administration of such a government, a portion of its citizens are deprived (from any such invidi-
ous causes) of an equal participation of the privileges and preroga-

tives of citizenship, the principles of republicanism are mani-
festly violated.[7]

Implied here is the simple, yet profound, truth that a denial of rights
to a given group on any arbitrary basis constitutes a threat to the
rights of all citizens. Garnet had already elaborated upon this theme
in petitions and in his personal statements before the legislature. Degradation among a section of the community, he showed, meant a relative
degradation to all. To the extent that Negroes were held in subordination, a direct proportion of whites were affected and would likewise be
victimized as objects of Negro crime.[8]

The Negro state convention which met the following year on 25
August 1841 at Troy acted in accordance with the sentiment expressed
in 1840. The chief issue remained suffrage restriction. In appealing to
the whole community, the Negro's plight was presented as affecting
everyone; by forcing blacks into second-rate citizenship, whites were
fostering crime. At this convention, Negroes echoed Garnet's determination to agitate until successful, and annual meetings were subsequently held, usually emphasizing equality of suffrage and showing a
decided sympathy with Liberty party ideals.[9]

Just as he played a significant role on the state level, Garnet also
exerted an influence on a national basis. National meetings among blacks
came back into vogue during the 1840s. Because Negro New Yorkers
and Philadelphians had decided to go separate ways in 1835, there had
been no national meeting for seven years in spite of numerous attempts
to assemble them. Under the radical third party influence, the convention met in 1843 to give direction and detail to Negro aspirations.[10] The
choice of Buffalo, New York, as the convention site was probably deliberate; the same city was to host the third National Liberty party convention later the same year.

The call for a Negro gathering in *The Liberator* was the signal for
opposition from those Negroes in Boston who distrusted the politics
of the New Yorkers. They did decide, however, to participate and to
vocalize their opposition. To the Negroes of New Bedford, the convention sponsors were deserters of the Garrisonian tradition, and to desert
Garrison was considered a heresy.[11] Regardless of this sentiment, the
convention met on 15 August 1843 at Buffalo. Controversy still persists
on the convention's ideas, the measures proposed, and their significance.
Central to the controversy is Garnet's role and his well-known *Address*.

Closest to his heart were two new stratagems that he wanted the convention to adopt: first, the endorsement of the Liberty party, and secondly, agreement to accept in principle the rightness of slave resistance. In view of the schism which Garnet's second goal was to generate, it should be mentioned that there was some unanimity at the convention. More than twenty resolutions passed with widespread agreement, particularly those condemning religious institutions and those pastors who accepted discrimination or who refused to take affirmative anti-slavery action.[12]

Opposition arose over those resolutions which were sympathetic to the Liberty party; they were adopted over the protests of Remond and Douglass. Of first importance was Resolution Five which stated "That it is the duty of every lover of liberty to vote the Liberty ticket so long as they are consistent to their principles." Douglass, William Wells Brown, Remond, and other Negro Garrisonians opposed this resolution on the grounds that all parties were necessarily corrupt and that their friends in Massachusetts would make no exception for the Liberty party.[13]

Resolution Sixteen, adopted without debate, expressed a view of government which strict Garrisonians had repudiated: "That we believe that it is possible for human governments to be righteous as it is for human beings to be righteous, and that God-fearing men can make the government of our country well pleasing in His sight, and that slavery can be abolished by its instrumentality."[14] This view of government was to prove infinitely more realistic than the Garrisonian view that government was corrupt a priori; there was simply no good reason to preempt established channels of change because the mechanism was subject to possible corruption. Clearly, Garrison's position was unworkable.

Resolution Twenty-five stated that the Freeman's party and the Liberty party were one and the same. Again, Douglass, Remond, and Brown voiced their opposition: they had faith neither in the party nor in the leaders of the party. They asserted that they would not support it or encourage others to do so. Resolution Twenty-six recommended that freemen throughout the nation organize Liberty Associations in their respective counties and nominate "tried friends of liberty" for office. Finally, Resolution Twenty-eight denounced both the Whig and Democratic parties as proslavery. In the judgment of the convention, these parties would keep the institution intact.[15]

In accepting these resolutions, the convention followed Garnet's lead. Douglass remained true to his Garrisonian principles for another five years; after the Free Soil party's convention of 1848, he began to accept political abolition as most free Negroes had by that date.[16] Quarles states that Remond "temporarily abandoned his nonvoting stance" in the same year when he voted for Stephen C. Phillips, the Free Soil candidate for governor of New York.[17] Brown remained consistently Garrisonian in orientation on this issue. He took just umbrage at Garnet's inaccurate statement that only Remond and Douglass had opposed the Liberty party during the Buffalo meeting. "When I see such quibbling by such men as Henry Highland Garnet," he wrote, "it makes me tremble for the fate of the slave at the hands of political parties."[18]

The second measure Garnet advanced in his address, the advocacy of slave resistance, failed in 1843 but in time became increasingly acceptable to both black and white abolitionists. Garnet probably began to turn to the idea of slave resistance between 1842 and 1843. For the white and black Garrisonians, it hit a vital nerve center, convulsing them and producing an "over-reaction." The impact this proposal had on the convention was significant.

The advocacy of slave resistance as a means to liberation was not original to Garnet or for that matter to David Walker, from whom Herbert Aptheker states Garnet borrowed many ideas. Aptheker has found another document containing a call for violence which was contemporaneous with Walker's *Appeal* of 1829.[19] This is a book of poems entitled the *Hope of Liberty* by George Moses Horton, a slave from Chatham County, North Carolina; the poems were published by Joseph Gales, editor of the *Raleigh Register*, in his newspaper. Horton expressed these thoughts:

> Oh Liberty, thou golden prize
> So often sought by blood—
> we crave thy sacred sun to rise,
> the Gift of Nature's God!
> Bid slavery hide her haggard face
> and barbarism fly
> I scorn to see the sad disgrace
> in which enslaved I lie.[20]

Stronger militance was also expressed in a pamphlet issued in February 1829 by a Negro New Yorker, Robert Alexander Young. Young prophesied the coming of a black savior who, by his invincibility, would be able to free his people.[21] The most important work promoting militancy was, of course, the *Appeal* by Walker.

David Walker was from the South and the son of a free woman, and he settled in Boston at the age of thirty or thirty-five. He immediately began antislavery activities which included the publication of his *Appeal* late in 1829. By 1830, the date of his death, it had already gone into a third edition and was widely discussed throughout the nation.[22] In some parts of the South, the *Appeal* created outright alarm. The governor of North Carolina denounced it as expressing subversive sentiments encouraging slave insubordination. The mayor of Savannah, Georgia, wrote to the mayor of Boston requesting Walker's arrest, while Richmond's mayor claimed several free blacks had the *Appeal* in their possession. The governors of North Carolina and Georgia took action against the pamphlet, while the Virginia legislature held secret sessions to suppress it. Four states—North Carolina, Mississippi, Georgia, and Louisiana—used the pamphlet as a pretext to enact severe restrictions on "seditious propaganda." At least one white man, a printer in Milledgeville, Georgia, was found distributing it.[23]

Most of Walker's work is in the religious vein. He predicted bloody retributive justice upon white slaveholders and bigots, and he saw this outcome as inevitable unless emancipation was not immediately declared.[24] Aptheker's assertion that Walker was ambiguous on the use of violence is correct.[25] Walker was speaking directly to the fears which motivated Garrison's agitation, yet, as Aptheker contends, his *Appeal* fell slightly short of Garnet's carefully condensed statement delivered in 1843 at Buffalo. It certainly did not receive quite the same reception in *The Liberator* as Garnet's *Address*. Garrison expressed a general disapproval of its spirit, though conceded that the *Appeal* contained "many valuable truths and seasonable warning."[26]

Another black abolitionist who accepted violence as a means of slave liberation was Charles Remond during his tour of England in 1840. Remond welcomed a war between England and the United States if the slave would thereby gain his freedom.[27]

The similarity in thought between Walker and Garnet is probably more obvious in a comparison of the *Appeal* with Garnet's 1842 *Address* before the National Liberty party's convention in Boston's Faneuil Hall. Garnet's *Address* expressed, as Walker's *Appeal* had, the sentiment that only reform would prevent divine retribution:

> I cannot harbor the thought for a moment that their [the slaves']
> deliverance will be brought about by violence. No, our country
> will not be so deaf to the cries of the oppressed; so regardless of
> the commands of God, and her highest interests. No, the time for a
> last stern struggle has not yet come (may it never be necessary).
> The finger of the Almighty will hold back the trigger, and his
> all powerful arm will sheath the sword till the oppressor's cup
> is full.[28]

Thus, both Walker and Garnet, while not directly advocating violence,
were making known the possibility of a bloody insurrection. They were,
in effect, deliberately threatening slaveholding interests on the one hand
and playing upon the Garrisonian abolitionists' fears on the other.

Walker's influence on Garnet's 1843 *Address to the Slaves* is more
subtle and detailed than described by Aptheker.[29] This influence will be
discussed presently.

Interestingly, Garnet rejected violence as a means of effecting the
slave's deliverance in early 1842, but by the summer of 1843 had completely reversed his stance. In addition to the more acceptable Garrisonian methods, he believed that political parties were merely one
means toward liberation. Garnet told his audience in 1842 that "the
slaveholders count upon numbers; we upon *truth* [author's italics], and
it is powerful and will prevail."[30] Yet, he was becoming increasingly
disillusioned with the possibility of enlightening the slaveowner by conventional means. He was undoubtedly aware that Southern newspapers
looked on West Indian emancipation as a failure, in spite of evidence to
the contrary. If Southern minds were closed, then propaganda by word
would never change them. Only the vicissitudes of power—so many
votes, so much pressure—would move them. In 1843, Garnet was to
point out to the slaveholder that there were three million angry slaves
in the South.[31]

Another possible influence in turning Garnet to greater acceptance of
violence was the 1842 Supreme Court decision in *Prigg v. Pennsylvania*.
In recognizing the national government's right to maintain slavery and
in thereby upholding the fugitive slave law of 1793, the court made an
essentially proslavery decision. During the time of its rendering, however, it was open to interpretation. The court's decision was decidedly
a setback to Liberty party spokesmen who had already accepted the
ideology of Joshua Giddings and Salmon P. Chase. Giddings had been

ejected from the House of Representatives in 1842 for his strong anti-slavery stand, and Chase had stated that slavery was a local institution with which the federal government could have no connection.[32] The "slave-power," to use their phrase, which was to become a national watchword, had simply gotten its way. Perhaps, then, Walker's admonition that victory in this country was impossible was proving to have relevance to Garnet. Walker's growing desperation is reflected in the following words from his *Appeal*: "For I pledge you my sacred word of honor that Mr. Jefferson's remarks about us have sunk deep into the hearts of millions of the whites and never will change this side of eternity."[33] While Garnet was becoming increasingly anguished, there is no evidence that he was yielding to Walker's abject despair. Although Garnet ultimately sanctioned resistance, nowhere did he specifically repudiate the possibility of eventual triumph in America; that is an essential difference between these two radical figures. Certain assertions in Walker's *Appeal*, however, were included in Garnet's 1843 *Address to the Slaves*: (1) Walker's statement that slaves were deliberately being kept in a degraded and ignorant state.[34] (2) His assertion that slavery was evil in the sight of God and that God was partial to the oppressed.[35] Since, according to Walker, submission to slavery was sinful, it was far better to die than accept submission.[36] Most of the *Appeal* elaborated upon these central assertions.

Garnet incorporated all of these ideas into his *Address to the Slaves*. He argued:

> In every man's mind the good seeds of liberty are planted and he who brings his fellow down so low, as to make him contented with a condition of slavery, commits the highest crime against God and man. Brethren, your oppressors aim to do this. They endeavor to make you as much like brutes as possible. When they have blinded the eyes of your mind—when they have embittered the sweet waters of life—when they have shut out the light which shines from the word of God—then, and not till then has American slavery done its perfect work.[37]

There followed the next statement rendered entirely in capital letters: TO SUCH DEGRADATION IT IS SINFUL IN THE EXTREME FOR YOU TO MAKE VOLUNTARY SUBMISSION.[38] Further on in the same paragraph, also in capitals, he continued: "NEITHER GOD, NOR ANGELS, OR JUST MEN, COMMAND YOU TO SUFFER FOR A SINGLE MOMENT. THEREFORE IT IS YOUR SOLEMN AND IMPERATIVE DUTY TO USE EVERY MEANS, BOTH MORAL, INTELLECTUAL, AND PHYSICAL, THAT PROMISE SUCCESS."[39]

The next few paragraphs were largely an invocation to the slaves to action and resistance, if not to insurrection. In this respect, Garnet's directions to the slave constitute his original contribution. Beginning with Lord Byron's famous phrase, "If hereditary bondsmen would be free, they must strike the first blow," Garnet urged the slave to go to their masters and to tell them of their determination to be free, appealing to the slaveholder's sense of justice. He advised that they entreat their masters to remove the burdens placed upon them and to compensate them for their labor: "Promise them renewed diligence in the cultivation of the soil, if they will render to you an equivalent for your services. Point them to the increase of happiness and prosperity in the British West Indies, since the act of Emancipation."[40]

If the persuasive approach failed, the slave was to refuse to work, to strike. "If they [the masters] then commence the work of death, they, and not you, will be responsible for the consequences. It is far better to die than live as a slave and to pass a degraded status on to children."[41] Further, he stated: "However much you and all of us desire it there is not much hope of Redemption without the shedding of blood."[42] Then, in the final paragraph, which is commonly cited in anthologies, Garnet exclaims:

> Let your motto be RESISTANCE! RESISTANCE! RESISTANCE!—No oppressed people have ever secured their liberty without resistance. What kind of resistance you had better make, you must decide by the circumstances that surround you, and according to the suggestion of expediency. Brethren, adieu. Trust in the living God. Labor for the peace of the human race, and remember that you are three million.[43]

Carleton Mabee accurately describes this statement as an encouragement of violence. Its "bite" on the black and white abolitionists was felt immediately. A heated floor fight commenced in the convention after Garnet finished speaking. Mabee contends that the wording was carefully chosen to appeal to Negro leaders, most of whom Garnet knew were committed to nonviolence. Since Garnet did not directly ask the slaves to revolt or to reply to white violence by mass nonviolent action, as James G. Birney had advocated in 1835, he hoped that the convention would go on record in favor of insurrection.[44]

At first glance, Mabee's view is credible. It would be quite unlikely for an uneducated bondsman to advise his master to heed the example of West Indian emancipation—let alone be informed on the subject. On the other hand, if Aptheker's information is correct and Walker's *Appeal* did in fact penetrate the South to slaveholder and to slaves, then perhaps Garnet was thoroughly serious in his attempt. Garnet was in contact with fugitives via the underground railroad, and in his Liberty party speech of 1842, he told his audience that slaves were well acquainted with developments in nonslave areas in their behalf. Certainly, he wanted the convention to accept his words; perhaps he actually wanted the slaves to have a copy of his speech.

Opposition to Garnet's stand came immediately from Frederick Douglass, a faithful Garrisonian, who objected to the excessive physical force advocated in the *Address*. Douglass urged the Convention to rely moral means a little longer. While Garnet's *Address* might not lead the slave to rebellion, he argued that the indirect result would be insurrection, and in no way did he wish to attach his name to that.[46] Another objection, raised by A. M. Sumner in the evening session, was that the speech would be fatal to the free blacks of the slave states as well as to those living on the borders of free states.[47] Eventually, by a vote of 19 to 18 the convention killed the effort to distribute Garnet's *Address*. Among the 19 were Douglass, Remond, Brown, and many of the same delegates who were against endorsing the Liberty party.[48]

In rebuttal, Remond cited the good already done by abolitionists, the example of peaceful West Indian abolition, and his belief that public opinion was coming around to emancipation in the light of new information.[49] He, too, was a faithful Garrisonian at the convention, perhaps, having forgotten his strong anti-Garrison statements which had been made overseas three years before.[50] Another Garrison disciple, William Wells Brown, waited until 1857 before he endorsed slave rebellions as the means to fight oppression.[51] Douglass did not wait quite that long; at a speaking engagement at Faneuil Hall in Boston in mid-1849 he stated that he had abandoned the pacific stand he had taken at Buffalo in 1843.[52] Although black abolitionists were temporarily stunned by Garnet's *Address* and at first refused to accept it, even in modified form, it made an enduring impression.[53]

A few days later, when a second vote was taken on whether to support the distribution of the speech, the resolution failed by an even greater margin. In the interval Garnet's teacher, Theodore Wright, who had supported it, changed his mind as had Charles B. Ray;[54] they found too much violence in Garnet's *Address*. Thus, so far as the Buffalo meeting was concerned, Garnet had lost. The matter was brought up again at the national convention of 1847, and again was defeated. However, Garnet published his *Address* and Walker's *Appeal* together two months later. Negroes in Ohio, meeting in a statewide convention in 1849, passed a resolution to have five hundred copies of the *Address* and *Appeal* distributed without charge.[55]

Garnet was successful in binding the convention to the Liberty party, but unsuccessful in having his speech adopted. He introduced another measure, which was to be accepted, recommending the sponsorship of a newspaper that would be the quasi-official voice of the Negroes. He and Ray presented to the convention a report calling for a press "in our own hand," to be used not only for purposes of counteracting hostile influence, but also as an instrument of positive good and elevation.[56] The report urged that if a newspaper were established by any individual enterprise, the enterprise had to be investigated and, if found suitable, should be given the patronage of the convention.[57]

Upon receiving the report, the convention passed the following resolution:

> That a committee of seven be appointed by this Convention to take measures, as soon as may be, to establish a weekly paper, devoted impartially to the welfare of our whole people, without regard to condition, and to the welfare of humanity universally—to appoint an editor and publisher, and to fix their salaries; or in the event that they should not establish a paper, and one should be commenced as an individual enterprise of a proper character, to recommend said paper as entitled to the patronage and support of the people.[58]

Garnet was named to this newly formed press committee. It may be
argued that Garnet had a selfish motivation—the desire for influence
and power. On the other hand, a black newspaper would be a valuable
tool, regardless of who was to publish it.[59]

In effect, this report set in motion a process which eventually ended
with the acceptance of Frederick Douglass's *North Star* in the later
1840s as the most important black newspaper. One of the reasons Garnet's personal influence declined after 1843 and throughout the early
1850s was that Douglass became his opponent and refused to give much
coverage in *The North Star* to Garnet's overseas activities.[60] Evidently,
Douglass believed that Garnet was running away from the fight. Better
coverage did appear in friendlier tabloids, but these were smaller in
circulation and ephemeral compared with Douglass's effort.[61]

Carter G. Woodson calls the convention of 1843 the high point of
Garnet's leadership among blacks and the years that followed the era of
Douglass.[62] While true, this statement requires some amplification.
Garnet's personal leadership in the New York State Negro convention
movement after 1843 continued relatively unchanged, as did his status
in the councils of state and national Liberty party organizations. Charles
Wesley asserts that "the Buffalo Convention of the Liberty Party was
the most significant convention in the history of the Negro's political
life in the United States prior to the Civil War. Several Negro delegates
were present. Among these were the distinguished public figures of
Henry Highland Garnet, Charles B. Ray and Samuel R. Ward."[63]

There is no question that Douglass was the dominant voice of the
Negro press from 1848 until 1858 in the United States. Even when he
was in command, Garnet scarcely gained a foothold among Negroes in
Philadelphia who had boycotted the convention of 1843 because they
were thoroughgoing Garrisonians.[64] It was easy, therefore, for Douglass
to gain their acceptance in the coming years.

Yet, personal leadership is by no means the measure of Garnet's full
impact. The Garnet faction helped lay down the strategy for Negroes.
It advanced political activity and organization, acceptance of violence to
free the slave, and finally, emigrationist activity.[65] Garnet provided the
ideas which even his rivals accepted by 1860. His strategies, then, if not
his personal leadership, were rather completely victorious. As previously
pointed out, Douglass, Remond, and Brown eventually reversed themselves on the issues of violence and political action, as well as on emigra-

tion. For Garnet no drastic reversal in thought was necessary; it was his opponents who had grown up in Garrison's camp who lagged behind him. Pressure from Garnet, the rush of events in the 1850s, and fear of loss of a constituency contributed to their changes in position. By 1860, political action, violent methods, and emigrationist plans had become the means of choice for many black abolitionists.

Garnet also had an impact on white abolitionists. Increasingly, as a result of the events of the 1840s and the 1850s, such as the admission of Texas to the Union, the Mexican War, and the Dred Scott Decision, more whites began to see the inevitability of physical force to destroy the peculiar institution. After 1858, radical Republicans began to fear the spread of slavery into nominally free states.[66] Standing almost alone in 1843, Garnet was thoroughly repudiated for his *Address*, particularly by the Garrisonian press. Both *The Liberator* and *Herald of Freedom* ran the same editorial condemnation signed by Maria W. Chapman:

> We say emphatically to the man of color, trust not the counsels that lead you to the shedding of blood. That man knows nothing of nature, human or Divine,—of character—good or evil, who imagines that a civil and servile war would ultimately promote freedom.

> Does he [Garnet] find that gospel in harmony with his address? Does he find his Divine Master counselling "war to the knife, and the hilt," when *He* addressed the weary and the heavy laden of the earth?[67]

This editorial evoked from Garnet his frequently cited denunciation of the Garrisonians:

> My crime is that I have dared to think, and act, contrary to your [Mrs. Chapman's] opinion. I am a Liberty Party man—you are opposed to that party—far be it from me to attempt to injure your character because you cannot pronounce my shibboleth. While you must think as you do, we must differ. If it has come to this, that I must think and act as you do, because you are an abolitionist or be exterminated by your thunder, that I do not hesitate to say that your abolitionism is abject slavery.[68]

Further in the letter he told her:

> But the address to the slaves you seem to doom to the most
> fiery trials. And yet, madam, you have not seen that address—
> you have merely *heard* [author's italics] of it. You say that I
> "have received bad counsel." You are not the only person who
> had told your humble servant that his humble productions
> have been produced by the *"counsel"* [author's italics] of
> some Anglo-Saxon. I have expected no more from ignorant
> slave-holders and their apologists, but I really expected better
> things from Mrs. Maria W. Chapman, an anti-slavery poetess,
> and editor *pro tem* [author's italics] of the Boston *Liberator*.

> In the meantime, be assured that there is one black American
> who dares speak boldly on the subject of universal liberty.[69]

While Garnet was condemned by white and black Garrisonians for
his stands on violence and political abolition, he found a warm reception among some white radicals. John Brown's contempt for slaveholders was nearly as great as Garnet's It would be difficult to estimate the
extent of Garnet's influence on Brown, who had published Garnet's
Address at his own expense.[70] "But the fact is," writes Stephen Oates,
"Brown was growing increasingly militant in his own denunciation of
slavery, and the passage in 'Sambo's Mistakes,' urging slaves to resist
their white oppressors sounds almost exactly like something Garnet
would say." Moreover, Oates continues, Brown was soon to quote
Hebrews 9, that "almost all things are by the law purged with blood;
and without the shedding of blood is no remission."[71]

When Brown was addressing his band of Gileadites, he sounded "emphatically like Garnet" in telling Negroes how to resist the "brutal
aggressions of Southern Slaveholders."[72] In retrospect, some of the
advice black militants gave Brown proved inaccurate. Oates states that
"Evidently his [Brown's] discussions with Negroes like Garnet and
Douglass—and his study of *The Liberator* and other abolitionist publications had convinced him that slaves all over the South were seething
with hatred for their white masters and were on the verge of mutiny."[73]
In the 1850s Brown had expected Garnet, Douglass, William Still, and

others to raise money and Negro recruits for the "coming revolution."[74]

It is also difficult to assess the effect of Brown's violence on the crusade against slavery. The massacres in the West and the Harper's Ferry episode were merely events in a chain leading to the election of Lincoln and to the secession of the Southern states from the Union. Although Mrs. Chapman and the Garrisonians had condemned violence, the Emancipation Proclamation was clearly a result of battlefield activities during the Civil War and Lincoln's fear of intervention by the British on the side of the South.[75] The extent to which the war liberated the slave is, of course, another important question, which goes beyond the scope of this study. It may be stated safely, however, that while Garnet's personal influence may have declined as that of Douglass increased throughout the later 1840s and 1850s, Garnet's impact on both Negroes and white radicals continued to be widely felt.

Upon the conclusion of the Negro national convention of 1843, Garnet led a state convention of Negroes assembled in Rochester. This group unofficially aligned itself with the Liberty party. However, Garnet did not make the minutes of this meeting available to the other Negro leaders of the New York City area until the state convention of the following year. When New Yorkers found out about this manipulation, they took steps to counteract the impression that the Rochester stand was representative of all blacks in the state.[76] In his defense, it may be stated that, like his opponents, Garnet was mortal and was capable of manipulation to get his programs officially sanctioned.

The Buffalo convention of the National Liberty party was held immediately following the two Negro meetings in August 1843. It adopted twenty-one resolutions, most of which condemned slavery and its effects both directly and indirectly.[77] When taken together, these resolutions provided an ideology of abolition within the framework of the Constitution and through the utilization of the political process. When the convention began, Garnet told the audience that both the national and state conventions had endorsed the Liberty party principles. He said further that only two opposing votes—by Douglass and Remond from Massachusetts—were cast.[78] Because of that false statement, William Wells Brown justly rebuked him.

As a member of the nominating committee, Garnet exerted considerable influence. He addressed the convention during the afternoon session of 29 August in favor of Resolution Three which was adopted. It read:

That the Liberty Party has not been organized for any temporary
purpose, by interested politicians, but has arisen from among the
people, in consequence of a conviction, hourly gaining ground,
that no other party in the country represents the true principles
of American Liberty or the true spirit of the Constitution
of the United States.[79]

This resolution represented an effort to bring harmony to the meeting
and to attract dissatisfied Garrisonians to their cause. The fact that the
party was small did not seem to bother most Liberty enthusiasts because the majority were ministers like Garnet who adhered to principle,
even though it might mean sacrifice of success in the elections.[80] Although the complete text of Garnet's remarks has been lost, a brief
description appeared in *The Emancipator and Free American* and in the
Cincinnati Daily Chronicle. Even the *New York Daily Tribune*, which in
1843 was politically Democratic, found Garnet one of the ablest speakers that its correspondent had "ever listened to."[81] Garnet, as usual, was
in his best oratorical form. Generally, his speeches were given effusive
praise in the press. One reporter marveled that he had never heard
Garnet make a bad speech. Reprinted here is one account of Garnet's
Liberty party speech written by a white correspondent for the *Daily
Chronicle*. The passage is instructive not only in the description of
Garnet, but also in illustrating his effect on the writer:

His skin is jet black, indicating an unmixed African descent,
but his head nearly approaches the caucasion formation, being
one of the finest, we ever saw on a negro. He is one of nature's
own noblemen, and his speech was infinitely the best both in
manner and matter that was made during the afternoon
session, and showed us conclusively, that some of the negro
race, if not all, in intellectual power are by nature fully
equal to whites.

To see him stand up in all the native dignity of manhood,
and listen to his thrilling eloquence, as he recounted the
wrongs of his race, was enough to awaken in every right
thinking mind, an indignant adhorrence of a system that
would hold him, or such as him in slavery. His remarks were
clad in beautiful language relieved by genuine sparkling wit,

or burning with fiery and indignant eloquence. His handling
of the famous line of Terrance,

    "Homo sum, et nihil humani a me alienum puto,"
at the close of his remarks, was very fine, and given with
thrilling effect, not impaired from the apparent unconscious-
ness that the sentiment was uttered eighteen hundred years
ago. "I am a man," said he, "and nothing which concerns
humanity is uninteresting to me."[82]

Such a performance, if it could not completely erase prejudice
among whites, could gain unqualified commitments to abolition. The
reporter for *The Emancipator* was even more sophisticated in his
praise of Garnet's powers. He commented:

The Rev. Mr. Garnet of Troy, a colored man of the darkest
hue, also advocated the sentiments contained in the resolutions, particularly the third. He too, had had experimental
knowledge, and had felt in his own person the crushing weight
of prejudice, and could vividly portray its blasting and withering influence. Mr. Garnet, is one of the few instances in which
resolute and manly independence and perseverence, has over-
come these obstacles, and despite their opposition, he appeared
before the convention, an elegant and eloquent speaker; successfully awakening those feelings of sympathy and philanthropy,
which are almost universally inherent in the human heart, but
which education and interest have in so many cases, well-nigh-
smothered.— Yet not for himself did he strive to awaken the
sympathies of his hearers, he gloried in the impress his maker
had put upon him, but feeling deeply for his race, who are still
in bondage, he would bring all moral and political influences
to bear upon slavery for its extinction. A large number of
colored persons were present. The principle part of the evening
was occupied by Mr. Garnet, much to the gratification of a
large audience, who, we presume from their appearance, were
seldom more highly entertained, and whose opposition to the
unjust demands and encroachments of slavery upon the nominally free, will henceforth be increased, and by whom new
resolves were made to resist more resolutely, watch more carefully this national curse; and to extinguish it, use of all proper
means.[83]

During the rest of 1843, Garnet lectured extensively throughout New York State in behalf of the Liberty party. It was not until December that he took time out to answer Mrs. Chapman. While it is true that his personal influence within the Negro national movement declined as a result of his *Address*, his political activities, his suffrage leadership in New York State, and his aid in rescuing slaves continued unabated. During the last week of December, he delivered an address at a convention held in Great Barrington, Massachusetts, on behalf of the slaves. The focus of his remarks was the endorsement of the Liberty party, which to him was the only viable alternative to slave insurrection—a situation that he felt would surely come, if political solutions failed. Thus, he considered the party the only hope of the slave short of violence.

Garnet's tactics may be summarized as follows: the key to full citizenship for free Negroes lay in achieving the suffrage in the nominally free states. Once the suffrage was won, the rest would follow. In order to gain the suffrage, petition and propaganda were viable approaches. However, for emancipation, the petition and other conventional methods were inadequate because of the Prigg Case, the expulsion of an antislavery congressman, and the likelihood of the admission of Texas. After all, the expulsion of Joshua Giddings from the House of Representatives in 1842 for suggesting that slavery was a local institution with which the federal government could not have a connection was a discouraging development for political abolitionists. So too would be the admission of Texas as a slave state, for the government would appear to be actually expanding the power of slaveholders.

Garnet probably believed that the official channels at the federal level simply were blocked. Therefore, outside approaches were necessary: namely, the continuing growth of third party pressure and the call of resistance in any "way that promised success" on the part of the slave. While maintaining these beliefs, Garnet continued his search for still other means toward abolition and self-realization for blacks in the later 1840s.

NOTES

1. In the well-known anthologies of Herbert Aptheker, Leslie Fishel, and Benjamin Quarles, Garnet seems to "pop out" as the voice of physical resistance to slavery. In the documentary type of history, distortion is commonplace. In

Ernest J. Miller, "The Anti-Slavery Role of Henry Highland Garnet" (Master's thesis, Union Theological Seminary, 1969), there is the assumption that Garnet's *Address* constituted his great contribution. The same supposition is also found in the recently published work of Earl Ofari, *"Let Your Motto Be Resistance": The Life and Thought of Henry Highland Garnet* (Boston: Beacon Press, 1972), p. x. Ofari's work, though weak in background data, contains an appendix of documents on Garnet which will be helpful to Garnet scholars. In his view of Garnet as a contributor to the onward movement of Negro Americans toward liberation, I agree wholeheartedly.

    2. Smith, *A Memorial Discourse*, p. 33, and in Crummell, *Africa and America* (Springfield, Mass.: Wiley and Co., 1891).

    3. Quarles, *Black Abolitionists*, p. 172. See chapter 4, pp. 68-77, of the present work, for additional discussion of the suffrage fight.

    4. Ibid., pp. 173-174.

    5. *National Anti-Slavery Standard*, 3 June 1841, p. 207; see also Quarles, p. 183.

    6. Howard H. Bell, *The Negro Convention Movement, 1830-1861* (New York: Arno Press, 1969), p. 66.

    7. *Minutes of the 1840 Convention*, p. 18.

    8. Bell, pp. 65-66.

    9. Ibid., p. 65. In *The Colored American*, 13 March 1841, p. 1, appears a full statement by Garnet of the arguments he presented.

    10. Bell, p. 69.

    11. Ibid., pp. 71-72.

    12. *Minutes of the National Convention of Colored Citizens* (New York: Piercy and Reed, 1843).

    13. Ibid., p. 16.

    14. Ibid.

    15. Ibid., p. 22.

    16. Quarles, *Frederick Douglass* (New York: Atheneum, 1970), p. 145.

    17. Quarles, *Black Abolitionists*, pp. 168-169.

    18. Farrison, *William Wells Brown*, p. 79; for Garent's erroneous statement, see *The Emancipator*, 7 September 1843, p. 74.

    19. Herbert Aptheker, *One Continual Cry* (New York: Humanities Press, 1965), pp. 27-28. Ernest J. Miller provides a discussion as to the origin of the idea in his thesis. It is largely based on Aptheker's research, pp. 65-66.

    20. Aptheker, "Militant Abolitionism," *Journal of Negro History* 26 (October 1941): 444.

    21. Ibid., p. 445.

    22. Aptheker, *A Documentary History From Colonial Times Through the Civil War*, p. 90.

    23. Litwack, *North of Slavery*, p. 234; Aptheker, *A Documentary History*, 1, p. 90.

    24. Loren Katz (ed.), *Walker's Appeal and an Address to the Slaves of the United States of America*, pp. 23-39.

    25. Aptheker, *One Continual Cry*, p. 58.

26. Ibid., pp. 50-51; Garrison cited by author.

27. Quarles, *Black Abolitionists*, pp. 224-225.

28. *The Emancipator and Free American*, 3 March 1842, p. 207.

29. Aptheker, *One Continual Cry*, p. 39.

30. *The Emancipator and Free American*, 3 March 1842, p. 207.

31. Katz, p. 96.

32. Eric Foner, *Free Soil, Free Labor, Free Man: The Ideology of the Republican Party Before the Civil War* (New York: Oxford University Press, 1970), p. 82. Garnet's fears of slavery being extended into Texas may also have been a contributory reason. He alluded to the Texas question briefly in the 1843 *Address*; see Katz, p. 95.

33. Katz, p. 39.

34. Ibid., p. 29.

35. Ibid., pp. 23, 30.

36. Ibid., pp. 23, 25. Walker said that whoever accepted slavery "ought to be kept with all of his children or family in chains, to be butchered by his *cruel enemies*" [author's italics].

37. Ibid., p. 92.

38. Ibid.

39. Ibid., p. 93.

40. Ibid.

41. Ibid.

42. Ibid.

43. Ibid., p. 96.

44. Carleton Mabee, *Black Freedom: The Non-Violent Abolitionists from 1830 Through the Civil War* (New York: The Macmillan Co., 1970), p. 60.

45. Quarles, *Black Abolitionists*, mentions Garnet's involvement in the underground railroad, p. 149; *The Emancipator and Free American*, 3 March 1842, has an account in which Garnet told the audience of slave awareness of events outside the South, p. 207.

46. *Minutes of the National Convention of Colored Citizens* pp. 12-13.

47. Ibid., p. 18.

48. Ibid., pp. 18-19.

49. *The Liberator*, 8 September 1843.

50. Quarles, *Black Abolitionists*, pp. 224-225.

51. Farrison, *William Wells Brown*, pp. 286-287.

52. Quarles, *Frederick Douglass*. pp. 115-116; also *Black Abolitionists*, pp. 227-228; Mabee, p. 294.

53. Quarles, *Black Abolitionists*, pp. 227-228, 238.

54. *Minutes of the National Convention of Colored Citizens*, pp. 23-24.

55. Quarles, *Black Abolitionists*, pp. 227-228; *Minutes of the Ohio State Convention* (Columbus, Ohio: n.p., 1849), p. 18.

56. *Minutes of the National Convention of Colored Citizens*, pp. 27-28.

57. Ibid., p. 28.

58. *Minutes of the National Convention of Colored Citizens*, pp. 25, 29.

59. Woodson, *DAB*, pp. 154-155.

60. Far greater coverage of Garnet's activities in the Free Produce movement is provided by the ephemeral *Impartial Citizen*. My suspicion is that Douglass feared Garnet would gain in prestige at his expense; also, Douglass believed black abolitionists could serve best by staying at home. I discuss this point in Chapter 5 below.

61. *The Impartial Citizen* was edited by Samuel Ringgold Ward who shared Garnet's radical views. The paper was printed in Canada and elsewhere, and only sporadic issues remain in existence.

62. Woodson, *DAB*, pp. 154-155.

63. Charles Wesley, "Negroes in Anti-Slavery Political Parties," *Journal of Negro History* 29 (January 1944): 44.

64. Mabee, p. 62.

65. The black New Yorkers were consistently in the vanguard of black abolition. For discussion of political abolition, see Chapters 2 and 4; for discussion of emigration, see Chapters 8 and 9 below.

66. Foner, p. 101.

67. *Herald of Freedom*, 29 September 1843, p. 125, and *The Liberator*, 22 September 1843.

68. *The Liberator*, 3 December 1843; letter reprinted in Carter G. Woodson, *The Mind of the Negro as Reflected in Letters Written During the Crisis 1800-1860* (Washington, D.C.: Association for the Study of Negro Life and History, 1926), pp. 194-195.

69. Ibid.

70. Stephen Oates, *To Purge This Land with Blood: A Biography of John Brown* (New York: Harper & Row, 1970), p. 61; also Quarles, *Black Abolitionists*, p. 238; and Woodson, *Negro Orators and Their Orations* (Reprint; New York: Russell & Russell, 1969), p. 150.

71. Oates, p. 61.

72. Ibid., p. 74.

73. Ibid., pp. 211-212.

74. Ibid., p. 241. In two recent works, Quarles provides information which suggests that Garnet advised Brown to delay in carrying out his raid at Harper's Ferry, because Garnet did not think the timing was correct. See *Allies for Freedom: Blacks and John Brown* (New York: Oxford University Press, 1974), p. 76; *Blacks on John Brown* (Urbana: University of Illinois Press, 1972), 29-30.

75. John Hope Franklin, *From Slavery to Freedom*, p. 280-284.

76. Bell, pp. 82-83.

77. Thomas V. Cooper, *American Politics* (Philadelphia: Fireside Publishing Co., 1882), Book II, *Political Platforms*, pp. 26-27.

78. *The Emancipator and Free American*, 7 September 1843, p. 74.

79. Ibid., p. 79.

80. Foner, p. 78.

81. *New York Daily Tribune*, 4 September 1843, p. 1.

82. *Cincinnati Daily Chronicle*, 7 September 1843, p. 2.

83. *The Emancipator and Free American*, 11 January 1844, p. 148.

84. Ibid.

4

Political Activism:
Second Phase

The years 1844 through 1848 witnessed the decline of Garnet's personal influence on a national level but a greater acceptance of his antislavery tactics. In the conventions of black New Yorkers which met throughout the mid-1840s, his views emerged triumphant. During this period, the Liberty party claimed an increasing number of black supporters. Then, in 1848, blacks began to shift toward the Free Soilers.[1] During this period, Garnet was also involved in the development of a newspaper which came to speak for the black community.

Early in January 1844, Garnet began to pressure the state legislature to eliminate voter discrimination. He addressed the assembly in a four-hour speech. Like so many of his documents, it has been lost, having been excluded from the *Legislative Journal* altogether. The *Legislative Journal* refers only to the several petitions which subsequently flowed into the legislature, were read, and then referred to the appropriate committee. By 1844, the petition campaign was creating considerable opposition from whites, as evidenced by a number of remonstrances sent to the legislature opposing the aim of the Negro petitioners.[2] Ignoring his opposition, Garnet pursued the franchise. He also spoke in behalf of the goals of the Liberty party in February at the convention of the Massachusetts State Liberty party in Boston. This speech also was probably never recorded. In it, Garnet admonished the convention that "if the hope which the Liberty Party held out for speedy and peaceful emancipation of the slaves was taken away, bloody revolution would inevitably

follow." At the same gathering, the Prigg decision was officially condemned as proslavery and as a denial of the fugitives' civil liberties.
Special concern was voiced over the slaves' right of habeas corpus.[3]

The Schenectady meeting of colored citizens in September 1844 was
largely a Garnet show. As chairman of the Central Committee, his name
appeared first on the call. Most of the convention delegates came from
areas other than New York City, where opposition to his position was
coalescing.[4] During the first day, Garnet was one of five members
appointed to the Business Committee.[5] That evening, the first trial of
strength occurred over the presentation of a petition from Negroes of
the Empire City who opposed the decision of the previous state convention to support the Liberty party.[6]

Led by James McCune Smith, the faction from New York City
wanted its protest received by the convention and inserted into the
minutes, so that there would be no question as to its opposition to the
Liberty party. Garnet rose in protest. After hearing the ensuing debate
in the afternoon and evening sessions between the two factions, the
convention sustained Garnet, 39 to 11. The New Yorkers, badly beaten,
promptly resigned those offices which they held at the convention.[7]
The Business Committee then offered the following resolution on the
suffrage, which met with unanimity:

> Resolved, that as the equal privilege of voting would, if rightly
> exercised, insure to our people an additional measure of protec-
> tion and respectability, and would open to us means and incen-
> tives to improvement now wholly lost to us, therefore, it is both
> our interest and duty to do our utmost to secure this privilege.[8]

With or without the leaders from New York City, Garnet proceeded
along his way.

The following morning, a series of resolutions implementing the suffrage resolve was passed. Among the resolutions was one for the circulation of petitions by committees appointed for that purpose. It was
also decided to publish the minutes of the convention in pamphlet form
and to hear reports describing the conditions of Negroes in the various
districts represented by delegates.[9]

In the afternoon session, Garnet's opponents inserted their reasons
for resigning from the convention. In refusing to record their protest,
the convention was denying them the right of petition. Further, the

precedent was established by which one convention should not inter-
fere with the work of another. Finally, the commitment of the colored
citizens of New York State to one of three political parties by the decision of the previous Rochester convention would be prejudicial to
their appeal for the franchise, which, in their view, had to be made to
the people as a whole.[10]

Garnet denied the protest for several reasons: the protest was presented on narrow grounds and was calculated to do no good; the convention wished to meet the sentiments of the protest in the form of a
resolution, but the minority behind the protest refused, the sentiments
of the protest were wrong inasmuch as it taught the "fearless, and
patriotic citizens of New York to stand before the world utterly destitute of any political opinion"; and finally, the Garnet faction did not
"crave the enjoyment of the right of suffrage from the hands of any
set of men who would deny us the Republican right, of thinking as we
please."[11]

Ironically, many of the upstate Negroes living outside of New York
City were already meeting the $250 qualification for voting and were
exercising this right. They had far less to gain in advocating the unrestricted franchise for all citizens. On the other hand, they had less to
lose if affiliation with the Liberty party by the convention should prevent the gaining of the vote throughout the state. That is why Smith
and other prominent New Yorkers were justifiably cautious and why
they repudiated affiliation with the Liberty party.

After these protests were lodged and answered, Garnet submitted to
the convention the Business Committee's *Report* on the best means of
promoting the enfranchisement in the state. No single class of means
would suffice, the report stated. Four proposals were set forth:

1. A general diffusion of Literary, Scientific and Religious
    knowledge among the people. This can be done, as it has
    already been done in some places, by the establishment
    of Public Libraries, Lyceums, and Public Lectures.

2. By careful education of our youth, and holding out to
    them additional encouragement, in proportion to the extra
    difficulties which they have to encounter.

3. By giving our children useful trades, and by patronizing those who may have engaged in useful handicraft.

4. The Committee would urge as first in importance the removal of our people from the cities to the country. Prejudice is so strong in cities, and custom is so set and determined, that it is impossible for us to emerge from the most laborious and the least profitable occupations.[12]

The rest of the *Report* elaborated on the fourth point. In the rural areas, there were no licensing arrangements and other regulations which restricted Negroes. As evidence of opportunity in the countryside, it was stated that more blacks possessed the franchise there than in the city. The countryside offered greater possibilities of property ownership and hard, honorable agricultural labor, which in turn would yield the greatest, quickest amount of personal happiness and uplift. While prejudice existed throughout the city and country, it was less in evidence in the country and by diligent labor could ultimately be defeated.[13]

Other resolutions that were passed proclaimed the example of West Indian emancipation as proof that such a policy was efficacious and that prejudice had no basis in fact. As mentioned before, the machinery for the petition campaign was put into operation. No resolves specifically mentioned the Liberty party, yet omission meant continued endorsement.[14] Garnet could claim the victory, yet by so doing, he divided the leadership from New York City.

Charles B. Ray, in a letter to the convention, urged the body to support the Liberty party in no uncertain terms. On the other hand, Garnet's fatherly teacher, Theodore S. Wright, disagreed. Previously, he had deserted Garnet over publication of the *Address to the Slaves* during the Buffalo meeting. On this occasion, Wright disagreed not as to ends but as to means chosen by the convention. He explained:

My confidence is in the principles upon which the Liberty Party is based.—I believe they are just. But were it my happiness to be a member of the Convention I would not be anxious for its formal identification with this party. I should not advocate it, unless an issue between this and one of the other parties were forced upon me, or some action was proposed to the dis-

paragement of the Liberty Party. I would then feel religiously
called upon to stand by liberty principles.[15]

This defection was to prove permanent. When the national convention
met again in 1847, the opposition, now composed of some leaders
from New York City and some older Garrisonians, turned away from
Garnet's personal leadership in favor of the more moderate Frederick
Douglass. The Philadelphia leadership, staunch Garrisonians, would
continue as before to boycott national meetings.[16] It would still have
been relatively easy for the moderates within the national leadership to
outvote Garnet. However, Negroes in Ohio and whites within and outside of abolitionist circles would begin seriously to entertain more
violent solutions to the slavery question.

After Schenectady, little is known of Garnet's activities until the
following July. During this interval, he probably continued in his welfare work as it related to his Troy congregation and worked on the
suffrage campaign throughout the state. On 4 July 1845, the one recorded occasion on which he broke his vow never to speak, Garnet
addressed an immense crowd in the city of Homer, New York. His performance on that day was given the highest praise in *The Emancipator
and Free American*:

> We wish all our fellow citizens, of whatever sect in religion, or
> party in politics, who have been self-abused by cherishing a
> prejudice against African character and endowment, could have
> listened to the "off-hand" oration of Mr. Garnet on Friday last.
> Those prejudices would have been dissipated, and if they had
> correct hearts, they might feel honored in taking his coal-black
> hand and calling him—BROTHER.

> If this compliment should meet his eye, his delicacy must sub-
> mit to our sense of duty and justice, in offering his feeble
> acknowledgement of sense of his high deserts. He is one of the
> brilliant stars of the 19th century, and scarcely surpassed if
> equalled by the most glorious lights of the age. Well might our
> excellent ex-governor Seward say, as a friend at our hand
> informs us, "I never listened to eloquence until I heard
> Henry H. Garnet."[17]

Garnet's informal address, as it was called, was entitled "The Wrongs of Africa." It began with humanistic references from the Bible and asserted that the Declaration of Independence was an outgrowth of biblical principles. In the second paragraph, Garnet marshaled forth his knowledge of contemporary history and pointed with personal pride to the successes of the American Revolution. Having evoked emotions of pride, patriotism, and hopeful expectation in his audience, Garnet then entreated them to examine American slavery:

There are at this moment three millions of slaves in the United States. Merciful God, what a vast number is this! Our proud New England does not contain more inhabitants. Besides this number in actual slavery, there are more than half a million free people of color in the nonslaveholding states who have been proscribed by law or abused by prejudice. Thus the government has placed its feet upon the neck of three and a half millions of Africo-Americans. Where there has been one tear shed in consequence of the oppressions of our mother country, or the perils of the revolution, there have been a thousand shed on account of the bitterness of that slavery which you tolerate. And for every drop of blood poured out in defense of American liberty, you can be pointed to streams drawn from the lacerated bodies of the descendants of Africa.[18]

Garnet then named the wrongs which he identified as having derived from some hundred and twenty-five years of enslavement:

In consequence of this condition, a mighty overwhelming current of prejudice has set against us.

My brethren, many of whom are members of the church of Christ, are sold like beasts in the shambles, and every tie of relationship is ruthlessly torn asunder.

Sons have been compelled to behold the mothers who bore them, withering beneath the lash; aye and more, they have sometimes been forced to apply the scourge on the labor-broken frames of their aged parents. Our sisters, daughters, and wives have been

driven into prostitution, and concubinage, and their unhappy
offspring have been sold by unfeeling fathers, and in order to
prevent these children from pleading the privileges of their Anglo-
Saxon blood, the American slave law declares that the child shall
follow the condition of its mother! [19]

Without becoming specific, he turned his guns on religious practices,
proslavery intellectuals, and finally the government as perpetuators of
oppression:

> The Holy Bible is a sealed book to all the enslaved with few ex-
> ceptions. Hence they are the most unfortunate of all heathens.
> They sit in darkness while light surrounds them. They die of
> thirst while streams of salvation are flowing through the land.

> In some parts of the country the most systematic efforts have
> been made to keep us in intellectual darkness; and the reason
> urged in favor of course is, that knowledge would reveal our
> condition to us more plainly, and would therefore make us
> discontented.

> Slaveholders and their apologists, say that we are ignorant and
> unprepared for freedom, and still they punish with imprison-
> ment and death every attempt to prepare!

> Our children that are born from day to day, and who might have
> as fair opportunity as any others to fill the most useful spheres
> in life, are thrown into the same ocean of degradation in which
> their father's rights have been engulfed.

> . . .

> All these iniquities are sanctioned by many of the professing
> Christians, and by many of the ministers in the land.

> The government of the country is likewise against us, and the
> degradation of this class of American citizens is considered by
> our national lawmakers to be an object of their highest
> ambition. [20]

After expounding on the theme of religious hypocrisy, intellectual dishonesty, and governmental opposition to the yearnings of the blacks for liberation, Garnet concluded with a list of complaints.

We complain that members of the church and ministers thereof, many of whom are slaveholders, and dealers, and slavebreeders—are held in fellowship by the nonslaveholding portion of the church, notwithstanding it is generally acknowledged that their deeds are evil.

We complain that this connection with sin hinders the growth of pure and undefiled religion, and exposes the church to the ridicule of infidels.

We complain that those who sit in Moses' seat do not rebuke this sin in the spirit of Jesus Christ—but rather cry Peace, Peace, where there is no peace.

We complain that the course of a large portion of the church furnished the state with an excuse for the wrongs which it inflicts upon us.

We complain that we are subjected to all these misfortunes and oppressions, without any crime whatever. Yes, we are hated without a cause!

In the name of humanity—for the sake of justice—in view of an approaching judgment—and in the name of an eternal God, we demand redress for these wrongs.[21]

This is an accurate summation of Garnet's antislavery views. He made use of various means for promoting liberation. Demanding social justice on public occasions was one way; another was the continuation of pressure on the New York legislature for equal voting rights.

After Schenectady, another state meeting on the suffrage was held the following year in Syracuse. Garnet personally presented the resolutions on suffrage and related topics to that convention. These resolutions included the following familiar premises: equality in voting was

the cornerstone of democratic government; the extension of the vote
to one group and its denial to another was a repudiation of basic democratic principles; and the exemption of Negroes from military service
provided no justification for disfranchisement, particularly since
Negroes never had chosen to be excluded from military service.[22]

Garnet felt that the $250 property qualification for Negroes drew
them into a caste system which on the one hand separated whites and
blacks and on the other, Negroes who had property and those who had
none. These divisions had persisted for twenty-five years. During that
time, public opinion had shifted so that individuals who currently
favored equality in suffrage were at last considered respectable. Finally,
in the event of a state constitutional convention, the convention should
support delegates who favored equal suffrage.[23]

As a copy of the Syracuse minutes is not extant, no further detail
of Garnet's activities at the meeting is possible. It is known that Garnet
offered resolutions providing for agents to be placed in the field in
critical areas in the event of a state constitutional convention. While
the meeting received favorable coverage in the local press, opponents
of Negro rights interpreted remarks made on the convention floor to be
unfriendly criticism. Much was made of the possibility that fifteen
thousand Negroes, if enfranchised, would then hold the balance of
power between the two major parties in the state.[24]

Such a possibility was based on reported contemporary press
accounts and commentary on the convention. *The National Anti-
Slavery Standard* contained some citations on this event from other
newspapers. An article in the *New York Globe* expressed concern that
Negro voting rights would encourage blacks from other states to move
to New York and thereby create economic conflict with whites over employment. Therefore, the writer for the *Globe* felt that enfranchisement
must be defeated; if not, New York would be thrown open to abolitionists who would encourage violence. The writer went so far as to assert
that by 1848 a Negro candidate would be running for the presidency of
the United States.[25] The *Eastern State Journal* of White Plains contained an article favoring the removal of all suffrage privileges from
Negroes because of their alleged inferiority.[26] From the *Morning News*
of New York City came the same bitter attacks, while the *New York
Tribune*, increasingly abolitionist in tone, came to the support of equal
suffrage.[27]

When it became apparent that a state constitutional convention would indeed be held, the Colored State Central Committee met and put into operation its state machinery which had already been assembled at Syracuse. Adopting a position favored by metropolitan Negroes, an appeal was presented to the entire electorate, regardless of party.[28] These efforts were to prove fruitless; New Yorkers refused to remove the Negro property qualification.

The franchise setback in his home state, the martyrdom of Charles Torrey (a New England political abolitionist who died in prison charged with aiding fugitives[29]), and the annexation of Texas followed by the Mexican War gave rise to heightened militancy and to a greater receptiveness of measures which Garnet had advocated several years before. This was to be reflected to a significant degree in the Negro national convention of 1847.

In the latter part of 1845, Garnet traveled to New England on behalf of temperance and abolition; some of his observations and activities during this trip were printed in *The Emancipator and Free American*. He was struck by the need for an agent to travel among Negroes generally, especially to encourage them to remain strong in the face of their difficult trials. He blamed religious institutions generally for keeping the Negro in a disorganized and segregated condition.

> In my visits to many of my brethren, I have found some of the best materials for good purposes scattered and dispersed. I have beheld them perishing by the wayside, and famishing for the waters of life under the very eaves of the sanctuary. The manner in which they are treated in many places by the prejudice which is tolerated by the church, drives them out from all public worship, and a most fruitful source of infidelity is opened. With a heart deeply affected I tell the American church wherever it tolerates caste—that it is doing more than all other things to drive the colored people into downright infidelity.[30]

Early in November Garnet spoke at least twice in Providence, Rhode Island. In these addresses, he expressed his anger that among the many churches of that city only three in which whites worshiped did not maintain the most rigid forms of caste. He noted that while three schools were maintained for black children, there was no high school.

Although one-third of the students at Prudence Crandall Philo's Academy were Negro, Brown University would receive no black students.[31]

In New London, Connecticut, which Garnet also visited at this time, he observed that, with the exception of the Roman Catholic church, every church in the city tolerated segregation of the worst kind.[32] The abolitionists and their co-workers with whom he associated in New England probably offered little help in easing Garnet's bitterness over the caste pattern which the religious institutions perpetuated.

A year and a half later, at the anniversary meeting of the American and Foreign Anti-Slavery Society held on 11 May 1847 in New York City, he told the assembly that every tear shed by the slave would be most fearfully avenged thereafter. Rather than an American civil war, he was referring to rising of blacks throughout the world. Speaking in metaphor, he proclaimed:

> The children of Africa scattered as they were all over the world, unnationed, appealed to America for redress—that America whose sails whiten every sea, and whose diplomatic parchment is lying in every court. Oh! that that proud America would cast her eye towards downtrod Africa, whose bony hand was outstretched, in tears and agony, imploring comfort in affliction.
>
> Bleeding Africa holds up her hand in imploring anguish, and cries to the world: Give me my children, and my rights! Nothing now could impede the progress of abolition; it has advanced too far, and "young Africa" is in the field, and he may be seen here today emerging from the dim clouds that so long have involved him in darkness and gloom. In one hand he holds the charter of his rights, and with the other grasps the brightest stars in the constellation of Liberty.[33]

Through these words Garnet revealed worldly concern for blacks that transcended national boundaries. Although Garnet's concern for blacks was vividly expressed in the above passage, along with his attitude toward violence, there is some earlier evidence of such sentiments. Late in 1846, for example, the Liberty Street Presbyterian Church elders passed the following resolution: "That inasmuch as our Pastor has determined to visit the island of Jamaica, W. I., that we concur in the measure and pray that God may prosper him in his journey."[34]

These pan-African feelings (the word *feelings* is used here because
there is no evidence of any carefully constructed program in Garnet's
writings) eventually crystallized into the African Civilization Society,
which will be discussed later. Perhaps the most significant aspect of his
remarks before the American and Foreign Anti-Slavery Society was his
understanding of the proslavery forces in the United States, an understanding which went beyond the indictment and the ideology of the
Liberty party. Again Garnet's language turned metaphorical, especially
in the use of the pronoun "he." His meaning was clear, however:

Here in the North, we hear a great deal said about Southern aggres-
sion, Southern ambition, and Southern ascendency in the government—Southern men we are told monopolize all the offices worth
claiming. He believed that the people in the Southern States, loved
honor and pride; and he wished he could say the same of the Yankees; the Southern man in Congress, says to his Northern brother;
"Make me a minister, make me a colonel, make me a great man,
and you may do as you please." Then Brother Johnathan comes
forward and says, "give me the money, and you may have the
power." He condemned the North for the puerile course it had
pursued on the question of slavery; it was more guilty than the
South, in the matter, because it was more enlightened in the
latter. We hear much said, too, of the horrors of war by these
same hypocrites. Who makes the very bullets that we are now
mowing down the poor Mexicans with?

These very prating Yankees; and who makes the cannon but those
same hypocrites who with their lips deprecate the war? They admit
that Slavery is wrong in the abstract, but when we ask them to
help us to overthrow it, they tell us it would make them beggars!
The work of freedom cannot go on till Northern hypocrisy first
gets out of the way, and allows the car of Liberty to roll on. Place
a bale of cotton or a barrel of sugar upon the confines of Pande-
monium, and these gentry would rush forward and seize it.
Patriotism or morality, with a Yankee, means *Money* [author's
italics] . Touch his pocket, and if that jingles, he is full of
patriotism.[35]

One month later, in October 1847, Garnet and other upstate New
Yorkers sponsored a call for another national meeting. Other promi-

nent Negroes—Douglass, Brown, Remond, and William C. Nell—also
signed the call, in hopes of winning the others to a moderate course.
Besides delegates from Massachusetts and New York, people from Connecticut, New Jersey, Michigan, Maine, and Vermont assembled in Troy
at Garnet's church.[36]

The great majority were from New York (46 of the 66 delegates),
and they were divided into two groups. One, the upstate faction, followed Garnet, and the other, the New York City faction, was led by
James McCune Smith. In addition to these two factions, there was the
New England group. Douglass forged an alliance of the New England
Garrisonians and the leaders from New York City, and that alliance
prevailed over Garnet's faction on crucial issues.

The issue on the agenda was the idea of a national press which had
been considered favorably in 1843. No serious opposition to the idea
developed, although William Wells Brown was dubious about its
financial survival.[37] The question of implementation was important
because three of the delegates had either published their own paper or
were about to do so: Garnet had coedited *The National Watchman*;
Thomas Van Rensselaer printed *The Ram's Horn*; and Frederick Douglass was about to bring out *The North Star*.[38] A proposal was made to
merge the *Watchman* and *Horn* into a national press. Douglass, fearing
that such a press would become the captive of a clique, opposed this
proposal and instead favored sustaining all three newspapers.[39] While
no specific paper was singled out for this role at the meeting, a resolution in favor of a national organ, which came from James McCune
Smith's *Report*, was decided in the affirmative 27 to 9. Garnet and
Smith had united forces on this issue. Garnet was elected home agent
for the new newspaper.[40]

On the second day of the meeting, the national convention focused
on Alexander Crummell's proposal for Negro institutions of higher
learning. This proposal, unlike the previous one, was not a critical issue
for the delegates; hence, Garnet and the Garrisonians aligned in opposition to the creation of an exclusive Negro college. Garnet's vote on this
measure was lost, as the convention decided to accept Crummell's *Report on Education* with the exclusive college provision included.

Infighting began when Douglass, as head of the committee to determine the "best means to Abolish Slavery and Caste in the United
States," read the committee report to the assembly. [41] Douglass pro-

duced a mild sensation by his grandiose condemnation of religion. He called upon the slaves to come out of their proslavery churches and stated that his right arm should wither if ever he worshiped in such company. At this point, the Garnet faction insisted on changing Douglass's phraseology slightly. Instead of "Religion sanctifying slavery," Garnet favored the phrase "religion, falsely so called;" also, he found the term "moral suasion" objectionable and favored adding the words "political action." In the first instance, Garnet, as a minister, felt that religion was being blamed excessively when represented as being entirely in favor of slavery. Therefore, he thought the phrase "falsely so called" would clarify the matter without doing injustice to Douglass's thought. Secondly, he took exception to reliance upon moral suasion as *the only means* of securing freedom for those enslaved. Political action, he pointed out, should also be included as a legitimate means. Garnet was successful in the early confrontation in having the *Report on the Best Means to Abolish Slavery and Caste* recommitted and modified in committee; it was adopted unanimously when reconsidered.[42]

The final *Report*, even with its modified condemnation of organized religion, was basically a moral suasionist document. It specifically condemned slave insurrection: "All argument put forth in favor of insurrection and bloodshed, however well intended, is either the result of unpardonable impatience or an atheistic want of faith in the power of truth as a means of regenerating and reforming the world."[43] Also, the two resolutions embodied in the *Report* called for the "unceasing assertion of our rights" and perpetual agitation until those rights were attained.[44] If anyone, the committee made up of Douglass, Crummell, John Lyle, and Van Rensselaer could claim the victory. Of the four, Douglass had contributed the most by initially heading the committee, by defending the *Report* before the convention, and in being reappointed as one of the members of the new committee.[45]

As in 1843 at Buffalo, Garnet repeated his *Address to the Slaves*, and while this time the audience listened with less trepidation, they refused to endorse it. An angrier mood pervaded in the 1847 meeting partly because in the intervening years public opinion had taken a more aggressive tone.[46] In addition, Douglass's encouragement of the use of education and propaganda had its influence in softening the "bite" of Garnet's message.[47] Nevertheless, the national convention did appoint a committee consisting of Garnet, Van Rensselaer, and Amos

G. Beman to draft an *Address to the Slaves*, and it passed a resolution advising Negroes to instruct their children in the art of warfare.[48] As mentioned earlier, the Ohio State convention of 1849 requested five hundred copies of the *Address*; John Brown is said to have printed the *Address* at his own expense.[49]

Garnet continued to support the earlier convention decision to encourage settlement of blacks in frontier areas. With the establishment of various communal experiments during the middle decades of the nineteenth century, the farm took on an exaggerated significance in the minds of many social reformers. Black leaders were generally optimistic about migration to the frontier, yet were aware of existing proscriptive laws in frontier states. For them, the decision of town versus countryside was probably a choice among evils. Opportunity would be greater, it was believed, on the frontier. They favored migration to upstate New York at this convention because Gerrit Smith had set aside homesteads for Negroes.[50]

During the Troy meeting, agriculture was viewed in the same favorable way, except for a new development. Gerrit Smith, the philanthropic and humanitarian Liberty party leader, had made land available in New York for Negroes for the asking. He placed 140,000 acres at the disposal of three thousand Negroes, and in so doing had for the first time made many of them eligible for the franchise.[51] This offer was enough to divert attention toward settlement of Smith's land. Although Garnet and other black leaders were to work hard in finding suitable recipients for the land, this project was not to become a great success.[52]

So far as the national press was concerned, Garnet's work bore positive results. He was in effect carrying out the original hopes of the Negro convention movement.[53] *Freedom's Journal* and its successor, *The Rights of All*, had attempted to play such a role in the late 1820s, and in the early 1830s *The Liberator* had assumed such a function. As Garrison moved toward other reforms and developed an ideology that divided abolitionists, Negroes once again sought an organ that would be exclusively theirs.[54]

From these efforts came *The Struggler* edited by Philip A. Bell, to be followed in January 1837 by *The Weekly Advocate*. After some reorganization, *The Weekly Advocate* became *The Colored American*, which for several years was the chief organ of the Negro people. After 1840, *The Colored American* became increasingly committed to political abolition, a move which left Negro leaders in Philadelphia and Massachusetts somewhat alienated. In 1840, Garnet published an ephemeral newspaper, *The Clarion*, "dedicated to aid the Negro in all aspects of his emancipation,"[55] ; no copies are in existence. In 1847, he published *The National Watchman* in Troy from which excerpts appeared in *The Emancipator* and other antislavery newspapers.[56]

At Troy in 1847, as at Buffalo in 1843, the subject of a press was discussed. James McCune Smith, backed by Garnet, led the way.[57] Opponents of the scheme, Douglass and Van Rensselaer, came in for some of Garnet's dry wit when he said of those men about to go into the newspaper business: "of course, there was nothing of selfishness in all this."[58] It may have been that Garnet was angling for an appointment as home agent for the same reason, a position to which he was elected.

When the final vote was taken, less than one-fourth of the voting members cast their ballots against the press. Sixteen of the twenty voting members cast their ballots against the press. Sixteen of the twenty voting New Yorkers voted in favor as did nine of the fourteen delegates from Massachusetts. Among those who did not vote were Douglass, Nathan Johnson, and William Wells Brown: Douglass was about to establish his own paper; Johnson was acting chairman; and Brown was a loyal Garrisonian.[59]

The new resolution recommended all of the existing black newspapers including the *Northern Star* (later *The North Star*), as worthy of community support. Also, the *Report of the Committee on a National Press* was adopted by the convention. It empowered a committee of eleven to begin raising funds and to appoint home agents to sell subscriptions and serve as correspondents. From that time forward, *The North Star* assumed the leadership of Negro publications. Its influence was to remain pervasive through most of the 1850s until challenged by *The Weekly Anglo-African* in 1859. Even then, in the eyes of whites and blacks Douglass remained the most renowned of his color.

Control of the press in some measure explains why Garnet's influence declined as Douglass's arose. Naturally, a personal and ideological rivalry arose between Douglass and Garnet. While it is not part of our purposes here, a case could be made against Douglass for excluding from his columns the antislavery activities of Garnet, the Crafts, and others who journeyed overseas in behalf of freedom in the 1850s.[60] By 1847, then, the powerful moral suasionists of the Douglass-Nell variety had triumphed over the militant, politically minded Garnet-Ray faction without alienating each other in the process, although the latter group had gained ground since 1843.

Garnet's exit from this country in 1849 is another reason why his influence in national convention circles declined during the early 1850s. (His impact in England and Jamaica was considerable and will be discussed in Chapter 6.) *The North Star* became the most important Negro newspaper during the 1850s until Douglass's nonemigration policy, in the face of greater repression and demands for emigration, gave way in importance to newer publications which were more willing than Douglass's to be governed by popular opinion.[61]

On the other hand, militancy persisted and grew more intense among Negroes after 1847. In that sense, Garnet was riding the crest of another new wave. The militancy which he advocated involved some risk, given the prevailing national sentiment against black abolitionists and particularly against pamphlets such as his. Rebuffed by the national convention, Garnet published his *Address* combined with Walker's *Appeal* a few months later. While the Ohio convention of 1849 refused to carry out its resolution to circulate five hundred copies of this publication, its militant attitude was unmistakeable. Then, too, five months later in a Boston speech, Douglass indicated that he had abandoned the pacific stance he had taken at the Buffalo meeting six years earlier. He told a packed audience in Faneuil Hall that he would welcome the news that the slaves had revolted and "that the sable arms which have been engaged in beautifying and adorning the South were engaged in spreading death and devastation there." His remarks produced something of a sensation, and he continued saying that a state of war existed in the South and that Americans should welcome a successful slave uprising in the same way as they had rejoiced when news of the overthrow of the French monarchy has arrived.[62]

Although the motion to form black military companies lost at Troy, it was a portent of increasing interest in that direction which culminated with the Negro troops marching off to battle under Union arms. Quarles traces in detail the course of this interest through local conventions, the formation of actual units, and the recruitment efforts of Douglass, Garnet, and others.[63] After 1847, then, the Douglass faction was compelled to give ground to the Garnet faction in order to maintain effective leadership among blacks.

NOTES

1. Quarles, *Black Abolitionists*, pp. 185-187.

2. *New York Assembly Journal*, 67th Session, 1844. Petitions in favor of the franchise appear on p. 1011 from Albany County, p. 328 from Duanesburgh, p. 333 from Troy; remonstrances against these petitions are listed on p. 359 from Erie County and on pp. 350-351 from Buffalo.

3. *The Emancipator and Free American*, 22 February, 1844, p. 168. No other reference to Garnet's remarks has been located.

4. *Minutes of the Fifth Annual Convention of the Colored People of the State of New York Held in the City of Schenectady, etc.* (Troy, N.Y.: J. C. Kneeland & Co., 1844), pp. 3-4, 8-9.

5. Ibid., p. 5.

6. Ibid., p. 10.

7. Ibid., pp. 10-11.

8. Ibid., p. 11.

9. Ibid., pp. 11-12.

10. Ibid., p. 13.

11. Ibid., p. 14. A clash also occurred over the presentation of the Schenectady minutes to the governor. The Smith faction held that the governor would act favorably upon them in his annual message. Garnet disagreed, stating that he had already seen those of Rochester and made up his mind accordingly. See *The National Anti-Slavery Standard*, 24 October 1844, pp. 81-82, and 17 October 1844, p. 79.

12. *Minutes of the Schenectady Convention*, p. 15.

13. Ibid., pp. 16-17.

14. Ibid., pp. 17-18.

15. Ibid., pp. 19-21. The quotation appears on p. 21.

16. Carleton Mabee, *Black Freedom*, p. 59.

17. *The Emancipator and Free American*, 6 August 1845, p. 60.

18. Ibid.

19. Ibid.

20. Ibid.

21. Ibid.

22. Ibid.

23. *The Republican*, 18 September 1845, p. 1, reprint of the original article which appeared first in the *Syracuse Journal*. These ideas were embodied in seventeen separate resolutions which Garnet presented to the assembly.

24. Howard Bell, *Negro Convention Movement*, 1830-1861, p. 84.

25. As cited in *The National Anti-Slavery Standard*, October 1845, pp. 69, 73.

26. Ibid., 11 January 1846, p. 121.

27. Ibid., 2 April 1846.

28. Bell, p. 85n.

29. Torrey was one of a number of abolitionists who was imprisoned for aiding fugitives throughout the antebellum period. As in the case of Lovejoy, the imprisonment evoked a stream of protest and antislavery writing.

30. *The Emancipator and Free American*, 19 November 1845, p. 118.
31. Ibid.
32. Ibid.
33. *The Emancipator*, 19 May 1847, p. 2.
34. *Session Book of the Liberty Street Presbyterian Church* (Philadelphia: Presbyterian Church Archives), p. 12.
35. *The Emancipator*, 19 May 1847, p. 2.
36. Bell, p. 86.
37. *Proceedings of the National Convention of Colored People, and Their Friends, Held in Troy, N.Y. etc.* (Troy, N.Y.: J. C. Kneeland & Co., 1847), p. 7.
38. Ibid., p. 6.
39. Ibid., pp. 6-7.
40. Ibid., p. 9.
41. Ibid., pp. 10, 13.
42. Ibid., pp. 14, 15; Bell, p. 88.
43. *Proceedings*, p. 31.
44. Ibid., p. 32.
45. Bell, p. 89.
46. Ibid., p. 90.
47. Ibid., also in *The Liberator*, 19 November 1847, p. 185.
48. *Proceedings*, p. 17.
49. James McCune Smith claimed that Brown had the document published at his own expense. Quarles disagrees on the grounds that no copies have turned up and that Brown himself didn't have the money. See Benjamin Quarles, *Allies for Freedom*, p. 67.
50. Ibid., p. 13; also the *Report of the Committee on Agriculture* which is attached at the end of the *Proceedings*. In Tyler, *Freedom's Ferment*, appear numerous examples of experimental farm communities scattered over the frontier. Bell, pp. 93-94, contains a discussion of the agricultural question at the convention.
51. Bell, p. 93.
52. Ibid., p. 94.
53. Ibid.
54. Ibid., p. 95.
55. Charles Wesley, "Negroes in New York in the Emancipation Movement," *Journal of Negro History* 23 (1939): 95. Garnet was also an agent in Troy for the *Palladium of Liberty* from 27 December 1843 to 27 November 1844. In the issues located in the Library of Congress, no articles by Garnet were found.
56. In the articles reprinted in *The Emancipator*, Garnet promoted Arthur Tappan and praised one of his convention adversaries, James McCune Smith, as a distinguished leader among Negroes. He did point out the fact, without great fan= fare, that Smith voted for the Whig party. See *The Emancipator*, 8 September 1847, p. 4; also in the 21 March 1844, issue appears Garnet's account of his escape from slavery. While it did contain some material excluded from Smith's *Memorial Discourse*, the occasion on which it was presented may have encouraged Garnet to indulge in a bit of poetic invention.

57. Bell, p. 96.

58. *Proceedings*, p. 6; Bell, p. 97.

59. Bell, p. 97.

60. *Letter*, Garnet to Tappan, 25 August 1849 (New Orleans: Amistad Collection, Dillard University).

61. *Proceedings*, p. 17; Bell, p. 99.

62. Quarles, *Black Abolitionists*, pp. 227-228.

63. Ibid., pp. 229-249.

5

Garnet Becomes
More Radical

From 1848 to 1850, militancy and political abolitionism became the dominant themes of the black emancipation movement. For many Negroes this brief period between the end of the Mexican War and the Compromise of 1850 confirmed long held suspicions that the federal government was indeed dominated by slaveholding interests. Garnet continued his ministry at Troy until 1848 and then at Peterboro and Geneva, New York, for a brief period. Besides his ministerial duties, he spent much time lecturing on the antislavery cause throughout western New York, and he attended at least six state and national conventions. At considerable risk he asserted his individual civil rights on trains and steamers. Finally, he commenced a lecture tour in England, Scotland, and Ireland.

During these years, the rivalry between Douglass and Garnet grew acute. In their favor, however, neither was willing to place personal advancement above the cause of freedom and equality. By 1850 when Garnet left the country for England, his mark had been left on Douglass who now became a convert to political abolition and militancy. Douglass had in turn influenced Garnet. Garnet had endorsed *The North Star* and altered his attitude toward religion to suit Douglass.

In February 1848, Garnet gave Douglass an unsolicited endorsement of *The North Star*. It came at an antislavery meeting held in Troy which Douglass was also attending. After the meeting, Douglass expressed his gratification: "I have long regarded Mr. Garnet as being quite liberal in his views and profoundly patriotic in his feelings. But considering his long and ardent attachment to the Liberty Party, and his intimate connection with the orthodox church, his manly commendation of the *North Star* was as unexpected and surprising, as it was gratifying."[1] While Garnet still disagreed with Douglass's stand on separation from the government and from the churches which Douglass considered proslavery instruments, Garnet now believed the higher purpose of abolitionism would be better served by an exclusively black newspaper edited by Douglass.[2] Another factor in Garnet's support of Douglass's paper was that Garnet's and William G. Allen's *National Watchman* was published only in 1842 and 1847 and probably had little more than shoestring support. At the time of Garnet's endorsement, Douglass promised the use of his columns to any and all men, regardless of viewpoint.[3]

Again in February, at a meeting of the Female Benevolent Society of Troy, Garnet delivered an address, *The Past and the Present Condition, and the Destiny, of the Colored Race*, one of the few Garnet documents which has remained intact.[4] This discourse was about eight thousand words in length. Its second part, "The Present Condition," also contained suggestions for the Negro community. Insofar as the address elucidates Garnet's antislavery philosophy, it will be treated in detail here.

The first part, "The Past," contains little information new to the student of Negro history. In later years, John Hope Franklin and Carter G. Woodson recorded the same information, though perhaps less eloquently. Garnet related the contributions of Africans to ancient Hebraic, Egyptian, and Roman civilizations and to the glory of Ethiopia. At the beginning of his address, he noted that in reality there was but one race since there was one creation; even so, he alluded to the achievements of representatives of the races, when the Anglo-Saxons were living in caves as barbarous brutes.[5] Garnet also mentioned Las Casas, the Roman Catholic priest, who brought blacks as slaves to the New World and unwittingly encouraged the lucrative slaving business which dissipated a continent. With much emotion he said: "If I might apostrophize, that bleeding country I would say, O Africa! Thou hast bled, freely bled, at every pore! Thy sorrow has been mocked, and thy grief has not been heeded. Thy children are scattered over the whole earth, and the great nations have been enriched by them."[6]

After praising emancipation in the West Indies and the successful
Haitian insurrection, Garnet detailed the brutality of American slavery
which "Hell itself cannot overmatch."[7] He praised the heroism of
Joseph Cinque on the *Amistad* and condemned Spain, which continued
to sanction slave trading, and Brazil, which held three million Negroes
in bondage.[8] For Placido, the martyred apostle of Cuban independence,
he had tender words and included in his remarks Placido's famous poem
of liberation.[9]

The second part, "The Present Condition," contained a plea for unity
among Negroes, which has an amazing relevancy to the ideological divisions of today: "How unprofitable it is for us to spend our golden
moments in long and solemn debate upon the questions whether we
shall be called *"Africans," "Colored Americans,"* or *"Blacks."* The question should be my friends, *shall we arise and act like men, and cast off
this terrible yoke* [author's italics] ? Many are too apt to follow after
shams, and to neglect that which is solid."[10] He then told his audience
that many among them had wasted their funds in extravagance and
spectacle instead of useful charity. *"The principles of progress,"* he told
them, *"in the ways of truth, and resistence to tyranny should be the
bases of all our public demonstrations, and numerical representations*
[author's italics].[11]

Garnet then touched on the significance of the late war with Mexico.
In his view, the American victory represented a successful but superfi-
cial triumph of slavery. He was optimistic:

> I would not despair of the triumph in the hemisphere, were Mexico
> to be annexed to this Union. For one I would welcome my dark-
> browned and freedom-loving brethren to our embrace. Aye! let
> them come with the population of seven and a half millions. One
> fifth of that number are white, and they are ultra abolitionists.
> Two fifths are Indians, and the other two fifths are of the black,
> and mixed races. I repeat it, I should not despair if they should
> come.[12]

For Garnet, the dominions of slavery were beginning to crumble.
Many Northern whites, he said, were beginning to realize that their own
freedom required the emancipation of the bondsmen, and in the West
he saw powerful indications of antislavery strength. "The Colored race,"

even though profoundly oppressed, was increasing in unprecedented numbers.[13] Based on a table giving the slave population in Louisiana, Missouri, Arkansas, and Texas for 1820, 1830, and 1845, Garnet concluded that Negroes, though transplanted in a foreign land, had grown with their oppressors as wild ivy about the forest trees. The degree of intermixture had made it perplexing for the Anglo-Saxon to decide how to draw the color line.[14] Garnet's inescapable conclusion was that *"this western world is destined to be filled with a mixed race* [author's italics].[15] "We are planted here," he said, "and we cannot as a whole people, be re-colonized back to our fatherland." Through the deepest ties, whites and blacks were inseparably joined in the New World.[16] Thorough intermixture was inevitable to Garnet, regardless of pressure and prejudice to the contrary. "It matters not whether we abhor or desire such a consummation, it is now too late to change the decree of nature and circumstances."[17]

It is important to keep in mind Garnet's qualifying statements about emigration. Later in his career when he advocated limited emigration to Africa and Haiti, he was being neither hypocritical nor inconsistent. The African Civilization Society which he founded was not the Negro version of the American Colonization Society, as some of his critics, past and present, have alleged. Nor in supporting emigration had Garnet turned his back on the possibility of equality in America. Garnet was to favor *voluntary* emigration abroad in the name of antislavery activities, such as establishing a cotton region in hopes of destroying the economic base of the Southern economy. He never advocated the wholesale exodus of black Americans; nor insisted upon compelling free blacks to leave against their will.

Perhaps his greatest mistake was his judgment on color prejudice outside this country. "Colorphobia is confined," he said, "almost entirely to the United States and the Canadas."[18] He believed that prejudice in other areas of the world was based on condition alone. Even today, many American sociologists and historians maintain this same mistaken notion. It is easier, however, to excuse Garnet who made his statement in 1848 before the development of social science.

For Garnet, the Negro American's destiny was to be found here among whites. In the last part of his speech, he was resoundingly optimistic. Negroes, he believed, would hasten the death of prejudice and and its effects through their personal virtues of temperance, frugality, and industry, through engaging in agricultural pursuits and acquiring knowledge of the sciences and the arts, and finally through resistance in the name of eternal justice.[19]

Despite Garnet's strong African sentiments, he accepted the American aspect of his identity. At the end of his speech, Garnet gave a ringing affirmation of the American creed:

> We must also cherish and maintain a national and patriotic sentiment and attachment. Some people of color say that they have no home, no country. I am not among that number. It is empty declamation. It is unwise. It is not logical—it is false. Of all the people in this wide earth, among the countless hordes of misery, there is not one so poor as to be without a home and a country. America is my home, my country, and I have no other. I love whatever of good there may be in her institutions. I hate her sins. I loathe her slavery and I pray Heaven that ere long she may wash away her guilt in tears of repentance. I love the green hills which my eyes first beheld in my infancy. I love every inch of soil which my feet pressed in my youth, and I mourn because the accursed shade of slavery rests upon it. I love my country's flag, and I hope that soon it will be cleansed of its stains, and be hailed by all nations as the emblem of freedom and independence.[20]

During the spring of 1848, Garnet journeyed throughout New England, becoming involved in a case of racial discrimination. (Ironically, he himself was to undergo such an ordeal later in the summer.) A Jeremiah Myers had purchased a first-class ticket on the Stonington Railroad in Rhode Island, but as he attempted to take his seat a conductor told Myers to sit elsewhere in a seat provided for "niggers." Myers, persisting in asserting his rights to the seat, was thrown bodily from the railroad platform without regard for his life. Immediately, handbills explaining the incident were issued, and a mass meeting attended by fifteen hundred persons was held at a hall in Providence. Garnet was appointed one of a committee of three to transact the business.[21]

As a result of the meeting, a petition was sent to the Rhode Island legislature urging a law to prohibit such denials of civil rights in the future. Garnet spoke at some length of similar experiences which Theodore Wright, Wright's father, Crummell, and he had been subjected to several years before on steamboats owned by the Stonington Railroad. Garnet recounted that in one instance during a severe storm, they had sought the safety of the afterdeck, were immediately ordered forward, remonstrated, and then Wright's father was seized by the throat and thrown to the deck. On that same line, Wright's wife, a woman of feeble and delicate health, suffered such great exposure that she died on her return home. It was also on the Stonington Railroad that Frederick Douglass had been dragged from the cars and beaten. To Garnet's knowledge, this was the only New England transportation company that permitted such barbarism. He therefore urged a common cause in defense of Myers and resistance whenever similar abuses occurred. He felt resistance would bring the black man respect from friends and enemies alike. Garnet refused to specify the kind of resistance but said that "he generally hugged the seats, and sometimes they would go with him as a whole or in part." He explained that "if every colored man who should be molested would give their assailants affectionate embraces, after the mode of a grisly bear, these upstarts would soon become weary of such manifestations of brotherly love."[22] Such tactics proved successful, he continued, in the case of the Utica and Schenectady Road which changed its policies after four men were required to remove forcibly the crippled Garnet. In any case, such oppression clearly violated the company charter, and, if not the charter, then certainly the state constitution and should be tested.[23]

Garnet again surfaced in April 1848 to speak out on the *Pearl* incident. After an attempt by seventy or eighty slaves in the District of Columbia to escape on board the schooner *Pearl* was unsuccessful, Garnet used the occasion to urge Douglass to a more militant position. If they had been whites, Garnet argued, telegraph wires would have been cut, railroad tracks torn up, and a cannon fired to slow pursuers. "Do you think friend Douglass," he wrote, "it would be an unpardonable sin for slaves to do the same?"[24]

Perhaps Garnet's most significant antislavery activity during 1848 was his role in the Buffalo meeting of the Liberty League, an offshoot of the Liberty party. The Liberty League had nominated Gerrit Smith for the presidency against the wishes of the main body. Douglass and Garnet spoke at the meeting, at which each adopted opposing interpretations of the federal Constitution. Douglass, faithful to his Garrisonian views, told the convention that the document was the offspring of slaveholders and was really a tyranny for all others. It had no regard for the rights of the slave, while it conferred political power upon the slaveholders according to the number of humans *they* could plunder and rob. This tyrannical control enabled the federal government to protect slavetrading for twenty years, conferred power upon the slaveholder to recapture his slave anywhere in the United States, and empowered the national armed forces to suppress servile insurrections. This view of the document, Douglass's indictment went on, was accepted not only by the original framers, but also by those who adopted it, all the legislatures and political parties, a large wing of the Liberty party included, and finally the overwhelming majority of Americans past and present.[25]

In rebuttal, Garnet, Beriah Green, and others stressed the objects for which the Constitutuion was written as stated in the preamble, the absence of the word *slave* in the document, and the use in its stead of the word *person*. They argued the impossibility of making a case for a slave's owing service in labor to the slaveholder, and finally that all doubt or ambiguity about the true meaning of any legal instrument was to be taken advantage of in favor of justice and humanity.[26]

Although both views have merit, in terms of strategy, the second view was better, for it provided a counterattack to the proslavery arguments within the framework of established institutions. The Garrisonian view, on the other hand, unwittingly strengthened the slaveholder interpretation of the Constitution and was of less political value.[27]

As a member of the Business Committee, Garnet prepared and defended on the convention floor an *Address of the Liberty Party to the Colored People of the Northern States*. This document, less than one thousand words long, was couched in language designed to arouse feelings of guilt and determination. It began with the statement that, as a group, blacks were hindering the emancipation movement.[28] "Nevertheless," the *Address* read, "it remains true, that, as a people, you are doing far less than you should, to shame the slaveholders out of their wicked and absurd doctrine, that the Negro is fit for slavery only."[29]

To become successful, Garnet said, Negroes could not be content with attainments equal to those of whites; they had to outperform them. That meant they had to excel in learning, work, thrift, and moral virtue. Nor should blacks cluster in large villages and cities and become resigned to menial occupations. "Had the colored people of this State been scattered over the state on farms or in mechanic shops," then "they would have been the equals of the white men among them— strong as is the prejudice against color, their respectability would have extorted from that prejudice the right of suffrage."[30]

The most significant collaboration with the enemy (and here Douglass emphatically agreed with Garnet) was the affiliation of many free Negroes with proslavery political and religious institutions. In Garnet's and Douglass's view, it would have been far better never to have seen a church or to have read the Bible than to have sanctioned enslavement by remaining a member of proslavery churches. Garnet's document stated that for every Birney vote cast by a Negro, five went to the proslavery Henry Clay. The *Address* ended by stating that slavery would cease to exist only after the Negro had established himself as a vigorous opponent of such institutions.[31]

After the Buffalo rally was over, the delegates began to disperse. Garnet, fresh from the convention floor and militantly assertive of personal constitutional rights, prepared for a speaking engagement in Canada on temperance. He was never to reach the lecture hall, however. Perhaps with Myers' experience in mind, he entered a railroad car of the Buffalo and Niagara Line bound for Canada. The conductor, James Graham, immediately ordered Garnet into another car. Garnet began to comply until he realized he was being placed in the car nearest to the engineer. He therefore returned to his original seat. Graham returned and insultingly ordered Garnet from the car. Again Garnet began to comply but verbally protested his segregation. "You shall go where I choose to place you," Graham replied. Garnet asked if he had performed any indecorus act to merit ejection from his seat. "Colored people," came the reply, "cannot be permitted to ride with the whites on this road, for Southern ladies and gentlemen will not tolerate it."[32]

Finding this reason unsatisfactory, Garnet walked toward his original seat but at this point the conductor seized him violently by the throat and choked him. Another passenger joined in the beating, continuing to choke and hit him with his fists. The crippled Garnet defended himself as best he could. A part of the time his one good leg was near the car wheels. Shouts rang out—"don't kill him, don't kill him!" Finally, a railroad officer broke up the attack, informed Garnet that the company could do as it pleased, and said that prosecution would be completely unavailing. The railroad officer called him a fool and told him to "go to the devil." Severely bruised and beaten, Garnet left and had to be placed under a physician's care.[33]

A short while afterward, Garnet recovered his strength and immersed himself in radical politics. By endorsing Gerrit Smith for president, he ostensibly broke with the regulars in the Liberty party who had nominated John Hale. Garnet probably backed Smith more from conviction than from friendship. To Garnet, Smith saw profoundly beyond chattel slavery toward even greater kinds of bondage. In this instance, winning seemed remote and less important to the social reformer than the presentation of new insight, to the electorate. Garnet defended Smith against the charge of being a pseudo-abolitionist. He agreed with Smith's assertion that, throughout the world, land monopoly was a greater source of suffering and debasement than slavery. Even without slavery in Ireland, he continued, land monopoly subjected the Irish to famine which swept away thousands. For Smith's part, he agreed with Garnet that, even when the American slave was finally freed, the attainment of equal status would still require some several hundred years. For Garnet, land monopoly formed the crux of the West Indian problem—slaveholders became the landowners after emancipation: "The chains of the last slave on earth may be broken in twain, and still, while the unholy system of landlordism prevails, nations and people will mourn. But the moment that this widespread and monstrous evil is destroyed, the dawn of the gospel day will break forth, and the world will have rest."[34] None had been as unlandlordlike than Smith who had freely given land to Negroes.[35]

With certain exceptions (Wendell Phillips for one) abolitionists as a group did not closely align themselves with the workingman's causes. Quarles has shown this weakness in Douglass's refusal to join forces with the Free Soilers. The above quotation from Garnet reveals a sensitivity to the larger aspects of the slavery question. While in the British Isles, Garnet participated in the radicalizing of large numbers from all levels of society. The Free Produce movement in Great Britain in which he worked after 1849 did in fact bring abolition to the masses.[36] Garnet, then, had more than just a fleeting commitment to the free white worker's problems.

For Negroes, perhaps the most significant event of 1848 was the national colored convention held early in September. Bell has called the gathering which assembled in Cleveland, Ohio, the "high point of an era" because it capped a decade of such meetings, witnessed the apogee of black hopes for equality before the law for the next fifteen years, and united Negro interests with radical third-party movements. It also officially recognized the importance of women's participation in the proceedings.[37]

Although Douglass was chosen convention chairman, the spirit of political abolition carried the meeting. Conversion of the convention to militancy graphically demonstrated how far blacks had moved from Garrisonian precepts toward greater involvement. Douglass went on record with a protest of this shift, but even without Garnet's presence he was plainly overridden. Two resolutions in favor of the Free Soil party were passed. The fact that they were moderate in tone is a testimony to Douglass's dissenting influence; yet even then he would not support the resolutions.[38]

Although Douglass's *North Star* received conventional support in another resolution,[39] Douglass, the acknowledged leader of the convention, had been rebuked. He was out of step with changing sentiment, and Garnet's political stance had been accepted. In the late 1840s, Douglass was also losing the battle over moral suasion versus violence. The convention voted, but did not carry out its resolve, to distribute five hundred copies of Garnet's *Address to the Slaves*.[40] Clearly, a crisis in leadership had occurred. Douglass had denounced the Ohio resolution which provided for the publication and distribution of the *Address* and had refused to talk at the Free Soil convention which met in August 1848 on the grounds that he had had "a recent throat operation."[41] But he was losing many of his black constituents. Garrison and some other white abolitionists proved to be unyielding. Under pressure from Garnet and other political abolitionists, from the knowledge of widespread conversion among Negroes, and also from the advice of Miss Julia Griffiths[42] who had recently become associated with *The North Star*, Douglass himself became a convert and grudgingly sacrificed his old commitment to Garrison. This decision helped Douglass to retain his popularity among Negroes.

Douglass, Garnet, Remond, Henry Bibb, and Samuel Ward attended the Free Soil convention in the same year.[43] Their remarks remain lost in history.[44] Garnet, loyal to the Smith faction of the Liberty party, could not, of course, lend his support to Free Soil, although he was no opponent of its principles. If blacks were not following Douglass's position on political action, neither were many following Garnet to Smith. On the other hand, they were not irrevocably involved in the political process as a means of improvement. Support for Smith was merely one of the many unpopular positions which Garnet was to take during the next decade. Other black leaders, after repudiating his position on emigration, would subsequently accept his views in a general way. Among Negroes, then, the pattern of the 1840s was to continue throughout the 1850s.

As the election of 1848 approached, black reformers such as Garnet, Douglass, Remond, and Martin Delany became heavily involved in political activities. About a month after the convention at Cleveland, these men shared an antislavery platform in Philadelphia. Garnet and Delany shook hands for the first time and began what was to become a working relationship in the years ahead. Unfortunately, Garnet's speeches in Philadelphia during the November rally have not been found. This convention followed the example set in Cleveland in voting its support of *The North Star*. Garnet, though more reserved than Douglass in his criticism of the role of religious institutions in slavery, generally accepted Douglass's view but stopped short of making a blanket indictment. Garnet's statement was recorded as follows: "Rev. H. H. Garnet followed our friend Douglass, and made a powerful and effective appeal to the common sense of the people, as holding any longer a proslavery connection in their Churches; he called upon all men to unite with the slave's friends in breaking every link which would connect the two contending parties."[45]

One reason for Garnet's movement toward accommodation with Douglass's indictment of the churches was probably a result of the struggle then raging between the New and Old School Presbyterians within the church polity. "No Communion with slaveholders" was increasingly gaining the initiative. Although the final rupture was still nine years away, when the Synod of the Western Reserve in 1857 took a strong antislavery stand, the ferment had spread throughout all four synods.[46]

According to the convention proceedings, Garnet was granted and then denied access to one Philadelphia pulpit for purposes of making an abolitionist speech. This refusal angered him greatly. Both he and Douglass specifically protested this rejection as "the greatest insult that

can be offered to a cause," and the convention endorsed their complaint.[47]

Perhaps the most significant document to come from the Philadelphia gathering was *The Address to the Colored Citizens of Philadelphia*
which Garnet and four other members of the drafting committee presented for publication. "If we should present our subject to you in a
single sentence," *The Address* read, "we should say—Equality, Brotherly Love and Liberty to all men" After this introductory acclama-
tion came a customary plea for unity which was followed by the main
body of the document. The essence of the document was an assault upon religious elements deemed to be proslavery. The fact that "elements"
were condemned instead of the entire religious establishment, given
Douglass's conviction, was something of a success for Garnet. In drafting *The Address*, Garnet carefully phrased his thoughts to give individual believers the option of deciding for themselves whether their particular religious connection promoted slavery. "Are you connected with
the gory institution of slavery in your ecclesiastical relations? Are you a
Presbyterian—a Baptist—an Episcopalian, a Methodist, or any other religious body that is in union with slaveholders? If so, we entreat you to
alter that relation."[48]

The document begged its readers to follow their consciences. It
quoted James G. Birney's statement that the American church was the
bulwark of slavery; yet the thrust was on proslavery elements. It named
ministers both North and South of the Mason-Dixon line who gave communion to slaveowners, and it asked them to withdraw from their
churches. In the committee's view, the American Board of Foreign
Missions and the Bible and Tract Societies were proslavery and should
not be supported.[49]

At Philadelphia, Douglass and Garnet were together on the same platform, united in opposition to proslavery elements in religion and in
support of *The North Star*. This comradeship was soon to disappear for
a number of years. In the months ahead their relationship turned to
bitter rivalry. For a brief period in the winter of 1848-1849, Douglass
faithfully reprinted in his newspaper Garnet's views and activities on
behalf of black people. Included in *The North Star* were accounts of
Garnet's travels throughout New York State, notices of his lectures on

temperance, and references to the school Garnet founded for free
Negro children in Geneva, New York.

While lecturing on temperance, Garnet named drunkenness as a rein-
forcer of white prejudice and stereotyping. A white could get drunk
without being noticed, he said, but all Negroes were held accountable
for the drunkenness of one black. For this reason, he urged sobriety as
a means of black elevation and improvement.[50]

To the same end Garnet established a school for children during the
winter of 1848. He operated the school during weekdays and preached
on Sunday in the Geneva Tabernacle at Geneva, New York, where he
had a ministry for a brief period. While residing temporarily at Peterboro in Gerrit Smith's home, he would journey to Geneva to tend the
needs of his parishioners. Among his students were three young girls
who had escaped from slavery. He wrote Douglass that the girls would
receive an education and would not be molested, "for there are yet two
places where slaveholders cannot come—Heaven and Peterboro."[51]

Garnet's other activities during the winter of 1848 remain obscure
except for a few articles and letters which found their way into *The
North Star*. More than anything else they reveal a mind constantly seeking other approaches and new alternatives for black advancement. Garnet traveled throughout western New York and found some thirty thousand Negroes living in areas west of Albany. Only six thousand of that
number were associated for worship, and virtually all were isolated by
the white caste system. As a result, much gambling and drinking, the
hallmarks of despair, were evident in Utica, Syracuse, Geneva, Auburn,
Buffalo, and Rochester. His observations were confirmed by another
black abolitionist, Mary Ann Shadd.[52]

The remedy, Garnet felt, lay in a proposed "Christian convention of
colored people and their friends," which would consist of a permanent
state society with paid missionaries to establish local churches. These
institutions would be used as welfare centers in addition to performing
more traditional functions. While Douglass objected to the word *Christian*, he liked the idea in principle. Garnet, however, went further and
questioned beliefs which Douglass and most Negro leaders had long held
sacred. Douglass, for instance, believed that blacks should not move
around, that free blacks should stay in proximity with slaves. In Garnet's
view, the greatest opportunity for Negroes after emancipation lay in the
West and South. There, he felt, blacks would quickly become artisans

and owners of lands on which they now toiled without reward. Because aristocratic traditions and monopolistic wealth were characteristic of the eastern and Middle Atlantic states, Negroes would have to migrate to western areas, following the good example of Douglass and William C. Nell, his associate, who had recently moved to Rochester. Therefore, Douglass's long held view that "we must banish all thoughts of emigration from our minds, and resolve to stay just where we are," was too categorically inclusive, Garnet believed, to serve the needs of Negro Americans. In a letter to Douglass published in *The North Star*, Garnet responded as follows: "Wherever other men immigrate, there should we be found. Emigration is often the source of wealth, prosperity and independence. Indeed, we do colonize where other people go but we generally wait until they have had the first choice, and then we come in for the scraps."[53] He went even further in the last part of his letter: 'I hesitate not to say, that my mind, of late, has greatly changed in regard to the American Colonization scheme. So far as it benefits the land of my fathers, I bid it Godspeed, but so far as it denies the possibilities of our elevation here, I oppose it. I would rather see a man free in Liberia, than a slave in the United States."[54]

Garnet clearly stated his position on black emigration in a published letter to his cousin Ward. First Garnet made the customary denunciation of Henry Clay's scheme, which included an emancipation of slaves coupled with their immediate exportation from the United States, their passage being paid for by the states and private philanthropy. Then he told Ward that he continued to favor enfranchisement here in America. On the other hand, he saw in an independent Liberia a valuable contribution to black liberation generally. The Liberian Republic would mean curtailment of slave trading on the African coast and the evolution of honorable black traders accompanied by the expulsion of their white counterparts. In addition, commercial treaties negotiated between the Republic and other nation-states would create respect for the race everywhere. He zealously predicted that Liberia would become the "Empire State of Africa."[55]

Any man who believed he could not grow in this country Garnet continued, should immediately go to Liberia. While he personally favored staying in America, he advocated colonization in another part of the United States, Mexico, the West Indies, or Africa—wherever freedom and enfranchisement were possible. Other peoples, he pointed out, had become great and powerful through colonization; therefore, blacks should go anywhere "where we can better ourselves."[56]

Among the black leadership, this statement was a bold and challenging one. Until this time, colonization had been scathingly condemned. Hence, Garnet's view, which laid down certain conditions when colonization and emigration would be desirable, was a dramatic departure for 1849. Few peers recognized the value of his proposal, most of them vehemently denouncing him and his position. Garnet's associates gravitated to this view only after another decade of abolitionist agitation, a period which saw the passage of the Fugitive Slave Law in 1850, the Kansas and Nebraska Act in 1854, and the Dred Scott Decision of 1857, all of which presented a stunning rebuke to abolition. By that time, Garnet had progressed yet another step: his African Civilization Society advocated aggressive, if limited, black emigration in the name of vigorous antislavery.[57]

During the winter months of 1848, Garnet devoted much of his energy to his school in Geneva. Little is known about this project; however, Henry Bibb visited Garnet's "splendid school" and church to deliver an antislavery speech. In April 1849, William C. Nell visited the school which at the time of his arrival was in the midst of a public exhibit. Nell, a perennial advocate of integration, reported that a large number of whites were in the audience and that the elocution class was composed of both juveniles and adults. A number of original compositions were heard, some of which he thought showed real evidence of genius. Many of Garnet's students also sang in the Geneva choir. According to Nell, the fact that Garnet held his exhibit after white schools in the area had been interrupted by ruffians on similar occasions was a personal triumph for the minister. Nell conlcuded that those who had seen black scholars perform would no longer believe that the Negro was unsuited for higher education.[58]

In the spring of 1849, New York's Negro leaders held a large anti-colonization meeting. Almost every prominent abolitionist living in New York publicly denounced colonization in much the same way as in the past. Two resolutions which George T. Downing introduced at the convention are representative of the intense antipathy its members felt toward colonization:

> That the testimony of our generation of the people of color is entirely, uniformly, and absolutely against the scheme of African

Colonization, and that this solemn testimony—peculiar in the history of this people, should be abundant evidence to all men that we will not remove to Africa except by the exercise of force.

That as natives of the sod we feel an affinity, an attachment thereto, which neither injury, oppression nor insult in the form of American Colonization Society or any other similar wicked scheme, can destroy, and it is our solemn determination while life lasts to be neither seduced nor driven from our homes.[59]

Just as Garnet had unnerved his Buffalo audience in 1843 with his speech inciting Negro slaves to civil disobedience, he again jolted his peers in January 1849 with positive remarks about limited emigration. They denounced him wholeheartedly a second time, evidently without realizing that his earlier views had gained wide acceptance. By 1848, political abolition had become the vogue for most Negroes, and so, too, had slave resistance. To the militancy of the *Ram's Horn*, edited by Thomas Van Rensselaer, and that manifest in the Ohio convention was added the voice of Charles Remond, who said in January 1849 that he would welcome any means that would abolish slavery.[60] Also in 1849, a convention of Negro leaders from Maine and New Hampshire debated whether they were bound to defend slaves if an insurrection broke out.[61] A similar respect for Garnet's emigrationist views would develop over time.

Douglass and Nell, however, taking a moderate approach, refused to sanction slave disobedience and violence. Douglass's and Garnet's diverging views on violence proved to be one important reason for the bitter antagonism which developed between them. Garnet's emigration proposal was probably another. Finally, a sense of rivalry developed from Garnet's proposed trip to England, for England was an important source of financial aid to Douglass's newspaper[62] and that source could be threatened by Garnet's presence.

The first of several skirmishes among the black leaders began over Bibb's speech before the American and Foreign Anti-Slavery Society in May. In this speech, Bibb advocated sending Bibles to slaves. Douglass branded his speech an "illogical display of cant phrases about the Bible," and the Bible's "power to abolish slavery if given to the slave."[63] While Douglass accepted the commonly held notion that the Bible was a revolutionary document, he believed that there was no way of getting it to

the slave except through his master. Hence, Douglass considered the
entire scheme very impractical.[64]

Unsatisfied with his response, Bibb, Garnet, and Ward invited Douglass to an antislavery meeting in New York City. Douglass agreed to
come, unsuspecting of the hostile reception awaiting him. There are
two versions of this meeting—one printed by *The Impartial Citizen* and
the other by *The North Star*. While the *Citizen* impugned Douglass's
veracity and integrity, the *Star* did the same to Ward, Garnet, and Bibb.
The meeting was ostensibly held to discuss the Bible question. The
Bibb faction accused Douglass of replying out of turn and of refusing
to give up the floor in violation of parliamentary procedure, and thus
it charged him with the responsibility for breaking up the meeting.
Douglass replied that he had no foreknowledge that Garnet, Bibb, and
Ward were to be the only people permitted to speak, and he denied
attacking Bibb on a previous occasion. He claimed that Bibb had misrepresented his religious faith, and that he had been deliberately
shouted down by Garnet and silenced by Ward. He stated that Garnet
had tricked him by asking a question and then shouting "I have the
floor—I have the floor," when he had tried to answer. Douglass denied
that he ever opposed giving Bibles to anyone. He concluded that his
adversaries had conducted themselves in such a fashion as to build up
their fame at his expense.[65]

The truth of these charges and countercharges is difficult to determine with the little evidence available. It does appear that there were
deliberate distortions on both sides: Douglass dealt harshly with Bibb,
while Garnet probably overstated Douglass's position on distributing
Bibles. This episode was merely the beginning of hostilities.

In June, Garnet wrote Douglass demanding an apology. His letter
ended with an insult: "Permit me, my dear sir, to say, that if I were as
ambitious of fame as yourself, I could pursue my course without advert-
ing to you, or without having the honor of your acquaintance, either
personally or by reputation."[66]

The antagonism between Douglass and Garnet deepened during the
summer of 1849 when Douglass discovered that Garnet was leaving the
country for Britain. In an article in *The North Star* entitled "Rev. Henry
Highland Garnet to leave the United States to lecture in the Free Produce Movement," Douglass sought to discredit him altogether in the
minds of his British and American readers. First, he said that Garnet had

no faith in "moral means for the overthrow of American Slavery," and
if Garnet advocated moral means in England it would be the "height of
hypocrisy." Secondly, he pointed out that Garnet had joined a cause
which he never advocated in America; therefore, he was a practical man
doing Free Produce work for practical reasons.[67] Douglass finished with
a warning to his readers: "we do not hesitate to say, that no reliance
may be placed upon any statements which he may make respecting *The
North Star* or its editor, should he condescend to notice either while in
England."[68] Douglass proclaimed Garnet the enemy: "We prefer an
open enemy, to one in disguise." The same editorial appeared in his
newspaper on at least two occasions.[69]

Douglass's charges were immediately challenged by the editor of the
Lynn Pioneer, a Mr. Bradburn, who denied that Garnet had no faith in
moral suasion. Bradburn wrote: "If Mr. Garnet has so declared himself,
then, we are happy to know, that Mr. Garnet's practice is better than
his faith, in that regard; for, to our certain knowledge, he has been,
during these many years past, busily plying moral means for the abolish-
ment of slavery."[70]

This disclaimer, printed in *The North Star* and truthful in detail, did
not satisfy Douglass who continued to denounce Garnet as a double-deal-
ing, unprincipled man.[71] At this point in their careers, both men openly
began searching for ways to discredit the other. For example, in 1849
Garnet and Ward were invited to speak at the Buffalo celebration of
West Indian emancipation. The celebration of West Indian emancipation was an annual occurence in the larger towns and cities of New
York and elsewhere. As a general practice, speakers were invited in
advance; handbills advertising them were printed and distributed, and
other arrangements were made to insure good attendance. They
accepted the invitation initially, but when they were offered a financial
remuneration to speak at Auburn, New York, both speakers had second
thoughts. Having already advertised Garnet and Ward in printed handbills, the Buffalo Committee was incensed, holding Garnet unfaithful
to his moral and legal obligations.[72] To the aggrieved committee came
Douglass, who, willing to discredit Ward and Garnet, published the
correspondence relating to the Buffalo arrangements.[73]

Garnet's and Ward's response to the Buffalo incident did not appear
until a month later in *The North Star*. Through *The Impartial Citizen*
Ward said that the Auburn Committee had offered them money whereas

Buffalo had not. The reason, he continued, for the black abolitionist's poverty was that nobody would pay them. Both he and Garnet had
remained silent for so long so as not to cause embarrassment.[74]

Garnet's remarks at Auburn, as reported in *The North Star*, damned
Douglass's leadership:

> Beware of the baneful and hell-born doctrines which are cunningly
> scattered among you, and that, too, with an industry worthy of a
> better cause. I speak plainly and pointedly, because the poison
> which I am about to analyze emanates from a high and respectable
> source, so far as talents and influence are concerned. Mr. Frederick
> Douglass tells us "we have no country."[75]

Douglass explained in the same article what the quoted phrase was intended to communicate, namely that the whites and the federal government considered Negroes to be outlaws in their own land. Therefore,
Garnet's statement misrepresented his intent. Douglass denied that he
had spoken contemptuously of the religious convictions of the colored
people, and he affirmed the inspiration of the Bible. Nor was he unstable
as Garnet had alleged. To Garnet's accusation that Douglass was forcing
Negroes to bow down to "the unreasonable and unnatural dogmas of
nonresistance," he countered that Garnet's actions regarding the Buffalo
convention demonstrated his own disregard of the Bible.[76]

Garnet's reply to Douglass, before his trip abroad, appeared in *The
North Star* on 7 September 1849. He accused Douglass of hostility
toward himself, Crummell, Pennington, and Bibb because they had
expressed views contrary to Douglass's own. Even more, he claimed
Douglass had fallen prey to envy: "Ah sir, the green-eyed monster
has made you mad. Pardon me, when I tell you that you never imbibed
a spirit so narrow from any dark son of our native Maryland, living or
dead." To Douglass's charge that he was an advocate of violence,
Garnet replied "*that political power ought to be used for that end, and
when rightly used, it is strictly moral*" [author's italic] . Garnet believed that slaves had a moral right to use physical power to obtain
liberty. "Do you, Frederick Douglass," he asked, "say otherwise?
Speak plainly—I am 'calling you out.' "[77] He denied that he was Douglass's enemy and that he would misrepresent him in England. Finally,
Garnet disagreed with Douglass's assertion that giving Bibles to slaves

was a cause unworthy of the attention of philanthropists. Before leaving for England, Garnet wrote Lewis Tappan, telling his patron and co-worker that Douglass wanted to "sit in St. Peters' chair and is haunted by the green-eyed monster."[78]

Despite letters from readers demanding an end to bickering among black leaders, Douglass remained hostile to Garnet. He asserted: "We neither forgive nor forget a man who insidiously seeks to destroy our character, and thereby, to stab the cause with which we are identified but we will hold him responsible for his conduct before God and man, until he shall repent."[79]

Douglass also impugned Garnet's motives to white abolitionists. While Garnet was abroad, Douglass told Mrs. Harriet Beecher Stowe that educated Negroes of the Russwurm, Garnet, Ward, and Crummell stamp had no stomach for continuing the struggle against prejudice and ignorance in this country, and thus it was that they sought more congenial places where they could live peaceful and quiet lives.[80]

Before Garnet left, he told Tappan that while lecturing in the Free Produce movement he intended to advocate the cause of freedom generally.[81] Garnet was to be faithful to that goal.

NOTES

1. *The North Star*, 11 February 1848, p. 2.
2. Ibid.
3. Ibid.
4. Henry Highland Garnet, *The Past and the Present Condition, and the Destiny, of the Colored Race: A Discourse* (Washington, D.C.: Moorland Foundation, 1848), newly reprinted by Mnemosyne Publishing Co., 1969. It can also be found in Ofari, pp. 160-183. My notes refer to the copy held in the Moorland Foundation.
5. Ibid., p. 12.
6. Ibid., p. 14.
7. Ibid., p. 15.
8. Ibid., pp. 16, 18.
9. Ibid., p. 17.
10. Ibid., p. 19.
11. Ibid., p. 19-21.
12. Ibid., pp. 22-23.
13. Ibid., pp. 17-19.

14. Ibid., p. 20.
15. Ibid., p. 21.
16. Ibid.
17. Ibid.
18. Ibid., p. 22.
19. Ibid., pp. 23-24.
20. Ibid., p. 24.
21. *The North Star*, 14 April 1848, p. 2.
22. Ibid.
23. Ibid.
24. Ibid., 28 April 1848, p. 3.
25. Ibid., 23 June 1848, p. 2.
26. Ibid.
27. Eric Foner, *Free Soil, Free Labor, Free Men*, pp. 138-139.
28. *Proceedings of the National Liberty Party Convention, Held at Buffalo, New York, June 14th and 15th, 1848; Including the Resolutions and Addresses Adopted by that Body, and Speeches of Beriah Green and Gerrit Smith on That Occasion* (Utica: S. W. Green, 1848), pp. 1, 4, 10-13.
29. Ibid., p. 10.
30. Ibid., pp. 11-12.
31. Ibid., pp. 12-13.
32. *The North Star*, 7 July 1848, p. 3.
33. Ibid.
34. Ibid., 15 September 1848, p. 3.
35. Quarles, *Frederick Douglass*, pp. 150-151.
36. Garnet's interest in the cause of freedom generally will be discussed in Chapter 6.
37. Bell, pp. 100, 104, 110.
38. *Proceedings of the Colored Convention in Ohio, September 6, 1848*, as cited in *The North Star*, 29 September 1848, p. 1; also Bell, pp. 106-107.
39. Bell, p. 102.
40. Mabee, p. 64; *The Ram's Horn* also advised slave resistance.
41. *The National Era*, 17 August 1848, p. 80.
42. Quarles, *Frederick Douglass*, p. 105. Julia Griffiths did much to keep Douglass's newspaper afloat through personal management and recruitment of necessary funds. She was extremely hostile to Garrison and convinced her husband to modify his stand on religion generally; she may have been a factor in Douglass's decision to champion political abolition.
43. Wesley, "Negroes in Anti-Slavery Political Parties," p. 52.
44. The writer could find no copy of the Free Soil convention minutes.
45. *The North Star*, 6 October 1848, p. 2.
46. William H. Roberts, *A Concise History of the Presbyterian Church* (Philadelphia: Presbyterian Board of Publishers, 1922), pp. 1-63.
47. *The North Star*, 6 October 1848, p. 2.

48. Ibid.

49. Ibid.

50. Roslyn V. Cheagle. "The Colored Temperance Movement: 1830-1860" (Master's thesis, Howard University, 1969), pp. 30-31.

51. *The North Star*, 8 December 1848, p. 1.

52. Ibid., 19 January 1849, p. 3; see also 23 March 1849, p. 3.

53. Ibid., 26 January 1849, p. 3.

54. Ibid.

55. Ibid.

56. Ibid.

57. The subject of black emigration in the nineteenth century remains controversial. Bell takes a positive view, as a new step in self-assertion. Other historians, Quarles for one, view it as giving up or as despair for equality in this country.

58. *The North Star*, 13 April 1849, p. 2.

59. Ibid., 4 May 1849, p. 2, and 11 May 1849, p. 2.

60. Ibid., 5 January 1849.

61. *Minutes of the Eighth Anniversary of the Maine and New Hampshire Historical & Agricultural Association, 1849,* as cited in Mabee, p. 64.

62. Thomas Harwood, "Great Britain and American Anti-Slavery" (Ph.D. dissertation, University of Michigan, 1959), p. 629. Many of Douglass's subscribers were British.

63. *The North Star*, 18 May 1849, p. 2.

64. Ibid.

65. Ibid., 15 June 1849, p. 2.

66. Ibid., 22 June 1849, p. 3.

67. Ibid., 27 July 1849, p. 2, and 7 September 1849.

68. Ibid.

69. Ibid.

70. Ibid., 10 August 1849, p. 2.

71. Ibid.

72. Ibid.

73. Ibid., 17 August 1849, p. 2.

74. Ibid., 14 September 1849, p. 2.

75. Ibid., 17 August 1849, p. 2.

76. Ibid.

77. Ibid., 7 September 1894, p. 3.

78. Garnet to Tappan, 25 August 1849 (Amistad Collection). In 1848, Garnet belonged to the Executive Committee of the American and Foreign Anti-Slavery Society for one year. See *The Liberty Party Almanac* for 1849, p. 16.

79. *The North Star*, 19 October 1849, p. 2.

80. Frederick Douglass, *The Life and Times of Frederick Douglass as Written by Himself* (Rev. ed.; New York: Crowell Collier Books, 1962), pp. 85-86.

81. Garnet to Tappan, 25 August 1849 (Amistad Collection).

6

The International Advocate

Black nationalism, as exemplified by Garnet's view that freedom in Africa was preferable to slavery in America, found more acceptance after 1847 and was more widespread throughout the 1850s. Once the initial fear generated by such a notion had dissipated, voluntary emigration increasingly became acceptable to black abolitionists. For many of them, the events beginning with the Fugitive Slave Law of 1850 suggested that they had little other choice. Douglass's denunciation of Garnet in the late 1840s is more comprehensible when viewed in the context of this fear.

The mere suggestion of voluntary exodus brought bitter denunciation for other reasons as well. One was the widespread Garrisonian dogma that blacks should stay in proximity with slaves, where, it was believed, they would do more good; and another was the personal economic motives among affluent leaders who wished to maintain their position and further their leadership within the community. As pressure mounted in the late 1850s and as they were pushed by the emigrationists and by events, these leaders were obliged to submit a plan of their own for a state-within-a-state organization. Although emigrationist fervor was not great in 1849, Garnet was not alone in advocating emigration from the United States.[1]

After Liberia was granted independence and the Reverend John B. Pinney was installed as agent and corresponding secretary of the American Colonization Society in 1848, interest in voluntary emigration among blacks increased. Under Pinney, copies of the *Liberian Advocate*,

African Repository, and later the *New York Colonization Journal* were distributed to every minister in New York City. The renewed interest in emigration was manifested in increased revenues and a tenfold expansion in numbers of emigrants. The New York Auxiliary took the lead over all others; it actually outfitted ships on which the parent society sent free Negroes. The state legislature went so far as to debate an appropriation of $20,000 to aid emigrants, but the measure drew effective opposition from Gerrit Smith, Garrison, and Negro moderates of New York. After the appropriation was killed, executives of the American Colonization Society began to reconsider and to reduce their emigrationist activity after 1852.[2]

During his first few years abroad, from 1850 to 1853, Garnet managed to sit on the proverbial fence between the radical schemes of the American Colonization Society and the stay-at-home philosophy of the moderates. It was a narrow, uncomfortable position, and he was severely berated, and most probably censored, by Douglass for doing so. In his tour of Scotland, England, and Ireland, Garnet repeatedly denounced the executives of the New York Colonization Society as proslavery conspirators. Here again, as he had on the issues of political abolition and militancy, Garnet was keeping his options open. Perhaps in his travels he would find a new direction.

When Garnet left the United States, he took with him a teenaged fugitive slave girl, whom he named Stella Weims and who had fled from the District of Columbia. She became his adopted daughter and lived with his family during its sojourn in the British Isles. Through the efforts of Charles B. Ray in New York and Garnet in England, money was raised to purchase the rest of the Weims family.

The Garnets arrived in England in August 1850. Henry Richardson, a Free Produce leader from Newcastle-upon-Tyne and an executive in the Friends of Universal Peace, and his wife Anna greeted the Garnets and took them into their home. Richardson and Garnet soon crossed the English Channel to participate in the annual peace conference held at Frankfort-on-the-Maine in August.[3] During the evening of the first session, Garnet addressed the convention. He told the delegates, most of whom were British and American, that their work was indeed vital and significant throughout the world, regardless of their scant numbers. He likened them to Christ in search of his disciples and urged the

assembly to persevere until victory had been attained.[4] Garnet's brief
remarks were translated by interpreters who were on hand for that
purpose; his was one of only a few speeches so honored.[5] He spoke
in favor of a general resolution which was unanimously carried. This
resolution read: "The Congress recommends all its members to labor
in their respective countries by means of a better education of youth,
by the pulpit, the platform, and the press, as well as by other practical
methods, to eradicate those hereditary hatreds and political and commercial prejudices which have been so generally the cause of disastrous
wars."[6]

In the press, reporters commented on Garnet's brilliance and his jet
black color. Intellectual brilliance and black skin generated great excitement in Germany.[7]

Garnet had other business at Frankfort. He and J.W.C. Pennington
spoke at a gathering sponsored by the Quakers at St. Paul's Church in
Frankfort on 25 August, recounting their personal experiences as American slaves and describing the evil effects of bondage. After gaining sympathy for the antislavery cause, they presented the Free Produce cause
as the best single means by which pressure could be brought upon the
institution in America. Garnet contrasted the difficulties he had experienced aboard ship in America to the gracious treatment he was
accorded in Germany. Pennington spoke of a little German boy who
befriended him on the street, an act which he took as a good omen for
antislavery in that country. Subsequently, a poem based on Pennington's experience was published in the local newspapers. The poem connected the incident with the longing of all people for brotherhood.[8]

Little is known of Garnet's work in Germany. In the *Report* of the
American and Foreign Anti-Slavery Society for 1849-1853, only brief
reference is made to Garnet's and Pennington's labors in Germany. The
small article merely states that meetings were held on the subject of
slavery and that, as a result, a German Anti-Slavery Society was formed
at Frankfort.[9] In addition, it reported an effort to organize free labor
stores in Germany.

After leaving Germany, Garnet returned to Newcastle-upon-Tyne
to begin his lecture tour in Britain. He next appeared in public on 16
September 1851 in the Scottish town of Gateshead where he spoke to
an overflow audience in what has been described as the "most spacious

apartment in the borough." He began by stating that he was appearing
before the English audience on behalf of a race oppressed and injured
in both America and Africa, and of the countless numbers of that race
on the islands of the ocean who lifted up "their fettered hands to
Heaven and prayed for liberty." He was speaking before them not only
as a full-blooded African but also as a man.[10]

Garnet then produced one of John Wesley's last letters which stigma-
tized American slavery as the worst in the world and urged a zealous
attack on the institution. Garnet proclaimed that three million people
were still its victims, and that there were thus as many human beings in
bondage in the United States as there were inhabitants in all of Scotland. While the physical horrors of slavery were profound, he considered the moral effects even more appalling:

> When he [the slaveholder] had blotted out from his victim the
> natural, inborn love of liberty, when he had extinguished within
> him all those high and holy aspirations and affections which gave
> dignity to human nature; then, with his foot upon the neck of
> his prostrate slave, he exulted in his work, and proudly pro-
> claimed that the crouching and abject serf was *content* [author's
> italics] ! But as a class, they were *not* [author's italics] content.
> If they were, how came it that thousands of them fled the house
> of bondage? The slaveholder bitterly complained of the loss of
> his property, he was angry that they sought and found an asylum
> in Canada, that, flying from the shadow of the Republic, they
> took refuge under the shelter of the English Monarchy. But what
> would have become of the United States, if the forty thousand
> Negroes now in Canada had been retained in bonds? Canada, in
> fact, was the safety-valve of American slavery, the protection of
> the Republic from a destructive explosion. Thither it was that
> the aspiring Negro, whose resolve was liberty or death, directed
> his fugitive feet; and woe to the United States, if no such asylum
> existed for the mounting and untameable spirits of his [Mr.
> Garnet's] race! Virginia and Maryland, Garnet stated, were
> states whose chief exports were slaves, and the average duration
> of an exported Negro's life did not exceed from five to seven
> years.[11]

At this point Garnet introduced with great effectiveness his proposals for a boycott of slave-manufactured goods. As it was described in *The Anti-Slavery Reporter*:

> Mr. Garnet exhibited one of the whips wielded by the drivers; a whip, he said, which had frequently been used in lashing men and women. He also produced the chains imposed upon the necks and limbs of slaves. But, he said, for these he was indebted, not to America, but to England. Yes! Birmingham was the place in which the shackles were forged which the man-stealer placed upon his prey.[12]

Garnet developed the theme of English guilt: "While America built the fleetest vessels in the world—the Baltimore clippers—to waft the poor Negro into slavery, Portugal and Spain supplied the crews, and England wove the fabrics that were given in exchange for the captive African, and forged his chains."[13] Garnet, though not a vocalist, then sang a song said to have been written by slaves and to have been sung by processions of the captured gangs. This piece recounted the slaves' longing for a better day.[14] Garnet visibly moved his audience by these simple expedients. He then told the group that Britain's most effective role in the emancipation of the American slave was by argument. The most powerful argument would be the discontinuance, as far as possible, of slave-labor products: As reported in *The Anti-Slavery Reporter*:

> A former generation gave up, for the sake of the Negro, the use of slave-grown sugar; and this was done when free-labour sugar was not to be had. A less sacrifice was now demanded of the British public. It was simply asked of them to prefer free-labour to slave-labour sugar, coffee, cotton, rice, and etc. This he believed, they would . . . do. He had been encouraged at Frankfort, while visiting that city as a delegate to the Peace Congress, by the request of the chief magistrate, that an anti-slavery meeting should be held. This suggestion was carried out, and it was resolved that free-labour stores should be established in Germany.[15]

Garnet then exhibited cottons and cotton prints, the products of free labor, which were currently on sale in Newcastle, Gateshead, and elsewhere. During the course of his address, he mentioned a slave law by which the Negro child was bound to follow the fate of its mother instead of the father. The motive of the law, he continued, was obvious; hence, there were many men and women in bondage who were as fair as any of the ladies and gentlemen whom he had the honor of addressing. To illustrate his point, he exhibited several daguerroetype portraits of fugitive slave girls, who for all their Anglo-Saxon blood were defiled by slavery.[16]

This creative presentation was to have a powerful effect. The number of speeches he gave in Scotland before the end of the year is not known. Garnet was in print again in September, calling attention to the case of William L. Chaplin, a middle-aged abolitionist and former friend of the martyred Charles T. Torrey. Like Torrey, Chaplin became a victim of laws incriminating those who aided fugitive slaves. Garnet castigated Daniel Webster, who had worked out the details of the Fugitive Slave Law, and the Reverend Professor Moses Stuart, an apologist for slavery associated with Andover Theological Seminary. Both of these men, he felt, would prove to be Chaplin's undoing, since they created the atmosphere which permitted his imprisonment and suffering.[17] The frontal attack, in which he named big names, was typical of Garnet's speeches abroad. He knew which members of the cloth accepted slavery or apologized for the institution, and he had no compunction about making their views public knowledge.

On 30 September 1851, Garnet and Pennington spoke at both sessions of a public antislavery meeting at Sunderland, England. They discussed slavery, depicting the institution as the very epitome of human misery. The slaves were treated as beasts of burden, family ties were disregarded, and whipping was a constant occurrence. Attempts to escape led to shootings. The abolitionists estimated the life of the slave on a cotton plantation to average some seven years. In their indictment, they included the new Fugitive Slave Law which had recently been enacted in the United States. Then they advocated free produce as a means of defeating the institution. Not only should slave-made American goods be refused in Britain but also that from Brazil and the Spanish colonies as well. They concluded by exhibiting a slave whip nine feet in length and manacles which were manufactured in Birmingham. This final gesture produced cries of "shame, shame," from the audience.[18]

In the following month, Garnet spoke at antislavery meetings in New-castle. By that date the significance of the Fugitive Slave Law was commonly understood within British antislavery circles, and scholarly critiques of it began to appear in British publications.[19] The law, with its full implications elucidated, provided another lecture topic for Garnet. He saw the new law as yet another illustration of the slaveholder's hypocrisy: the slaveholder expected all to believe that Negroes were happy in slavery and at the same time insisted upon a law designed to drag slaves back into bondage.[20]

According to Garnet, Henry Clay's notion that whatever the law declared to be property was property—regardless of duration, regardless of two hundred and fifty years of servitude—constituted the underlying assumption of the new slave law. Now, any slaveholder's oath would allow federal officials to deliver the slave without a trial. "He could send his oath and his agent—and that was enough. Once returned, he could demand a jury, a jury of slaveholders."[21]

According to the new law, Garnet continued, states and individuals therein to which slaves escaped were now responsible for the fugitives. Two-thirds of Garnet's congregation in Geneva, he went on, were escapees. Under the new bill, his own family might be seized. Garnet then introduced his proposal to boycott slave goods. Only when slavery was rendered economically unprofitable, he said, would the institution be abolished without internal violence. To those who heard the addresses, slavery stood condemned not only for the reasons Garnet gave, but also because it reduced men of his stature to the level of brutes.[22]

Printed materials, including propaganda tracts, were the mainstay of the Free Produce movement. Until Garnet toured the British Isles, the movement had had no regular lecturers. Nor was the movement financially well endowed; it was relatively small and never achieved its goal of rendering slavery unprofitable, though it succeeded in keeping the antislavery issue before the public.[23] In both America and Great Britain, Free Produce was a long-term movement, as old as the beginning of postrevolutionary abolition which harked back to the early decades of the nineteenth century.[24]

While in Britain, Garnet maintained correspondence with his co-workers in America. Free Produce material found its way into Ward's *Impartial Citizen*, beginning in the fall of 1850. Also, a letter from

Garnet was read before a Free Produce convention convened in Salem, Massachusetts, on 19 November 1850. In addition, Garnet served as a foreign correspondent for Henry Bibb's newspaper, *The Voice of the Fugitive*, throughout most of its short life in Sandwich and Windsor, in western Canada.[25] By the end of 1850, new impetus was visible in the movement in both the United States and Great Britain. "About twenty-six 'Free-labour Associations' have already been established," wrote Mrs. Anna Richardson, "chiefly in consequence of the lectures of H. H. Garnet."[26]

During the last few months of 1850, Garnet spoke at a number of meetings in Peckham, Stoke Newington, and London. At London, he met with different groups of women who warmly espoused the cause.[27] He addressed a large gathering on 6 November, and some of his remarks on that occasion were printed and paraphrased through the reporter. Although Garnet's themes had by then grown familiar, they still moved his audiences to feelings of guilt and antislavery sentiment. Of Garnet's speech on 6 November, one reporter remarked:

> He [Garnet] did not speak figuratively when he said, that the cotton which we used, the sugar with which we sweetened our tea, and the rice which we ate, were actually spread with the sweat of the slaves, sprinkled with their tears, and fanned by their signs, whilst the brutal driver goaded them to desperation, until an early grave relieved them from their misery. Could we then consent to give power to the arm that whirled the lash, and help to drive the iron into the soul of the poor bondsmen?[28]

According to the reporter, Garnet then took his seat amidst continuing applause. Those assembled passed the following resolution which fully incorporated Garnet's views:

> Resolved, That this meeting holds with abhorrence the still existing institution of slavery, and concurs in the expression of the sentiments of our coloured friend, H. H. Garnet [*sic*], on the importance of the free-labour movement as a check to this barbarous system. Although this country has set the example of liberating the slave in her various colonies, yet in her large commercial connexions with the United States of America

and Brazil she is virtually the upholder of slavery to a very considerable extent, and in this view of the case ought to exert her-
self to the utmost in its extinction. The recent oppressive law
in the United States, and the high price of cotton in this country,
have turned increasing attention to the loss of the slave, and an
attempt to ameliorate his condition will perhaps at this time,
above all others, be successful.[29]

Garnet devoted the entire year of 1851 to lecturing throughout Scotland, England, and Ireland in the Free Produce cause. In the large industrial cities of Birmingham, Newcastle-upon-Tyne, London, Belfast, and
Dublin and in the numerous surrounding smaller towns, Free Produce
associations were already in existence. He probably found it easy to
arrange his itinerary to include those towns with active associations in
addition to other cities where associations were being organized. In the
middle of January, he arrived in Belfast from Whitehaven and began a
marathon speaking tour: 15 January, the children of the Frederick
Street Ragged School; 18 January, the Ladies Anti-Slavery Association
of Free Produce; 19 January in the morning, at a Presbyterian church
and in the evening at the Independent Chapel. The Independent Chapel
was so crowded that great numbers had to be turned away. His sermons
were said to have made a deep impression. Returning to the Presbyterian
church on 21 January, he spoke for an hour and a half. The following
day in another Presbyterian church in Belfast, he again hammered away
at the evils of American slavery and stressed the moral and religious
state of the bondsmen. He told his audience that slaves were prevented
from use of the Bible and were forbidden by their masters from acquiring such education as was available to free men.[30]
     On the following evening he spoke at Ballymena, a town twenty-four
miles from Belfast. On this occasion, he expressed his indignation over
the Fugitive Slave Law and tied it in with the necessity for boycotting
slave-manufactured articles. At the end of this performance, he recited
a moving antislavery poem which was said to have been written by Dr.
G. Gamelial Bailey of Cincinnati, Ohio, an editor of several antislavery
papers in America. It was supposedly based on an incident in Tennessee
involving the sale of a slave woman and her blind child in which the
slavetrader did not want the mother and the slaveholder did not want
the child. Eventually, the youngster was sold to a third party for a

dollar. The poem, entitled "The Blind Slave Boy," though an artistic failure, is said to have brought an audience of some fourteen hundred to its feet. It told of the helplessness and anguish of a blind, black slave boy living in a world with strangers.[31]

Three days later, on 26 January 1851, he spoke first at the Primitive Wesleyan Church and later in a Presbyterian church on behalf of the Presbyterian Home Mission. Between the two sermons, both of which were to overflow audiences, he spoke in several sabbath schools to about fifteen hundred children. On the following day at the Institute for the Deaf and Dumb and Blind, a boy told him "a slave is one who is whipped and made to work without wages."[32]

Garnet lectured again on 28 January in the town of Newtonards, some eight miles from Belfast, where he spoke in the largest Presbyterian church in the area on the slave law. Here he added a new element to the usual resolutions condemning slavery. Ministers in Northern churches were singled out and condemned as proslavery apologists. Although the resolutions did not name individuals, they stated that it was "the bounden duty of all Christian Churches to hold no fellowships with any church admitting slaveholders to their communion."[33] Garnet had evidently shifted his attack to include certain Northern ministers who had made proslavery statements; later, he also denounced ministers who were executives in the New York auxiliary of the American Colonization Society.

In a two-hour address at a public meeting in Belfast on 30 January Garnet told his audience that the Irish, while repudiating the institution at home, often became slaveholders or their apologists in America. He also exposed the misconduct of certain ministers in America, particularly the Reverend Dr. Cox of New York City, who was an executive in the American Colonization Society. For the next few days, he lectured on the relationship between slavery and American religious institutions. Garnet cited proslavery sermons, named names, and produced resolves against elements he deemed to be tainted with slavery. At a gathering of the Primitive Methodist Chruch on 5 February, resolutions were passed expressing sympathy for those sections of the Christian church which had already separated themselves from communion with slaveholders. In this connection, the American Missionary Association was endorsed over the American Board of Foreign Missions. It was also decided to give up use of slave-made goods. Finally, a resolution was passed attributing the slave trade to the bad faith of the Spanish and Brazilian governments, and a petition was to be sent to Parliament asking enforcement of treaties between the Crown and these governments. After Belfast, Garnet left on 7 February for Dublin and spoke the same evening in the famous Rotunda.[34]

Returning to England in March, he preached at Birmingham to two thousand people. Another large meeting was held in Leamington at which time he shared the platform with distinguished local clergymen. Garnet publicly denounced religious leaders in America whom he deemed proslavery.[35] In Carlisle, after lecturing on the Fugitive Slave Law, he elicited a strong free produce resolve from the audience.[36]

Garnet made his greatest impact in Scotland and Wales, where the masses were more actively involved in the religious institutions. In England and Ireland, millions of workers did not attend any place of worship and were consequently cut off from the moral movements of the age.[37] The conversion of large numbers of people in the British Isles during the decade preceding the American Civil War in no small way influenced British foreign policy after the firing on Fort Sumter in 1861. When the Confederacy did mount its propaganda campaign in Britain in the 1860s, its agents could not make any headway. English abolition as supported by Douglass, Ward, the Crafts, William Wells Brown, and Garnet had done its work successfully.

The British and Foreign Anti-Slavery Society sponsored a soiree in London on 19 May at which Garnet, Pennington, Josiah Henson, and Alexander Crummell all participated. When he rose to speak, Garnet was greeted with loud cheers. He painted a carefully refined portrait of slave oppression in America. Included in his indictment of proslavery forces was the American Colonization Society which he attacked harshly:

May we not judge people by the company they keep? May we estimate the American Colonisation scheme by its president and officers? Who are its chief supporters? Slaveholders and their apologists. Who is its president and great supporter? A slaveholder! and the most consistent hater of the black race in all the land. Yes, and more, the advocate of the late Fugitive Bill—Henry Clay of Kentucky. This man is the popular president of the American Colonization Society. This Society had encouraged outrage and oppression towards the coloured people, and in their afflication they deceitfully come up, and with smiles say, "Now had you not better go to Africa?" And when the coloured man replied that he would rather remain in his native country, they would urge the matter more presuasively, saying, "But don't you see that the laws are against you, and therefore you had better go?" Why, who had made these laws? The very men who would be first to transport them! The Daniel Websters, and Henry Clays, and such-like men, slave-owners, with their hundreds of slaves—these were the men who made the laws, and would then transport the black man that he might be freed from their operation![38]

At this time, free Negro emigrationists were increasing in number in the Northern part of the United States,[39] and the American Colonization Society and its New York affiliate were promoting emigration to a free Liberia. Nevertheless, Garnet continued to blast away at Dr. Gardner Spring, Dr. S. H. Cox, and other ministers associated with the American Colonization Society as enemies of Negro freedom. Although Garnet thought it would be better to struggle free in Liberia than to live enslaved in the United States if these were the only options, he felt there must be other alternatives besides the involuntary emigration of the newly freed. Thus the Colonization Society remained a dangerous threat. Most of Garnet's remarks were directed against the American Colonization emigration scheme: "I speak in the name of the mass of the free American blacks, and would warn our English friends, that whoever asserts that the coloured people or their true friends entertain any other sentiments toward the Society than the deepest contempt and abhorrence, assert that which is entirely false."[40] After denouncing the colonization scheme and expressing his hopes that a free Liberia would become a viable state, Garnet turned to a more optimistic subject. He mentioned the many friends of abolition he had met in Ireland, England, Wales, and especially Germany. He had learned that Germans settling in the slave states had universally refused to become slaveholders.[41]

The energies of the black race, he continued, had not been crushed by slavery and were constantly moving upward. Once the turning point on slavery was reached, he thought the fetters of degradation and ignorance would quickly be broken. British public opinion had to be mobilized on the subject, and action against cotton produced by slaves was vital to force an end to slavery. Once slavery became unprofitable, it would die and America would in fact fulfill its democratic destiny.[42]

In their reports on the antislavery soiree, the editors of the *Nonconformist* made special reference to Garnet and other Negro visitors. They thanked the Fugitive Slave Law for sending among the British such a band of "zealous and intelligent witnesses against slavery, who will not allow public feeling here to subside on the question." The article joined in Garnet's scathing denunciation of the Reverend Dr. Spring of New York, a proslavery clergyman and executive in the American Colonization Society.[43]

During May 1851, the Congregational Union of England and Wales held a large meeting in London at which Garnet spoke. His remarks were carried in both *The Anti-Slavery Reporter* in England and in *Frederick Douglass' Paper* in the United States. Garnet began by telling his audience about the nature and operation of the Fugitive Slave Law and its rewards and punishments which worked to the benefit of the slaveowner and required every citizen to aid in the recapture of the slave. He added that fines were imposed for merely providing food, shelter, and clothing for the fugitive. He said that the law had already created great excitement in America; the president devoted his attention to it, and in one incident the army was called out when ten to fifteen blacks tried to rescue one slave.[44] Shaken as he was by the slave law, Garnet was naturally not as patriotic in 1851 as he had been in 1848. He told the audience that he was no longer particularly patriotic for the United States, great as the nation might be; he was simply a lover of liberty, and where it was in the greatest abundance there he was the happiest.[45]

Again turning his ire against proslavery religious leaders, such as Spring, Moses Stuart, Storrs, and Cox, he publicly denounced the Negro pew: "It was the offence given by this system which caused the secession which formed this church." When ministers used the Bible to defend slavery, he continued, it resulted in an altered view of the Message; hence, the ministers and the Holy Word were simultaneously being rejected.[46]

The next platform speaker, Mr. Campbell, quoted part of Garnet's denunciation of Dr. Spring who was alleged to have said that he would not emancipate the slaves if only a single prayer from his lips were necessary to do so. Garnet's references to Reverend Spring and others seemed to arouse great poignancy that evening. Campbell presented a resolution in the name of the assembly which would

deem it our duty to renew their solemn and indignant protest
against slavery as still existing among the American Churches;
and, in particular, to express their great surprise and deep
regret at the conduct of those Ministers of various denominations who have given either their direct countenance or their
tacit support of the Fugitive Slave Law recently passed by the
American Legislature.[47]

In the summer, Garnet addressed the annual meeting of the British
and Foreign Anti-Slavery Society at Exeter Hall in London. Since he
belonged to the American and Foreign Anti-Slavery Society in America,
which had for some years been affiliated with the British gathering, it
was not unexpected that Garnet should be asked to deliver an address
before it. Ward, Pennington, and Josiah Henson also enjoyed the
British and Foreign associations' support for perhaps the same reason.[48]
Because the association was more popular and stronger than the Free
Produce association, Garnet undoubtedly attained a larger following
than would have been possible on the Free Produce circuit alone.
Garnet, both because he was a truly black orator and was considered a
fugitive in his native land, thereby impressed large numbers of audiences.[49]

Conscious of the temperament of his audience, Garnet began his
address with references to the Exeter Hall battlers of yesterday—Wilber-
force, Clarkson, Buxton, and Sharpe. Others assembled there that evening had stood side by side with these illustrious men and were ready to
make the same triumphant contribution. He then addressed himself to
American slavery, beginning with the American Revolution before a
British audience, Garnet pointed to the hypocrisy involved in blaming
the English for slavery, fighting a war of independence, and then maintaining the institution intact.[51]

Garnet then attacked ministers in the United States as the very perpetuators of American slavery, stating that without the support of religious institutions slavery could not be kept alive a single day. While
America had initially followed the example of republican France, he
continued, France had proclaimed emancipation throughout her
colonies, while during the same period America passed a fugitive slave
law. The worst part for Garnet was that religiously trained men such
as Reverend Moses Stuart of Andover College, Dr. Cox of the American
Colonization Society, and Dr. Lord of Buffalo, New York, sustained

such an evil. Garnet quoted Dr. Lord as having said and acted upon the
rule, "when a slave comes to me, it is *Prima facie* [author's italics]
evidence he is a bad man." But why so? "Because he has run away."[52]

Once the successful fugitive had reached Canada, Garnet continued,
he could never be forced back into bondage across the border. When an
individual in the crowd asked him if English churches in the dominion
would receive the fugitive, Garnet replied that no Englishmen would
suffer them to enter an English church or to sit at their communion-
tables. It was not possible, he said, to make slaveholders realize their
comtemptible hypocrisy in kicking, driving, and hunting slaves in
bondage while publicly avowing their love and care for their souls. He
ended optimistically by stating that Americans were beginning to take
the subject into their own hands—the franchise was being broadened,
and the day would soon come when America would no longer hold her
head in shame.[53] Commenting upon Garnet's performance, a writer for
the *British Banner* reported that such a speech would have done honor
to the most gifted of England's sons.[54]

In addition to his antislavery speeches during the summer at conventions held in London, Garnet also served as a delegate to the World
Peace Congress which met in that city, although his name was not mentioned in the major newspapers. His wife Julia presided over the Free
Labor Bazaar which accompanied the convention.[55]

The fall and winter of 1851 were also months of heavy speaking engagements for Garnet. At five meetings in Glasgow, in addition to large
numbers of working people, many of the city's most privileged citizens
attended. In Edinburgh, the Ladies Emancipation Society sponsored
two meetings. Garnet also spoke in the surrounding towns of Paisley,
Ellensboro, Hamilton, Falkirk, Kirkialdy, and Dundee. After hearing
Garnet speak, the Ladies Emancipation Association of Glasgow, selected
the New York Committee of Vigilance as the principal recipient of their
funds. He spoke again at Whitehaven and at a soiree held in his honor at
Newcastle-upon-Tyne upon his return from Whitehaven.[56]

Between three and four hundred people turned out to welcome him
upon his return to Newcastle. The sentiments of those assembled at the
meeting were expressed in a long resolution which declared slavery the
most abominable wickedness on the earth's surface. The resolution
hailed Garnet as a successful fugitive from oppression, and it reassured
him of the sympathy, confidence, and love of the assembly. The great

design of the Fugitive Slave Law, it went on, was to supply the world markets with slave produce in competition with free goods; therefore, increasing the boycott of slave goods was indispensable.[57]

By 1852, not only individuals but institutions as well had begun to take an interest in the black Presbyterian minister and antislavery lecturer. The governing body of the United Presbyterian church was sufficiently impressed with Garnet to send him as its first Negro missionary to Jamaica, West Indies. For him this was his opportunity to realize a long-standing desire, namely to observe the effects of emancipation at first hand. Then, too, the United Presbyterian church in Jamaica had been a going concern for at least twenty-five years; Garnet would not be starting without a power base. As early as April 1852, Garnet received feelers of a possible appointment from Andrew Somerville, secretary of the Committee on Foreign Missions. After reviewing his credentials and interviewing him personally, the governing board officially designated Garnet as its missionary for Jamaica on 19 October in a ceremony held for that purpose in Edinburgh.[58]

After some delay because of illness and the need to secure appropriate traveling accommodations, Garnet, his wife, his adopted daughter, and his infant son left for Jamaica late in the same winter. They disembarked early in the new year under a veil of tragedy: Garnet's son had died on the way, and the minister's first act upon the island was the burial ceremony.

In January 1853, Garnet attended his first Presbyterian meeting and, as was customary, was invited to "sit and correspond,"[59] On the unanimous call of the people, Garnet was inducted at Stirling on 31 March. By that date, he was well into his religious duties, holding four classes during the week and one on the Sabbath afternoon.[60]

The Stirling post was located in the center of a good sugar district in Westmoreland, the most southwesterly of the Jamaican counties. The Stirling congregation was (and remains) in Grange Hill, a small village found only on the largest maps. It is approximately eight miles north of Savanala-Mar and thirteen miles south of Lucca. The old stone church in which he preached is still standing.[61]

Garnet began his work as a clergyman at Stirling with his customary vigor. By the end of 1853, he had revived the day school, doubled attendance at services, opened a Female Industrial School, which was operated by his wife and a Mrs. Lucas, and started another day school five miles away. Garnet's typical activities were as follows: on Sabbath day, religious school began at 9:00 A.M. and continued until 10:30 A.M.; one hundred and fifty students usually attended, an increase of 200 percent from the original number. After class, Garnet conducted services which were followed in the afternoon by catechetical instruction to his congregants, also numbering about a hundred and fifty persons. As he was short of staff, Garnet had to do most of the work himself.[62]

On weekdays Garnet taught all classes himself except for one which his wife directed. He offered an evening class on Wednesday for members and one on Friday morning for members, candidates, and the children of the Female Industrial School. Garnet held one Bible class on Thursday evening for young men and another very early on Saturday morning for people in the neighborhood. He gave instruction in sacred music every Monday evening.[63]

Garnet relied on funds from the Scottish church for support of the Grange Hill School, and on funds from friends in Jamaica and Britain for the Female Industrial School. Fortunately, neither school was expensive to operate. In spite of its pretentious name, the Female School met upstairs in the Grange Hill day school, and such mundane subjects as reading, sewing, and deportment were offered. It was simply a school for Christian homemakers.[64]

A second aspect of his work in Jamaica involved the Africans. Occasionally, the Royal Navy brought cargoes of captured slaves to the island, and a colony of about a hundred and fifty unassimilated Africans was located not far from Stirling. Garnet labored to convert them to Christianity but as of January 1854 had only modest success. On 15 September, he reported to the Presbytery that a Mr. Atkins, an elder at Stirling, had "for some time past" been acting as a Scripture reader among the Africans.[65]

In 1855, Garnet visited a place called Whiston Hill and started a new cause among the Presbyterians there. After some difficulties over land, this church became a reality, but not until Garnet had already left the island.

As Garnet's labors on the island commenced, events in the United States which were to have a profound effect upon him were getting underway. Martin R. Delany, the man most influential in promoting the nationalist-emigrationist position among free Negroes, published

his well-known pamphlet in April 1852.[66] Delany's plan for a black
empire in the Caribbean area became his consuming passion, and he
devoted more than a decade of his life to Negro emigration and nationalism.[67] Delany was not alone in his emigrationist views; Henry Bibb
was advocating emigration to Canada as a refuge and James T. Holly
also favored emigration. After the Fugitive Slave Law of 1850, the
notion of leaving for personal reasons became respectable among black
leaders.[68]

Both black and white abolitionists disapproved of Delany's move,
Douglass by ignoring it in print and Garrison by picturing it as the same
as the American Colonization plan except for the location.[69] The process of converting the Negro community to emigration and the creation
of a free black state would have to be undertaken without the aid of
the newspaper which Douglass had once proclaimed to be accessible to
the entire Negro community. To popularize his views, Delany and other
Negro nationalists called a series of conventions, but the meetings were
given negative coverage in the press. Floyd J. Miller, an authority on
Negro nationalism, has written that "Douglass' control over the most
influential black newspaper of the period was vital to the development
of anti-emigration sentiment, and his paper recorded letters, reports of
meetings and resolutions passed—almost all condemning Delany's call
and the upcoming National Emigration Convention."[70]

During his ministry in Jamaica, Garnet was likely aware of the growing nationalism among Negro Americans.[71] There is no evidence, however, showing a close relationship between Garnet and Delany on
Delany's scheme for a Caribbean empire.

When Garnet published a request for Negro emigrants to Jamaica in
June 1853, Douglass sought to discredit such a proposal. Garnet's
appeal for seventy laborers from America was published in the *New
York Tribune* and *Frederick Douglass' Paper*. Based on requests from
two local planters, one for thirty and one for forty laborers, Garnet's
appeal was primarily a business proposal which he believed would be
valuable for the laborers he hoped would emigrate. One request was
from a sugar planter, in Westmoreland parish, George Porteus, who
advertised for thirty laborers to whom he promised constant employment, a high salary, and temporary dwellings. Timber privileges would
also be given to those who wished to build permanent homes. The other
request was from an estate owner in the vicinity who was anxious for

forty American laborers and offered them yearly employment. They
would own the land after working on it five years and paying a reasonable fee thereafter.[72]

Garnet explained why black Americans were wanted in preference
to local people:

> The Creole is naturally indolent, and the climate and soil is so
> productive, that a livelihood can be secured without much
> exertion, and they seem to be destitute of sufficient physical
> energy to impel them to hard labor. Then they have some very
> ridiculous and silly notions about labor: for instance, a person
> of mixed blood will not work in the field, although he may be
> suffering for the commonest necessaries of life. The American
> would not be so foolish. Then, again, the work which they
> actually accomplish is very small, as they finish their day's
> work *before breakfast* [author's italics] , or by 10 or 11 o'clock.
> It is proper here to remark that, by that time, they do as much
> as they did for a whole day's task in the time of slavery. They
> might easily do three times the amount of work which they
> now accomplish, and an able-bodied American would do four
> times the amount. Therefore the planters are anxious to get the
> example of our people's industry and "go-ahead" enterprise.
> The time once was when too many planters were jealous of the
> advancement of the masses, and therefore did but little to en-
> courage them, but it is to be hoped that a better day has
> dawned upon us. These gentlemen whose names have been
> mentioned would do all in their power to promote the welfare
> and happiness of their hands. I would be willing to do what I
> can for any who may come, by way of advice, and as a minister
> of Christ.[73]

Garnet also listed the disadvantages for those who might be ready to
accept his offer, the main disadvantage being that the social condition
of the working classes was worse in the West Indies than in the United
States.

Garnet's correspondence evoked an angry response from Douglass.
Falling back on the old Garrisonian notion that it would be best for
the cause to have free Negroes in close proximity with the enslaved, he

categorically opposed the emigration of any free men to Liberia, Canada, or Jamaica. As he had done two years before, he told Garnet (whose name he consistently misspelled in print) to come home immediately and renew his agitation for freedom.[74] On the following page of the same issue, Douglass printed a small article stating that yellow fever was ravaging Jamaica and carrying off many ship crews.[75] Perhaps this was a coincidence and perhaps not, but such was Douglass's antipathy toward emigration in 1853 that he may have deliberately inserted the notice. He refused to examine Garnet's scheme on the basis of its personal merits, and a hostile response to any Garnet proposal was characteristic of Douglass for a number of years.[76]

Perhaps the most important published document bearing Garnet's name written during his years on the island was his eulogy of Stella Weims who succumbed to fever while living in Jamaica. It was printed in *Frederick Douglass Paper, The Voice of the Fugitive,* and the *Missionary Record.* A simple yet eloquent statement, it must have produced a wave of sympathy for the bereaved, for those who had raised money in Britain and the United States to purchase freedom for the family, and for the antislavery cause in general. It read as follows:

> When I told her that her race was nearly run, she paused for a moment and then said, "there is only one thing I wish for in this world—I want to see my mother." She paused again, and then continued, "I do not wish to live, I want to go home. In my Father's house there are many, many mansions. This world is shallow—there's nothing in it." She was visited by four of our ministers, and conversed with them calmly with great faithfulness. Her remains were followed to the grave by a large number of weeping friends, and they planted flowers around her lowly bed. She was the child of sorrow, but she will suffer no more. The cruelty and inhumanity of slavery exiled her from her native land and doomed her to die far away in a land of strangers, but she is free now; and God has wiped all tears from her eyes. She is the happiest and freest of all the Weims family, and in the heavenly world there are no slavehunters—no mourning captives— no dear, dissevered ties of nature, and no necessity for making appeals for the purchase of God's children. Although John Weims and his wife must be deeply affected to hear of the death of their

beloved daughter, still they must rejoice when they reflect that
she is beyond the reach of tyrants. May God bless those kind
friends in Britain who so nobly contributed towards emancipating that poor slave "mother," for whose sake her dying daughter
only wished to live. [77]

Stella Weims died in the winter of 1855 of a disease described as
"bilious fever." Garnet, also striken, requested sick leave in New York
City. He was granted permission and funds by the Scottish Church.
After consulting physicians and receiving mixed opinions, he left Jamaica sometime between the middle of December 1855 and the beginning
of February 1856. [78]

NOTES

    1. M. R. Delany and Robert Campbell, *Search for a Place: Black Separat-
ism and Africa, 1860* (Ann Arbor: University of Michigan Press, 1971), pp. 5-7.
Bell, *Negro Convention Movement, 1830-1861*, pp. 131-136. Bell's statement
that Garnet's "significant contribution to history from 1850 to 1865 lay in the
realm of emigration" (p. 134) appears to be overstated. The diversity and scope
of his contribution from 1850 to 1865 will be enumerated in the pages which
follow. It truly may have been Garnet's intention to seek a place abroad for
Negroes; however, just as he used institutions to further his goals, the reverse was
also true. The ramifications of Free Produce led to contributions in areas other
than black emigration. The same can be said for his relations with the Scottish
Presbyterian church, the American churches in which he worked, the missionary
organizations he joined, the relief activities in which he participated, and the private protest organizations he led.
    2. Eli Seifman, *A History of the New-York Colonization Society* (New
York: Phelps-Stokes Fund, 1966), pp. 115-130. Some $29,472.84 was collected
in 1847, and fifty-one emigrants were sent to Liberia. In 1851, the amount
reached $97,443.77, and the number of emigrants 676. See the *Liberia Bulletin*
(February 1900): 28. In 1859 and 1860, when emigration reached a new level of
acceptance among blacks, the American Colonization Society took in over
$100,000.
    3. Garnet did not take his entire family with him initially. Because of
financial hardship, his wife and children stayed behind. One of them died of illness. Through the aid of Gerrit Smith, the family was reunited in England. See
Ofari, "*Let Your Motto Be Resistance*," pp. 64-65. Quarles, "Ministers Without
Portfolio," *Journal of Negro History* 39 (January 1954): 33-34, identifies Richardson as a peace leader.

4. *Verhandlungen des dritten allegemeinen Friedenscongresses, gehalten in der Paulskirche zu Frankfurt a/M am 22., 23. und 25. August, 1850* (Frankfort am Maine: F. D. Gauerlander's Berlag, 1851), pp. 8-9.

5. *The Manchester Guardian,* 28 August 1850, p. 2.

6. *The Illustrated London News Supplement,* 7 September 1850, p. 213.

7. Ibid.; also *The Anti-Slavery Reporter* 5 (October 1, 1850): 160 and *The London Times,* 27 August 1850, p. 5.

8. Details of Garnet's harassment were printed in *The Impartial Citizen,* 12 October 1850, p. 4. For Pennington's talk, see *Verhandlungen des dritten allegemeinen,* p. 94.

9. *Report of the American and Foreign Anti-Slavery Society* (New York: American and Foreign Anti-Slavery Society, 1849-1853), p. 95; also *The Anti-Slavery Reporter,* p. 161.

10. *The Anti-Slavery Reporter,* p. 160.

11. Ibid.

12. Ibid.

13. Ibid.

14. Ibid., p. 161.

15. Ibid.

16. Ibid.

17. Ibid., p. 160.

18. Ibid., p. 175.

19. One of the most scholarly articles appeared in *The Eclectic Review* 1 (January-June 1851): 661-679. The article mentioned articles in other journals on the same subject.

20. *The North Star,* 31 October 1850, p. 1.

21. Ibid.

22. Ibid.

23. Ruth Nuermberger, *The Free Produce Movement* (Durham, N.C.: Duke University Press, 1942), in *Trinity College Historical Papers,* Vols. 23-25, pp. 4-137. The statement that the Free Produce had no permanent lectures is incorrect. See also Thomas Harwood, "Great Britain and American Anti-Slavery," p. 672.

24. Quarles, *Black Abolitionists,* p. 74.

25. *The Voice of the Fugitive* (Washington, D.C.: Rare Book Room, Library of Congress). Although Garnet is listed as a foreign correspondent, there were no articles written by him in those issues on file.

26. *The Slave, His Wrongs and Their Remedy,* January 1851, p. 1 (Washington, D.C.: Howard University, Moorland Foundation).

27. *The Anti-Slavery Reporter,* January 1851, p. 9.

28. Ibid., p. 15.

29. Ibid.

30. *The Impartial Citizen,* 17 May 1851, pp. 2-3.

31. *The Slave, His Wrongs and Their Remedy,* January 1851, p. 2, contains the poem. *The Impartial Citizen,* 17 May 1851, pp. 2-3, discusses the impact of the poem.

32. *The Impartial Citizen,* 17 May 1851, pp. 2-3.

33. Ibid.

34. Ibid.

35. Ibid., 10 May 1851, p. 2.

36. Ibid., 31 May 1851, p. 4.

37. Samuel R. Ward, *Autobiography of a Fugitive Slave* (Chicago: Johnson Publishing Co., 1970), p. 229. Ward made this observation while lecturing there himself.

38. *The Anti-Slavery Reporter*, 2 June 1851, pp. 86-87.

39. Bell has traced the increasing interest in emigration throughout the late 1840s as evidenced by the statements to that effect by Thomas Van Rensselaer in his newspaper, the journeys of A. M. Sumner and S. S. Ball overseas as representatives of Negro groups, and finally the interest in emigration among Garnet, Ward, Delany, and Henry Bibb. See pp. 130-135.

40. Ibid.

41. Ibid.

42. Ibid.

43. As cited in *The Anti-Slavery Reporter*, 2 June 1851, pp. 89-90.

44. *Frederick Douglass' Paper*, 20 June 1851, p. 1; also *The Anti-Slavery Reporter*, 2 June 1851, p. 102. This was one of the few times in which Garnet's activities were reported by Douglass.

45. Ibid.

46. Ibid.

47. Ibid.

48. Thomas Harwood, in his "Great Britain and American Anti-Slavery," pp. 672-673, examines the relationships of the various antislavery societies in Great Britain to those in the United States. In Britain, there were parallel divisions which corresponded with those in the United States. *The Voice of the Fugitive*, 4 June 1851, pp. 2-3, describes Garnet's impact.

49. *Frederick Douglass' Paper*, 21 August 1851, p. 1.

50. Ibid.

51. Ibid.

52. Ibid.

53. Ibid.

54. As cited in *The Anti-Slavery Reporter*, 1 August 1851, p. 130.

55. Harwood, p. 672.

56. *Frederick Douglass' Paper*, 11 March 1852, p. 4.

57. Ibid.

58. Somerville to Garnet, 19 April 1852, and 7 October 1852 (National Library of Scotland); see also *Missionary Record of the United Presbyterian Church*, November 1852, pp. 187-188.

59. Somerville to Garnet, 27 October 1852; also 5 November 1852, and 15 February 1853.

60. *Missionary Record*, July 1853, p. 328.

61. For the background information, the writer is indebted to Dr. Geoffrey Johnson, University of the West Indies, and Carleton Mabee who recently visited

the site of Garnet's ministry. Dr. Johnson's letter is dated 12 November 1971.

62. *Missionary Record*, May 1854, pp. 84-85.

63. Ibid.

64. Somerville to Garnet, 15 February 1854, and 14 March 14, 1854; also *Missionary Record*, March 1854, pp. 38-39; Dr. Johnson provided material on the offerings of the Female Industrial School.

65. *Missionary Record*, May 1854, p. 85; Johnson to Schor, 12 November 1971.

66. Floyd J. Miller, "The Search for a Black Nationality: Martin R. Delany and the Emigrationist Alternative," (Ph.D. dissertation, University of Minnesota, 1970), p. 63.

67. Bell, *Negro Convention Movement, 1830-1861*, pp. 134-135.

68. Ibid., p. 136.

69. Miller, pp. 76-77.

70. Ibid., p. 100.

71. Throughout the early 1850s, Garnet was in contact with Samuel Ward and Henry Bibb. He had also made the acquaintance of Horace Greeley during his visit to Great Britain.

72. *Frederick Douglass' Paper*, 10 June 1853, pp. 2-3; 20 August 1853, p. 2, and 2 September 1853, p. 2.

73. Ibid.,; for the quotation, see *Frederick Douglass' Paper*, 31 July 1851, p. 2.

74. *Frederick Douglass' Paper*, 2 September 1853, p. 2.

75. Ibid., p. 3.

76. Douglass refused to become a convert to emigration and black nationalism until the eve of the Civil War. His gradual change of mind will be discussed in the chapters which follow.

77. *Missionary Record*, 1 March 1856, pp. 36-37; also *Frederick Douglass' Paper*, 21 March 1856, p. 2; *The Voice of the Fugitive*.

78. *Missionary Record*, 2 June 1856, pp. 104-105. Discussion of Garnet's illness appears in Somerville to Garnet, 16 November 1855; 15 December 1855; 30 June 1856; and 12 September 1856. Garnet resigned officially on 13 January 1857. In the summer of 1855, Garnet wrote Somerville of his desire to transfer his ministry to an African post, possible Liberia. Somerville replied to his inquiry that the board maintained no mission in Liberia, and he generally discouraged Garnet's interest. It is possible that Garnet was thinking of an African commercial project supervised by Negroes as early as July 1855. The letter to Douglass for emigrants to Jamaica may in that sense have been a kind of trial balloon to test opinion among free Negroes within the United States. There is one reference to Garnet in the United States before December 1855; it appears in *Frederick Douglass' Paper*, 31 August 1855, p. 2. Garnet spoke to a Canadian audience on the topic of raising money to redeem slaves from bondage. If the story is correct and if in fact he spoke in Canada before December 1855, then he did so while on a visit to the United States. Garnet was being examined by physicians. It is unlikely that he was living in Canada at that time as Bell supposes. See Bell, p. 206.

7

The Black Republican

As he convalesced, Garnet found himself in an altered environment from the one he had left five years before. During his absence, both black and white America had changed for the better. By 1856, he foresaw as inevitable a national confrontation over slavery. While abroad, he had denounced Webster for joining Clay in producing the Compromise of 1850, and he had condemned the Fugitive Slave Law provisions before many thousands of Europeans. He was part of a larger process which in the years ahead swept the British masses into the antislavery ranks.

In the United States, the immediate effect of the Compromise of 1850 was to purchase a two-year peace between the sections. One historian has called the period the second "era of good fellings."[1] Perhaps a more appropriate description would be the quiet before the approaching storm. While slavery had received national attention before 1850, it had been superseded by issues such as temperance. Certainly, the prosperity of those years contributed to the antislavery lull. Moreover, abolitionist feeling as measured in political parties and votes seemed weak. Political abolition could look in the sole direction of Free Soil as the future vehicle of its hopes; yet the ineffectual showing of its candidate, John P. Hale, in the election of 1852 cast a long shadow. The election suggested that the electorate might want a respite from the issue. As for the Democrats, the Hunker and Barnburner Democrats had mended their fences behind the dark-horse candidate, Franklin Pierce, who became president. The Whigs, however, were not as fortunate with their candidate, General Winfield Scott, who garnered only a few votes in the Southern states.[2]

Divisions among the Whigs after their defeat at the polls, proved to be a portent of sectional difficulties. They never recovered as a national party after 1852, and they became known as "cotton," or proslavery, and "conscience," or Pro-emancipation, Whigs. The Democrats emerged as the only national party—the only remaining political organization in which Northern leaders were still seeking to smooth out sectional disagreements for the sake of party victory.[3]

The brightest event of the early 1850s for abolition was the publication of Harriet Beecher Stowe's *Uncle Tom's Cabin* (1852) which depicted the separation of families, maternal loss, and other evils inherent in slavery. Nothing which the apologists for slavery produced was able to counteract the effect of this monumental propaganda piece.

The slavery issue was revived by the transcontinental railroad ambitions of Stephen A. Douglas, senator from Illinois and floor manager of the 1850 Compromise. In order to garner Southern votes for his railroad scheme, Douglas proposed a bill in January 1854 which would allow the status of slavery in the Kansas-Nebraska region to be settled by popular sovereignty or by the settlers of the territory themselves. Originally the idea of Lewis Cass, popular sovereignty was not new. Nonetheless, the abolitionists were outraged.[4]

In a widely disseminated tract entitled "Appeal to the Independent Democrats," antislavery men attacked Douglas's argument that the 1850 Compromise had replaced the principle of geographical division with popular sovereignty. Neither party to the dispute was entirely accurate, yet in tampering with the Missouri Compromise, Douglas was the more reckless. Undeterred, he obtained President Pierce's backing and managed to push the Kansas-Nebraska bill through both houses of Congress.[5]

Douglas's victory proved shortlived, for in arousing indignation of such magnitude, he dealt his party a great blow. While the Whigs remained too weak to exploit the public reaction and the Republican party had not as yet emerged, the Democrats suffered a severe setback in the North. Perhaps the most damaging result of the Kansas-Nebraska Act was that it did not create a basis for stability in the new territory, and so began a bloody episode between abolitionist and proslavery supporters in the Kansas territory. Only a strong president would have been able to preserve order there, and Pierce was weak. Instead of backing his governors in Kansas when they needed his support, he remained indecisive, thereby aggravating the already tense situation. The natural propensity of frontier violence was therefore exacerbated by the sectionalist forces and by Pierce's inept leadership. Kansas ended up with two governments: a proslavery one at Lecompton, legal but not honest and an antislavery one at Lawrence, honest but not legal.[6]

After Pierce denounced the Free Soil government at Lawrence as illegal, the proslavery forces set up a grand jury, got the desired indictment, and rode in an armed "posse" to the town. Miraculously, only one life was lost as the Free Soil printing press was destroyed and property looted. Four days later, events took a grimmer turn when John Brown killed five unarmed proslavery settlers in the vicinity of Pottawatomie Creek. Then came terror and violence which killed perhaps two hundred before federal troops restored order four months later.[7]

The events in Kansas were verbalized in the Senate by Charles Sumner of Massachusetts who delivered his famous oration, "The Crime Against Kansas," which bitterly castigated the slave power and the elderly senator from South Carolina, Andrew P. Butler. After Sumner's speech, a nephew of Butler in the House of Representatives, Preston Brooks, caned Sumner severely. As handled in the Northern press, Sumner became a martyr, and Southerners were given a barbaric image. Southerners, on the other hand, made Brooks a hero and all Yankees rabid fanatics.[8]

Many of Pierce's proslavery policies, as revealed in the Gadsden Purchase of 1853, the Ostend Manifesto of October 1854, and the filibustering expeditions in Latin America, accentuated sectional passions. By the end of his term, even Southern Democrats knew he could not be reelected. As their candidate, they chose James Buchanan of Pennsylvania who as one of the signers of the Ostend Manifesto was particularly acceptable to the South. A remnant of the Whig party nominated Millard Fillmore to oppose Buchanan. The principal opposition came from a new party—the Republican—formed by "conscience" Whigs and anti-Nebraska Democrats. The new party bypassed its regular leaders to nominate a dashing but politically inexperienced newcomer from the Far West, John C. Fremont.[9]

For the leaders of the free Negroes, the events after the Fugitive Slave Law produced new and more profound tensions. Their effects on the growing nationalistic and emigrationist movement were explosive. Militancy had also increased, and Garnet's call to resistance now had greater respect. Although Garnet himself had echoed, as late as 1848, the patriotic sentiments shared by Douglass, Nell, Smith, and other Negro leaders, after 1850, Douglass was cast into a new role—that of the moderate who was to hold the line as long as he could against those, like Garnet, with more radical plans. Early in 1851, he bared his feelings in a letter to Gerrit Smith: "I really fear that some whose presence in this country is necessary to the elevation of the Colored people will leave us—while the degraded and worthless will remain behind—to help bind us to our present debasement."[10]

During Garnet's absence from the United States, the growing interest in a black homeland was revealed in state and national conventions of the 1850s. These meetings, more than *Frederick Douglass' Paper*, best served as a barometer of the Negro community's feelings. The developments within the convention movement, as regards emigration, prior to Garnet's return to New York will now be reviewed briefly. (For a full history of emigrationist thought, see Bell's authoritative study.)[11]

By 1854, an estimated 20 to 25 percent of Ohio's Negroes favored emigration. Lewis H. Putnam, a promoter of emigration in New York in the early 1850s, formed an emigrationist organization and won a favorable response from Governor Washington Hunt to his plea for state funds for his colonization scheme. Putnam's challenge was immediately met and successfully countered by established leaders, but his new emigrationist society, impotent as it proved to be, had alarmed the established leaders. There was more reason for them to fear the success of emigration than was generally admitted. In Maryland and New Jersey as well, emigration was receiving a good deal of attention. Increasing numbers of blacks from Pennsylvania, Maryland, Ohio, the District of Columbia, and Vermont emigrated to Canada, to the settlements already in operation across Lake Michigan.[12]

As early as 1849, Delany, like Garnet, had seen some favorable potential for emigration to free Liberia. By 1852, he was advocating the formation of a black empire in the tropical regions of the Western Hemisphere. Perhaps the high point in Delany's activity before 1856 was the National Emigrationist Convention held in Cleveland, Ohio, in August 1854. It precipitated an editorial battle between the Douglass forces and J. M. Whitfield who favored emigration and nationalism. According to Bell, the battle of the pens worked to the advantage of the emigrationists who went ahead with the meeting. The philosophical rationale for the emigrationists was embodied in Delany's well-known pamphlet,

"The Condition, Elevation, Emigration, and Destiny of the Colored
People of the United States, Politically Considered," which was
accepted by the convention. It denied the citizenship rights of Negro
Americans and contended that freedom existed only where a racial
group constituted the majority. Hence, the answer to the dilemma lay
in emigration, first to Canada as a way station and ultimately to the
West Indies. Central and South America and the West Indies, it was
believed, would welcome Negroes but would refuse admission to
whites.[13]

The national convention at Cleveland represented a minority action
in 1854; that minority was still strong enough to command a far wider
participation than had several of the general national conventions of the
1830s and 1840s. From 1854 until its peak in 1861, emigration gathered fresh momentum. The members of the national convention at
Philadelphia in 1855 were the first in many years to listen with respect
to a plea to come to Canada. Treated with less seriousness, but not
buried in committee as had been likely in the past, was a letter urging
attention to the lure of Liberia. Soon, established Negro leaders would
be forced into a defensive holding-action as they progressively yielded
to the emigrationist forces.[14] Thus, when Garnet returned to America,
he arrived in the midst of a leadership crisis among his peers and immediately immersed himself in it.

After December 1855, Garnet's name disappeared from the Presbytery records of the Jamaican synod; *Frederick Douglass' Paper* mentioned his arrival in its issue of 21 March 1856. It is likely that, for the
first two months of 1856, Garnet was regaining his strength. Douglass
used the occasion of his return to articulate the familiar homilies in
favor of staying home. Douglass's article stated that this country was
the proper theatre to fight and that Garnet was needed here to refute
prejudice. "Well do we remember his thrilling words upon the platform,
a few years ago in Liberty Hall, New Bedford. He exclaimed, on that
occasion, " 'America is our home; Here [sic] will we live, and here will
we die. And should we die during the battle, we shall die struggling to
be free.' "[15]

This was the Garnet that Douglass wanted to promote; as a strict
Garrisonian, Douglass would stay home and fight. So long as Douglass
held the reins of power among his associates, he could afford to be
charitable to Garnet. His views probably were not seriously challenged

by Garnet during the first year of his return; therefore, a period of rapprochement, perhaps even of mutual admiration, existed for about a year. At this time Douglass seemed to be more flexible. He so far forgot his anti-emigration principles that he proposed transplanting a thousand Negro families to the plains of Kansas to help make the area safe for freedom.[16] However, this aberration proved to be temporary.

By March, Garnet was again lecturing before large audiences. He spoke three times in one week in Boston on the effects of emancipation in Jamaica.[17] On a number of occasions throughout the year, particularly in August, Garnet discussed Jamaican independence. He told an audience of seven to eight thousand at Clifton Springs, New York (which was perhaps the largest assembly anywhere in the state that year) that Negroes celebrated the first of August because the American people had given them no worthy occasion to celebrate. In the detached manner of a social scientist, he contrasted conditions among Negroes before and after liberation in Jamaica, concluding that matters had improved. He demonstrated to the reporter present the falsity of the past declarations concerning "the ruinous effects of Emancipation in the West Indies."[18]

Having had to observe developments of the past six years from beyond the borders of the United States, Garnet claimed a detachment and objectivity on domestic developments. The first of these developments concerned political changes. By 1856, black New Yorkers would be choosing between the two antislavery parties, the Republican and the Radical Abolitionist. Of the two, the Republican party had become a national movement by 1856, except in the South. Its commitment to antislavery, however, applied only to the national territories; it would do nothing to disturb slavery elsewhere. In contrast, the Radical Abolitionists, which consisted of old Liberty party stalwarts and political abolitionists scattered throughout New England and New York, were scarcely a serious political contender on the national level. They took an antislavery view of the Constitution and proposed to use the federal government as a means of abolishing slavery throughout the country.[19]

In New York State, Negroes formed the New York State Suffrage Association in 1855, an organization designed as a Negro political party for the state. Its officers came from the Albany-Buffalo area and the metropolitan region, and Douglass became its head. As early as 1854, he threw his support to the Radical Abolitionists.[20] When the Republican party met and prepared its platform early in 1856, Douglass vigorously denounced it. He attended the Radical Abolitionist convention sponsored by Lewis Tappan, Gerrit Smith, James McCune Smith, and William Goodell in May. Garnet did not attend, despite his obvious sympathies for them.[21] At the Radical convention, Douglass confessed some sympathy for the Republican party; "but [he said] they do not give full recognition to the humanity of the Negro."[22]

Garnet spoke at a meeting of abolitionists held at Dr. Pennington's church on 7 May 1856 in New York City, and when he touched upon domestic politics, he expressed optimism at recent events. After tracing the course of proslavery legislation, he pointed to the great spread and intensification of antislavery feeling. Although Kansas was about to be admitted to the Union with a provision excluding Negroes, it was certain, that if Kansas came in as a free state blacks would ultimately be permitted to enter the state. The most promising sign to Garnet that slavery would die was that people were beginning to talk, vote, and pray for abolition. He likened the North to a coward in the corner, pounded by the South, who when forced to a coward's extremity said, "If we must fight, here's at you! And when a coward does fight he is always dangerous."[23]

As regards domestic politics, Garnet said there was nothing as good or as safe as radical abolitionism. The fact that the movement had a variety of branches was evidence of the inherent strength of the root, and the time was approaching when the goodly tree would extend itself over the land, bringing freedom beneath its branches.[24]

People were too much engaged in president-making, Garnet continued, and in territorial expansion, extension of churches, tract distribution, and home and foreign missions, so long as they did not touch slavery. Meanwhile, man's first duty—that of extending humanity, freedom, and justice—was forgotten. He singled out President Pierce for his promotion of slavery in Kansas:

> And if Mr. Pierce, by his devotion to Slavery, led to the shedding of blood in the cause of freedom in Kansas, the historian on whom would devolve the duty of recording the bloody events which would follow and by which the country would be involved in a consuming Civil War, would feel his limbs tremble beneath him and his cheeks grow pale at the fearful nature of the task.[25]

Like Douglass, Garnet had endorsed the principles of radical abolition, yet he refrained from attending the Radical Abolitionist convention held later in May in Syracuse. He saw public opinion as moving in
his favor; the bleak days of 1840 when political abolition had broken
new ground were far behind. Five years of detachment in Europe and
Jamaica had made him more optimistic as to the course of emancipation. His conviction that the North would indeed turn and fight may
have led him to embrace the Republican party.

As leader of the upstate Suffrage Association, Douglass had become
so intensely involved in the association that he fell into a personally
embarrassingly position in mid-August when he abruptly broke with the
radicals in favor of the Republican John C. Fremont and William Day-
ton. None of his friends was prepared for the shock of Douglass's complete shift in position.[26] By September, meanwhile, Garnet was openly
supporting the Republicans.

During the summer, Garnet maintained a busy lecture schedule,
speaking in June at a meeting in Philadelphia to denounce Brooks'
attack on Sumner and again in July at Dr. Pennington's church in New
York City. He lectured on the anniversary of abolition in New York
State at Auburn and also spoke at Skaneateles, Geneva, Conandaigue,
Penn Yan, and Buffalo. He shared the lecture platform with Douglass
in July and August, particularly when the subject was Jamaican emancipation.[27]

At the Philadelphia meeting, Garnet, Senator Stephen A. Douglas,
Howell Cobb of Georgia, Lewis Cass of Ohio, and other political leaders
spoke from the same platform. In the view of one reporter, E. D.
Bassett, Garnet produced the finest speech of them all.[28] Following his
remarks, two resolutions of commendation to him for his antislavery
efforts were passed unanimously. They read as follows:

> Resolve, 1. That in the Rev. Henry Highland Garnet, of eloquence,
> classic and unsurpassed; of fame untarnished; of character, pure
> and brilliant, we recognize an able, eloquent, and fearless cham-
> pion, standing in the foremost ranks of the hosts of that Freedom
> which now seems about to proclaim itself universal, living every-
> where in the hearts of men; and of his own people, the colored
> race, a weighty and faithful exponent of whom we, as colored,
> men, are proud to claim kindred.

[Resolve] , 2. That our unfeigned, heartfelt thanks are due, and
we hereby tender them to Mr. Garnet, for the series of able dis-
courses with which he has favored us during the present week; and
particularly, do we desire to give expression to our high appreciation of his searching and masterly exposition of the true relations to us, as exemplified in British Slavery and Emancipation,
and of the designs of that accursed institution which has so long
crushed and disfranchised our people, trampled down all laws
between man and man, and outraged those of the living God.[29]

Of Garnet's Auburn address on emancipation in New York, one
reporter wrote that he remained eloquent; Garnet's character, learning,
and ability, coupled with his Congo features, gave a powerful refutation
to beliefs of Negro inferiority.[30] The Clifton Springs speech led one
reporter to write that "there could not have been one selected who
could have spoken more eloquently upon the subject." His address
gained wide approval and was heard with deep attention. "I venture to
say," the reporter concluded, "that Mr. Garnet never was more eloquent
than on that day on such an occasion."[31] Unfortunately, no recording
of his remarks has been discovered.

In the late summer and fall of 1856, black New Yorkers renewed
their suffrage fight, first holding local conventions, then a single convention for the entire state. As in the 1840s, Garnet was one of the
movers behind these efforts. An estimated one hundred and fifty delegates assembled for the state meeting at Syracuse. They represented
five to six thousand voters and met for three days. Garnet's words were
summarized in both *Frederick Douglass' Paper* and the *New York Daily
Tribune*. Here he endorsed the Republican candidate. The account read
as follows:

> He [Garnet] wanted to say something about voting. They would
> soon be called upon to exercise what little of elective franchize
> they possessed, and he wanted to see measures taken to insure
> its greatest good. There were in the state some 5,000 or 6,000
> colored voters, about half of whom lived in New York or Brook-
> lyn. In these days, 6,000 voters were of some importance. He
> believed the coming election would be closely contested, and
> every colored man ought to vote right. Our people, said he, have

of late been seized with the spirit of do-nothing. Many do not
see the necessity of voting at all. There are not many inducements
for colored men to take part in politics, unless upon the broad
ground of principle; but they ought to act with those who come
nearest to liberty and justice, and he believed those were the
Republican party.[32]

After he was applauded, he proceeded to qualify his approbation:

That party [the Republican party] was not all they desired, but
so far as it goes it was right. Its great principle was to stop the
progress of slavery—to prevent the vast territories of Kansas and
Nebraska from being cursed with Slavery. White men would not
do their work for them, but they ought at least to help themselves now that there is an opportunity, regardless of the unkind
things uttered by some of the Republican leaders. He [Garnet]
remembered that the party leaders and the masses were distinct
classes. The leaders are governed by policy, but the sentiment of
the masses was at this moment opposed to slavery. In the West
our brethren are aroused.—These are the true intelligent friends
of Liberty. Let us co-operate with them.[33]

Garnet ended his political remarks on a note of indignation. As summarized in a news article, he said:

I cannot vote, Sir. I have labored to benefit the country, but I
cannot be permitted to vote for even a pound-keeper. Never
mind that. Let every man who can do all he can do to promote
the cause of Liberty. They extend civil rights to foreigners,
who then become our oppressors. They have got out of prison
themselves, and they forget Joseph. The oppressed Irishmen,
once naturalized, are the loudest shouters and bitterest foes
of the Negro. Of all things, he [Garnet] hated to see a black
Democrat; but he was sorry to say there were some colored
men so ignorant and misguided as to favor these avowed
supporters of the enslavement of their race. So, too, there
were some deluded men among them that go to Fillmore,
that man who jumped from his seat with indecent haste

to sign the Fugitive Slave bill, and has never regretted the
deed. He [Garnet] hoped before the election these men
would all see their errors, and give what little of suffrage
was permitted them to the cause of Liberty and Justice.[34]

Before the convention adjourned, it passed familiar resolutions to
form an organization to collect petitions for the franchise, with power
to appoint speakers and agents to facilitate their goals. A specific
appeal was made to Negro clergymen of the state to take a monthly
collection for the voter drive, and a resolution was unanimously
adopted endorsing the Republican party.[35]

Garnet's financial status improved in September when he was called
to the pastorate of the Shiloh Presbyterian Church in New York City.[36]
Previously, this had been the church of his teacher, Theodore Wright,
whose recent death had created the vacancy. Garnet preached the
eulogy for Wright; he did so, reported James McCune Smith, while in a
state of shock.[37] The Shiloh appointment, coupled with a generous
income supplement from the American Home Missionary Society, provided him with a new base of operation.[38] The American Home Missionary Society grant lasted only one year,[39] but it gave Garnet the
opportunity to revitalize the Shiloh congregation so that he could
continue his crusade for several years.

In September, he delivered an address before the Colored Odd
Fellows' Twelfth Annual Meeting. The Odd Fellows had been denounced by the editors of the *National Anti-Slavery Standard* as being
"Black trash," but to Garnet they represented a valuable kind of voluntary association. He alluded to the general advantages of Odd-Fellow-
ship to the members themselves and to their families.[40]

During the early months of 1857, the Dred Scott case shook the
community throughout New York and free Negroes elsewhere. Among
white abolitionists, it generated an outrage which was expressed in
meetings, large and small, throughout the cities of the North and Northwest. Pages were set aside for the case in the *New York Daily Tribune*.
The Supreme Court's decision fed the nationalistic and militant fervor
within the black community, so that by 1861, emigration outside of
the United States had won general approval.[41] While Douglass continued to fight the emigrationist surge, he was no longer doing so publicly; only the outbreak of the Civil War saved him from full commit-

ment. "By the middle of the year [1861]," Bell has written, that "no Negro leader of first rank, with the possible exception of George Downing, was publicly championing the traditional stay-at-home-at-any-cost beliefs; most of them did not look unfavorably upon emigration—or championed it as the true road to progress."[42]

Early in 1857, Garnet appealed to Gerrit Smith and probably to the Tappans for financial aid so that he could become even more independent financially.[43]

Garnet arranged a large Negro antislavery meeting at his church to denounce the Supreme Court decision. Beriah Green, his old professor from Oneida, Douglass, Garnet, and others spoke on that occasion.[44] Douglass and Green made long speeches and Garnet played the role of host. While he did not speak formally, he did make the following bitter comment: "Our people will not always consent to be trodden under foot; they will arm themselves some day, if need be, to secure their rights. It will not be a costly armament, neither a cent a piece will do it; armed with a box of lucifer matches, the black man will have the power in his hands."[45] He appealed to the whites in the audience: "I appeal to my white friends present—would not you do it? Am I wrong in saying it? I think you would. I would."[46]

Douglass also talked in violent terms. He considered Justice Taney's performance a "judicial lie," and he was confident that Taney's descendants would feel ashamed of their name. Douglass concluded that if freedom was to be obtained for Negroes in America, and if they themselves were not the chief instrumentality, they would never gain respect.[47] He had come a long way from his 1843 nonresistant position in black convention debates.

In the fall, Garnet held another meeting at Shiloh to raise money to purchase the freedom of a Methodist Episcopal clergyman. It is not known if the $1,000 necessary to obtain the man's release was raised.[48]

Garnet was involved in another fugitive case in September, in which a Negro slavehunter, Egan Brodie, had decoyed two fugitives back into slavery. In August 1858, Brodie promised to help the two runaways return to Kentucky in order to secure the escape of some relatives. Instead, they were given over to their original owners and received a hundred lashes. When Brodie returned to Cincinnati, Garnet discovered what had occured and informed the Negro community he was then visiting as to Brodie's identity. He exhibited a pair of manacles such as those the two victims wore and a bull whip as used in severe floggings. Brodie was given a trial of sorts, most of which Garnet attended. Except for Garnet's intervention, the man would have been dismembered. As it was, Brodie escaped with three hundred blows from a paddle, one for each dollar he had made from returning the enslaved. He was put in jail for his own protection, since blacks wanted to tear him apart, and was the cause of a minor riot when he returned home to Detroit.[49]

Having been called to the Shiloh church in September, Garnet was installed by the Third Presbytery of New York in November.[50] His acceptance of the post did not entail a compromise in principle, for in the same year Southern Presbyterians had withdrawn their affiliation with "New School" synods of New York and the Western Reserve as a result of the latter's strong antislavery stand.[51]

Even before his installation at Shiloh, Garnet became involved in the organization of Negro clergymen to promote common goals. A meeting was held in Philadelphia to facilitate the religious education of blacks, to give financial aid to poor churches, and to further the struggle for emancipation. Antislavery resolutions were adopted, the most notable of which praised the New School Presbyterian stand against slavery and denounced the Dred Scott decision. This resolution read as follows:

> On motion of Rev. A. N. Freeman, it was resolved, that we hail with great satisfaction and delight the recent secession of the Southern churches from the General Assembly of the New School Presbyterian Church in the United States of America, as a result of the recent action of that body on the subject of Slavery.[52]

> That the recent decision of the Supreme Court of the United States in the case of Dred Scott, the evident design of which is, to degrade and rid the free people of color of civil and political rights, to perpetuate Slavery, and dishearten true philanthropy in the United States: is alike a sin against God, and a crime against humanity; and that Judges Curtis and McLean, who dissented from the infamous decision are worthy of all praise.[53]

Garnet was elected to the Executive Committee of the new organization and planned another meeting for New York the following year. In the interim, he promoted an organization for Negro youth similar to the Young Men's Christian Association. The Young Man's Christian Society, as it was called, grew out of a meeting held at Shiloh in February 1858. In spite of rain, about two hundred people assembled to hear speeches by Garnet and some members of the Young Men's Christian Association. How far Garnet succeeded in this project is not known. At the time of its creation, the editors of the *New York Daily Tribune* were highly optimistic: "This is a newly organized Society, and promises to be of no little benefit to the rising generation of colored people."[54]

When the suffrage campaign began again in the fall of 1858, Garnet journeyed to Troy to speak at the New York State Suffrage Convention. He warned the delegates to be chary of the Republican gubernatorial candidate, first, because Gerrit Smith, who was running as an independent candidate, was his close friend and stood unequivocally for political equality for blacks; and secondly, because Garnet believed that the Republican candidate would not remove the suffrage restriction.[55] Unfortunately, the convention endorsed the Republican candidate over his objection.[56] Later, Garnet wrote Smith of his disappointment with the action of the Colored Suffrage Convention and proposed a second convention to countermand the decision.[57]

In October 1858, another meeting of Negro clergymen was held, this time in the New York City area. It adopted a new name, the Evangelical Association, and produced a series of resolutions on temperance and emancipation. Garnet added a third group to the New York and Philadelphia associations which came from Newport, Rhode Island.[58] While the full impact of this organization cannot be determined for lack of evidence, it was one of many avenues Garnet was exploring in the first few years after his return to America. Suffrage was another and the Republican party a third. For his communicants and for those who cared to listen, Garnet gave his interpretation of the events of the day as they related to the abolitionist crusade.

Garnet's chief interest in the latter half of 1858 became the African Civilization Society, an emigrationist association that he and Delany established to develop an industrial colony in Africa. The goals of the association were to eliminate the slave trade at its source and to create a cotton industry to compete with American fibers. It was to claim the greater part of Garnet's energies for the next five years. It was perhaps the most ambitious scheme of its kind in the entire antebellum period.

NOTES

1. Theodore Clark Smith, *Parties and Slavery, 1850-1859*, Vol. 18 in *The American Nation: A History*, ed. by A. B. Hart, 28 vols. (New York: Harper and Brothers, 1904-1918), pp. 28-29.

2. Ibid.

3. Ibid., pp. 36-38, 265.

4. Ibid., pp. 95-97, 281.

5. Ibid., pp. 98-107.

6. Ibid., pp. 109-135.

7. Ibid., pp. 149-151, 164-166.

8. Ibid., pp. 156-160.

9. Ibid., pp. 11-12, 79, 87-88, 146-147, 161-164.

10. Douglass to Smith as cited in Bell, *Negro Convention Movement, 1830-1861*, p. 138.

11. A full statement is given by Bell throughout the second part of his essay, pp. 120-274.

12. Bell, pp. 140-149.

13. Ibid., pp. 157-158.

14. Ibid., pp. 160-161, 179.

15. *Frederick Douglass' Paper*, 21 March 1856, p. 2.

16. Bell, p. 206.

17. *Frederick Douglass' Paper*, 11 April 1856, p. 1.

18. Ibid., 15 August 1856, p. 3. The funds to sustain Garnet during the early months of 1856 probably came from his friend Gerrit Smith to whom he wrote for money to lecture on 25 March 1856 (Gerrit Smith Miller Collection, Syracuse). Later money came from the Tappans through the American Missionary Association (AMA). Garnet was elected a member of the Executive Committee of the AMA and served from 1856 until 1860. On 1 September 1856, he was appointed a home missionary for the Shiloh Presbyterian Church of New York City. This means a supplement of $250 annually to his pastor's salary.

19. Quarles, *Frederick Douglass*, pp. 156-160.

20. Ibid., p. 155.

21. Ibid., p. 159.

22. As cited in Quarles, p. 160. There is no reference to Garnet in accounts of the Radical convention either in the *New York Daily Tribune* or in the *New York Daily Times*.

23. *New York Daily Tribune*, 7 May 1856, p. 5.

24. Ibid.

25. Ibid.

26. Quarles, pp. 161-162.

27. *Frederick Douglass' Paper*, 11 July 1856, p. 2.

28. Ibid., 27 June 1856, p. 1.

29. Ibid.

30. Ibid., 18 July 1856, p. 2.

31. Ibid., 15 August 1856, p. 2.

32. *New York Daily Tribune*, 24 September 1856, p. 3; *Frederick Douglass' Paper*, 3 October 1856, p. 1.

33. Ibid.

34. Ibid.

35. Ibid.

36. *New York Daily Times*, 26 September 1856, p. 8.

37. Smith, *A Memorial Discourse*, p. 55.

38. See note 18 above.

39. *New York Daily Tribune*, 26 September 1856, p. 7; *New York Daily Times*, 26 September 1856, p. 8. Both articles referred to Garnet's new ministry at Shiloh.

40. *New York Daily Tribune*, 5 September 1856, p. 7.

41. Bell, pp. 223-224.

42. Ibid., p. 223.

43. Garnet to Smith, January 8, 1857 (Gerrit Smith Miller Collection, Syracuse).

44. *New York Daily Tribune*, 18 May 1857, p. 5.

45. *New York Daily Times*, 18 May 1857, p. 1.

46. Ibid.

47. Ibid.

48. *New York Daily Tribune*, 27 October 1857, p. 7; *New York Daily Times*, 3 November 1857, p. 4.

49. *The Liberator*, 17 September 1858, p. 151.

50. *New York Daily Tribune*, 27 October 1857, p. 7.

51. William Roberts, *A Concise History of the Presbyterian Church* (Philadelphia: Presbyterian Board of Publishers, 1922), pp. 1-63.

52. *Minutes of the Second Presbyterian Congregational Convention* (New York: Daley Printers, 1858), p. 10.

53. Ibid., p. 11.

54. *New York Daily Tribune*, 31 February 1858, p. 4.

55. *The Liberator*, 1 October 1858, pp. 158-159; also *Troy Daily Times*, 15 September 1858, p.2.

56. Bell, pp. 189, 204. Also *Troy Daily Whig*, 16 September 1858, p. 3.

57. Garnet to Smith, 10 September 1858 (Gerrit Smith Miller Collection, Syracuse).

58. *Minutes of the Third Presbyterian and Congregational Convention Together with the Organization of the Evangelical Association of Presbyterian and Congregational Clergymen of Color in the United States* (Brooklyn: Book and Job, 1858), pp. 10-11, 15.

8

Africa and America

Before discussing Garnet's role in the African Civilization Society and his civil rights projects after 1858, it is necessary to elaborate on two points previously stated: the success of emigrationist social philosophies among Negro leaders, accompanied by nationalistic fervor—a deep-seated yearning for another country or place in which to live; and the events in American history which were largely responsible for its success. The rivalry among black abolitionists that resulted from these developments will then be discussed briefly.

Garnet was neither the founder nor the sole leader among the nationalists, but represented the leading edge of a decades-old movement which reached a peak in 1861. By that date, most of the front-ranking Negro leaders had been won over to emigration; the exception was George T. Downing,[1] the perpetual foe of emigration.

Bell has labeled the period 1858-1861 that of Emigration Triumphant among a number of black leaders within the convention movement.[2] By that phrase is meant the desire to seek a home abroad, although the motives and goals of emigration were frequently more complex than is suggested by this simplistic categorization. Black emigrationists of Garnet's stature were to qualify and quantify their proposals. There is no evidence that Garnet advocated more than a limited number of colonists in his African project. His scheme was one of a number.[3]

The enthusiasm for emigration might best be revealed in the Negro response to the project discussed by Frank P. Blair, Jr., in January 1858 before the United States House of Representatives. Blair, a congressman from Missouri and himself a believer in the incompatibility of Negroes with whites, was motivated by personal humanitarianism and economic expansion. He proposed that free Negroes be used to colonize territory in Central America, which would be held as an American dependency. Negro emigrationists were generally favorable to this plan.[4] James T. Holly, James M. Whitfield (whose interests in emigration dated to the late 1830s), J. D. Harris, and Alfred V. Thompson were all eager to support Blair if funds were forthcoming. Delany expressed some interest, though he was hesitant to accept money from whites.[5]

Another resurgent emigration project was the Haitian emigration movement, which was given a strong impetus in 1858, when the Haitian government renewed its official invitation to Negro Americans. Other proposals favored settlement in Central America and Africa, while a group of Negroes in Louisiana was reported to be developing a colony in the area of Vera Cruz, Mexico. Emigration to Canada had continued throughout the 1850s to the point that some were claiming that Canada had as many as fifty thousand inhabitants by 1860. Dr. J. S. Prescott's proposal that Negroes settle in certain frontier areas of the United States was seriously considered in Washington, Philadelphia, and Pittsburgh. The British were still trying to bring black laborers to Jamaica and as an inducement were reportedly offering Crown lands after three years of labor. Lewis Putnam was reviving his Liberian expatriation scheme in 1859, and the American Colonization Society was still promoting colonization of the same area.[6] For those who wanted to retain their American ties and still live outside the United States, Blair's scheme for using Negroes for peaceful penetration of Central America was available.[7]

The emigrationist surge is best understood in its historical context. The Fugitive Slave Law, mitigated by the passage of personal liberty laws, had placed the burden of proving one's freedom upon the accused. Then too, the Dred Scott case of 1857 which declared the Negro to be property seemed to many blacks a complete and categorical denial of his humanity. Although many Negroes looked to the Republican party as their political hope, and although the party grew at a phenomenal rate in the late 1850s, its commitment to Negro rights was limited to the territories. In the face of these developments, Garnet and other

emigrationists led new challenges to Douglass's leadership. They succeeded briefly in winning him to a more favorable attitude toward
emigration, if not to their particular proposals.

In 1859, Douglass, as editor of the most prominent Negro organ of
the period and the only general newspaper for part of the time, retained
a commanding influence. He was in no mood to retreat from his stand
on colonization:[8]

> Upon one point we wish to be especially explicit, and that is,
> upon no consideration do we intend that our paper shall favor
> any schemes of Colonization, or any measures the natural
> tendency of which will be to draw off the attention of the free
> colored people from the means of improvement and elevation
> here. Now, and always, we expect to insist upon it that we are
> Americans; *that America is our native land; that this is our*
> *home; that we are American citizens* [author's italics] ; that
> it is the duty of the American people so to recognize us.[9]

In expressing such sentiments, Douglass was no longer representing an
undivided Negro viewpoint. In 1859, a new publication appeared, and
its editor, Thomas Hamilton of New York, was less doctrinaire than
Douglass had become. The new paper, *The Weekly Anglo-African*, was
to have a leading role in giving both sides of the emigration story to the
public. In so doing it brought the issue out into the open—perhaps more
so than necessary—and *The African* was on occasion as nationalistic as
Delany would have been.[10]

For Douglass, it would be necessary to endure a painful flight from
the United States immediately after Harper's Ferry and to witness Lincoln's declaration in 1860 in favor of Union rather than interference
with the established order. By that time, the Haitian offer of free passage to black immigrants and aid in getting established, as well as renewed interest in Africa, proved very attractive to both white and
Negro abolitionists.[11]

This is not to say that despair alone provided the chief motivation
behind emigrationist programs. Without becoming enmeshed in the
literature of black nationalism, it is a safe assertion that this phenome-
non was complicated and that, during the late 1840s, it was related to
the European fervor unleashed by the revolutions of 1848 and by the

Hungarian statesman Louis Kossuth's well-publicized visit to America.[12] Yearnings for self-determination among Eastern European minorities were readily appreciated and supported by American abolitionists of every stripe.[13] Some Negroes were attracted to Liberia after it attained independence in 1847 and after Reverend Pinney's personal campaign in New York in the early 1850s, while others remained skeptical of any relation to colonization.[14]

The African Civilization Society harked back to another era for Garnet and represented a culmination of his personal experiences over the past twenty years. In a recent article, Richard MacMaster treats some of the more immediate causes for the formation of the society.[15] When Garnet was immersed in the New York suffrage campaign of 1841, articles began to appear in *The Colored American* discussing the newly formed African Civilization Society. Garnet probably read them, since the same newspaper was the touchstone of the suffrage campaign which he led. Originally the brainchild of Lord Fowell Buxton, a wealthy British philanthropist, the African Civilization Society proposed African settlements of black missionaries to teach local natives, to institute agricultural improvements, and to educate them against the folly of participation in the slave trade.[16] Buxton went to some lengths to differentiate his organization from the American Colonization Society. While he was not opposed to voluntary emigration or to the constitution of the American Colonization Society, he strongly disapproved of "the practical tendency of the institution itself to soothe American slaveholders by calling slavery a necessary evil and as such obstructing the efforts at immediate abolition." Furthermore, to facilitate black emigration, the American Colonization Society utilized various coercive measures, thereby making Liberia a place of exile. Finally, Buxton believed (as did many American abolitionists of the period) that the withdrawal of free Negroes from the proximity of those still in bondage would mean the loss of natural allies.[17]

The newspaper editors reacted favorably to Buxton's scheme. On another page in the same issue of *The Colored American*, they endorsed the proposal that educated Christian missionaries, recruited from among the "sons of Africa," be sent overseas. They also supported Buxton's desire to instruct West Africans in agriculture and to bring about development, which in turn would result in a turning away from "war, plunder, and the slave trade."[18]

Thus, years before publication of Benjamin Coates' pamphlet on cotton-growing in Africa and before Garnet's lectures in the Free Produce movement, Garnet was familiar with a number of ideas which became incorporated into the African Civilization Society when it was re-formed in 1858, having died earlier. Additional factors culminating in Garnet's embrace of the society were his personal sense of attachment for his ancestral home which was manifest at an early age,[19] and his acceptance, as early as 1849, of certain kinds of immigration under particular conditions.[20] Moreover, Free Produce efforts abroad and in the United States led to his understanding of the international implications and interrelationships that would be involved in bringing sufficient pressure to bear against American slavery. Finally, like Delany, Garnet read the column in *The Colored American* written by "Augustine" whom Floyd J. Miller has identified as Lewis Woodson of Ohio. In Miller's view, Woodson was "the father of black nationalism."[21]

The Free Produce movement, which was so important in the development of Garnet's approach to the emancipation effort, was involved in several influential activities: first and most well-known was the boycott of slave-grown cotton and sugar. A considerable literature was circulated by the Free Produce leaders to achieve these ends.[22] Secondly, Garnet and Pennington unquestionably advanced the cause of Free Produce abroad. Third, the industrialists connected with the association began experimenting with West African cotton. In 1850, Liberian President John J. Roberts welcomed an English agent sent to the African Coast by some textile firms for that purpose. Roberts discussed a plan for growing cotton in Africa with a Philadelphia Quaker, Benjamin Coates, who became very enthusiastic.[23]

When Garnet returned from Jamaica, convinced that England's cotton market was supporting the slave markets of America, both he and Coates became enthusiasts of Reverend Thomas Jefferson Bowen, a lecturer and Baptist missionary who had also recently returned from Africa in poor health. Bowen had worked in the Niger Valley and had established a mission at Abbeokuta in Nigeria.[24] Bowen's lectures, in which he dispelled notions of African barbarism, stressed the advanced civilization of the Yoruba towns, and described the agricultural methods and the local weaving, dyeing, and clothmaking industries, created a great sensation. One of Bowen's constant themes was that civilized black settlements would both reap great commercial benefit and bring the Christian message to the African continent.[25]

Then in 1858, Coates published his pamphlet, *Cotton Cultivation in Africa.*[26] This document of fifty-two pages contained a concise proposal which, when later combined with Coates' own financial support and money from other sources, became a living organization. The pamphlet revealed that Thomas Clegg and the Cotton Supply Association of Manchester, England, had researched and demonstrated that cotton could be grown inexpensively in Africa. Production of the African fiber would reduce the wealth of the South and would thus reduce the power of the slave system. Intelligent and educated Negroes would be the logical leaders of the African cotton industry. Coffee and rice could also be grown which would eventually aid in creating free labor for the area. A general exodus of colored people was not desirable; approximately fifty thousand over a ten-year period would suffice. He pointed to the success of Liberia in self-government and suggested the support of American and British abolitionists in his proposed society. He hoped this organization would supersede all of the currently existing anti-slavery and colonization societies. As to the means of colonization, Coates suggested emigrant aid societies of the Kansas variety to send deserving emigrants to Yoruba, Sudan, and other areas, where the climate was believed to be better than on the coast.[27]

A letter Coates sent to Crummell some years later contains a clear statement of his approach:

Such was the deep seated prejudice in the minds of nearly the entire colored population against the colonization enterprise, that they would not listen with patience to any arguments on the subject and the very name of Liberia was obnoxious to them. It was almost labor lost to talk on the subject even to men like Delany and Rob[er]t Campbell or William Whipper or Frederick Douglass, all of whom had a personal regard for me. But after Livingston and Barth had attracted some attention to Africa—and Bowen had shown the comparative healthfulness of the high table of the interior of Africa in the Egba, Yoruba country, I thought it best to direct attention to that region, knowing full well, that an interest once created in Africa, must accrue to the interest of Liberia, even should a successful and prosperous settlement be made elsewhere—as a matter of *expediency* & *policy* [author's italics] , therefore I suggested a new organization avoiding the obnoxious term colonization—and the result had not dis-

appointed my expectations—indeed my hopes were more than
realized—for as Mr. Garnett [*sic*] very justly remarked before
he left for England, that if not a single person went to Yoruba,
at this time, a strong interest had been awakened in Africa,
the result of which you have experienced in your intercourse
with our colored population—which had your visit to America
been two years earlier you could hardly have had a hearing
in many places where you have been now most favorably
received.[28]

Three meetings were held in the summer of 1858 in New York to
discuss the conditions of black Americans and the practicability of a
distinct nationality. At the third meeting, on 9 August at Spring-Street
Hall, Garnet presented his views. He told the audience that while
Negroes abhorred slavery and intended to fight it to the last, no man
should deprive him of his love of Africa, the land of his ancestors. He
gloried in her ancient glory, her science, and art and was proud to trace
his origins to Africa, the land of early civilization and powerful empires.
Love of country, he continued, was an essential part of man's nature,
and a void would exist until that was filled. He hoped to view a national
flag of which he would be proud. Dwelling at some length and in glow-
ing terms on the economic potential, he said that he hoped Negro citizens would not allow the whites to get too far ahead of them in Central
Africa. A few thousand intelligent and enterprising men would be
enough to plant a Christian nation which would be a center for moral
and religious as well as commercial and social influence for Africa.
White men could not do this work as well as the black, and God called
upon the Negro race to join in this object. "Let those who wish to stay,
stay here," he said, "and those who had enterprise and wished to go,
go and found a nation, of which the colored American could be
proud."[29]
    When it came into existence, however, the African Civilization
Society was a predominantly white organization in New York City and
Philadelphia, with Garnet as the president. Its constitution as signed by
Garnet stated that the primary aim of the society was "the civilization
and Christianization of Africa, and of the descendants of African ancestors in any portion of the earth, wherever dispersed."[30] It hoped to
promote Christian missions, using evangelical sects, and to destroy the

slave trade by promoting cotton and other industry in Yoruba, using primarily native labor. Garnet looked to the Negro churches of America to send out missionaries necessary to perform the task.[31] As the organizer of the Evangelical Association of Negro Ministers, Garnet would be in a commanding position to recruit missionaries for the new project. It was no coincidence, then, that seven of the nine ministers within the association became acitvists in the African Civilization Society.[32] This may partially explain why he came to regard the society as a missionary crusade, and, as will be shown, why Delany at first wished to work independently of Garnet.

Garnet was not the only Negro to be interested in the Niger Valley. As suggested earlier, Delany also had been involved in projects for the area. Before Garnet held meetings in New York in 1858, a convention had been held in Chatham, Canada, to establish a separate nationality for Negro Americans under Delany's direction. Steps had already been taken to send out an expedition to determine if the area was suitable for commerce and agriculture, particularly cotton.[33]

The Canadian movement was largely a continuation of the Emigration Convention of 1854 held in Ohio.[34] Although Garnet and Delany were friends and were interested in the same kind of commercial development in Africa, they clashed on emigration. For one thing, neither was temperamentally suited to serve in a subordinate capacity. Then, too, Delany's deep sense of nationalism prohibited him from accepting white participation and financial support.[35] Finally, Delany had an intense distrust of Christian religion, possibly because he lived in an age which used Christ's teachings to justify slavery.[36] Garnet, on the other hand, had a more ambivalent attitude toward Christianity. Delany's and Garnet's organizations used similar names, however, and each solicited funds from the American Colonization Society which repulsed men like George T. Downing. Each was to go his own way until 1861, when, after many setbacks and defections of personnel, Delany joined Garnet's organization.[37]

The response to Garnet's project was immediate and generally hostile. *The Liberator* at first reacted favorably to Coates' pamphlet but expressed doubt that the five thousand black emigrants a year could be raised.[38] Two articles which appeared on cotton-growing in Africa in the Garrisonian *National Anti-Slavery Standard* in the fall were likewise an endorsement,[39] but the *Standard* later became uncertain.[40]

George T. Downing wrote an angry letter of rejection to the *New York Daily Tribune*, which had printed several letters in praise of the African Civilization Society and Coates' pamphlet.[41] He denounced the organization as an offshoot of the American Colonization Society. Africans were already producing cotton themselves, he wrote, and if Africans could do such a good job, why was it necessary to send five thousand Negro Americans overseas to cultivate the crop? The real object of Coates' proposal, Downing wrote, was to rid the United States of free Negroes. So far as Garnet's role was concerned, he was needed at home. Downing continued: "Our friend Garnett [sic], it must be remembered left his country for Europe, afterward left Europe with his family for the West Indies, which was to have been his future home; afterward returned to his native home and settled himself down; and now we find him engaged in what I call a wild goose chase in Africa."[42]

Downing's blast drew an immediate response from Garnet, who in a friendly tone, made an effort to reexplain and persuade, but the explanation was doubtlessly rejected.[43] Again, Garnet had incurred not only Downing's resentment but that of other black intellectuals as well.

Frederick Douglass found seven reasons for opposing the African Civilization Society, and in so doing, he gave Garnet's program widespread publicity through the pages of *Douglass' Monthly*. In Douglass' objections, there was little new; they had been far more effective in the 1840s than they would be in 1859, and Garnet knew that a restatement of them would have little effect on the decision to stay in America or to emigrate.[44]

Douglass made little effort to examine Garnet's program on its own merits and stated his usual objections to emigration. He said that the program would take funds away from the domestic struggle and would keep the idea of a homeland alive, an idea which increased the black man's torment.[45] Douglass's analysis simply went no further on this point. He took no survey to determine the eligibility and skills of free Negroes in the United States; he made no inquiry into Garnet's sources of revenue in America or in England; and, he apparently made no effort to satisfy his curiosity about African cotton. In retrospect, Douglass appeared to be as defensive as he had been several years earlier when Garnet had advertised for American laborers in Jamaica.[46] Coates was probably correct when he wrote Crummell that the great majority of blacks and their leaders were unable to give the project a fair hearing in 1858.

So ended the period of rapprochement between Garnet and Douglass. They were to remain in different camps until Douglass's partial capitulation in 1861. Even when he modified his position, Douglass thought Haiti would be a better place for blacks because of its proximity to the United States; personally, however, he would stand his ground in America. Evidently, he retained the Garrison notion of "proximity" until the end.

Soon after Douglass's opposition was published Garnet was asked to defend his new scheme in the open forum. Meanwhile, as a minister, an abolitionist, and a fighter for justice, he remained close to people. Late in 1858 and again in 1859, meetings were held at Shiloh to commemorate the passing of two grand contributors to the antislavery cause, Samuel Cornish and William Jay. Appropriate eulogies were delivered on both occasions to mixed audiences; Douglass delivered the eulogy for Jay, and Garnet read the opening hymn at the Cornish service, "Servant of God, well done."[47]

In December 1858, a meeting of the African Civilization Society was held at Shiloh, called in response to the threatened reopening of the slave trade. Garnet chaired the meeting. Campbell, Delany and Garnet addressed a large number on that occasion.[48] Soon after, Delany and Campbell launched their exploration party into the Niger Valley.

While adverse reaction to Garnet's scheme came immediately from Downing, Douglass, William Wells Brown, Nell, and others, Garnet soon found friends. *The New York Colonization Journal* came to his defense. In an editorial reply to Douglass dated February 1859, the *Journal* stated that Douglass did not understand Garnet's plan. More could be done, it was argued, by using a fulcum than by trying to lift too much directly. By developing Africa, the Negro could attain higher status in this country then by working at home. The editorial excoriated Douglass for his lack of interest in African people.[49] Articles which appeared in the April and July issues cited rapid changes of opinion among Negroes regarding Africa. The *Journal* looked forward to the first anniversary of the African Civilization Society to be held on 11 May 1859.[50]

Other early supporters of the new society included R. R. Gurley, Reverend Pinney, and Theodore Bourne, all of whom were associated with the American Colonization Society. They constituted part of a "Yoruba cabal" within the organization, but were unsuccessful in convincing the board of directors to give the project full support. Through Bourne who had become the secretary-treasurer of Garnet's organiza-

tion, the American Colonization Society maintained a watchful eye.[51]
One black supporter of the new organization was Reverend J. Sella
Martin, a young antislavery minister.[52]

The new organization was reasonably well established by the autumn
of 1859. Conservatives, searching for a way to combat the growing
trend toward emigration, agreed upon a traditional convention with
speeches, resolutions, and memorials as the desired means. As Negro
Garrisonians represented the largest segment of conservative opposition,
the logical site for their meeting was Boston. Suffrage was listed as the
chief reason for the call, but the instructions given to the New Bedford
delegation to oppose colonization may have been closer to the actual
motive for the meeting.[53]

Williams Wells Brown set the tone by denouncing the African Civilization Society. Downing, the president of the "suffrage" meeting, followed suit. In his anxiousness to slay the monster of emigration, Downing was unwilling to devote time to the then defunct National Council
which the Bostonians were trying to revive and dominate. When the
African Civilization Society was challenged on the convention floor,
Reverend J. Sella Martin and Reverend J. B. Smith, both new to the
Negro convention scene, defended it ably. They championed the
approach favoring a home beyond the United States—even in Africa—
while the old guard remained loyal to their traditional beliefs.[54]

Eventually, the convention reached a compromise, admitting that
any Negro had the right to emigrate either for personal ambitions or in
a true missionary cause. But Garrison wanted a strong condemnation of
Africa and to make the African Civilization Society appear to favor
mass emigration, which, of course, was not the case.[55] This reaction was
predictable in 1859 when the abolitionist press was geared to keep all
Negroes as close to the slave as possible.

Garnet saw an opportunity to turn criticism into gain.[56] He scheduled
another meeting, or a return bout, for 29 August 1859. His chief lieu-
tenant, Reverend Martin, engineered a vote of confidence in Garnet's
past performance and commitment to the Negro. While it said nothing
of the African Civilization Society, the resolution passed with little
opposition or with a great deal, depending on the respective versions
printed in *The Liberator* and *The Weekly Anglo-African*.[57]

At this meeting, Garnet had things largely his own way. In one of his
first statements, he accused the New England convention of conspiring
to attack the African Civilization Society generally and to misrepresent

his views specifically.[58] Nell immediately protested the charge. Garnet continued, impugning the motives of Nell, Downing, and Reverend L. A. Grimes, a minister who had not volunteered his church for Garnet's use.[59] If Garnet's criticism was unduly harsh, he did succeed in clarifying his personal expectations of the new organization. After championing free discussion among his peers and colleagues, he singled out Downing, who was not present, as a special target. He wanted Downing to know that he was *not* a colonizationist. "Any man that says I am a colonizationist," proclaimed Garnet, "behind my back is an assassin and a coward; any man that says it to my face is a liar, and I stamp the infamous charge upon his forehead!"[60]

Having denounced the American Colonization Society for its stand on forced emigration of the newly freed, Garnet cited his expectations for the new organization. A first objective was "the immediate and unconditional abolition of slavery in the United States and in Africa, and the destruction of the African slave-trade both in this and that country."[61] His second objective was "the destruction of prejudice against colored people in the United States, especially in the nominal free states of the North; and we propose to do this by urging upon the abolitionists and the friends of humanity of every grade the necessity of giving trades and employment to ourselves and to our children." Third, he proposed "to assist in giving the Gospel to Africa, and thus render obedience unto the unrepealed command of Jesus Christ, to go into all the world and preach the Gospel to every creature." Fourth, he proposed "the civilization of Africa, by the introduction into that country of lawful trade and commerce; by the cultivation of cotton to supply the world from dependence on the cotton raised in the Southern states by slave labor, and by this means to strike the death-blow to American slavery."[62]

Garnet's next point was his most controversial one: "to establish a grand center of Negro nationality, from which shall flow streams of commercial, intellectual, and political power which shall make colored people respected everywhere." When asked if this state would be in America or Africa, he replied that he hoped it would be formed in the United States, especially if the slave trade were reopened. The American South seemed to him to be the likely place to build a black nationality; that region lay closest to the island of the Caribbean, "and we shall have every island in the Caribbean Sea."[63]

Garnet hoped "by the power of money and union of action in this country, to encourage our professional men of every occupation in arts and sciences of every grade, and thus keep the colored people here from the disrespect and contumely shown by others, and the despondency and despair felt by themselves by too many circumstances." Finally, all of these objectives were to be achieved through the voluntary cooperation of the friends of universal freedom, regardless of color, by working either here or in Africa.[64]

Such was Garnet's program. The antagonisms it generated in Boston were echoed by Douglass in October, and were intensified the following spring.[65] On a more positive note, Garnet had touched many wellsprings of motivation—economic advancement, missionary zeal, real estate on which one could be free, equal, and secure, and the more traditional aims of abolitionists. If Garnet's input provided the carrot of emigration among blacks, then events within the larger society in October provided the stick.

During September 1858, Garnet participated in the annual meeting of the Evangelical Association of Colored Ministers of Congregational and Presbyterian Churches held in New York City. While the meeting had been called largely to promote churches and church operations throughout the country, Garnet used the meeting as a forum for antislavery lectures. On one occasion he discussed the relationship between the churches and slavery, condemning American churches as sustainers of the institution. He mentioned that many ministers in Brooklyn declared men to be property and that some black clergymen were little better. Without becoming specific, he accused the clergy of making infidels of youth and poisoning their minds before they had an opportunity to bloom. True success in the ministry, be believed, depended on an uncompromising regard for truth, justice, and righteousness. Ministers had to assume these obligations.[66]

By mid-October 1858, Garnet had lined up a number of Anglo-African lecturers to aid in the promotion of a reading room open to all, with literature on current events and intellectual entertainments.[67] One of the first to visit the new facility, Horace Greeley, editor of the *Tribune*, expressed his approval. The reading room seems to have survived only eight months, closing in June 1860 at a small financial loss to Garnet.[68]

While he was actively promoting the African Civilization Society, Garnet maintained his interest in the advancement of black New Yorkers. In a long letter to S. S. Joscelyn, his old colleague in the American

Missionary Association, for funds with which to carry out these objectives, Garnet said that emphasis should now be placed on helping those who were already free. The large towns and cities along the banks of the Hudson, Garnet thought were ripe fields for missionary work. Black and white leaders were cognizant of the need, he continued, and had advocated the employment of a home missionary. "Let it not be forgotten that wherever we live, there is missionary ground, and will be such till slavery and its many evil effects are done away."[69]

Garnet wrote two letters to Joscelyn for funds, both which revealed his interest in his brethren's welfare at a time when black intellectuals were accusing him of giving up the struggle for rights in America. In the second letter, he proposed to establish a Sunday school in his own Shiloh Presbyterian Church, to open prayer meetings in localities with the greatest need, and finally to continue his Anglo-African reading room largely for the benefit of Negro youth. Finally, he proposed to serve as a city missionary himself in connection with the Association.[70] Although the reading room was unsuccessful, his Sunday school thrived. Garnet also performed some city missionary work and by March 1860 was able to report the opening of a school.[71]

In the larger society during this time, sectional polarization was rapidly continuing. If the Dred Scott case had convinced many Northerners that freedom was dangerously threatened by a conspiracy of the "slave power," John Brown's raid on Harper's Ferry on the night of 16 October 1859 had a similar effect below the Mason-Dixon line. Brown's action, over in thirty-six hours, had touched the South at its most sensitive nerve—its fear of slave insurrections. The South's alarm and resentment might have been lessened if the North as a whole had denounced Brown (as many Northerners did, including Lincoln). Brown, however, had the financial backing of some of the most respected figures in Boston, and his execution date became the occasion for public mourning in New England. Emerson declared Brown a martyr;[72] Theodore Parker and Douglass left the country. Douglass went to England, where he stayed until the heat cooled down, and his flight prompted Garnet's witty remark that Douglass was "fighting it out" under the protection of the British lion[73]—an obvious allusion to Douglass's slurs when Garnet went to England ten years earlier.

Brown was also praised by the New York abolitionists. Early in November, large audiences began coming to Shiloh Presbyterian

Church to pray for Brown. Garnet had held a preliminary prayer meeting at his home beforehand in which the principal participants were women. He visited the Siloam Presbyterian Church in Brooklyn on 24 November and delivered a eulogy before an interdenominational audience.[74]

On 2 December 1859, Garnet held another antislavery meeting at Shiloh for Brown who was about to be executed. He told his audience that the day of Brown's demise was at hand and would be known by subsequent generations as "Martyr's Day."[75] While he himself was not a man of vengenance, Garnet continued, he saw signs of divine retribution—"*For the sins of this nation there is no atonement without the shedding of blood* [author's italics]." It was no coincidence to Garnet that slavery should receive the most damaging blow to date in Virginia, the place in which slavery began in this part of the New World. "When he dies," Garnet continued, "he will leave behind him no greater apostle of liberty in all the land." After stating that Brown's motivation was the carrying out of the Golden Rule, Garnet saluted Brown as a hero whose "deeds will be inscribed on marble, and his grave will be visited by troops of pilgrims."[76]

After his eulogy, Garnet read a short poem which he had written. In three simple stanzas it stated the contribution which Brown's martyrdom was going to make to human liberty and the appreciation that thousands would have for him as a result of his sacrifice.[77]

Such were Garnet's efforts during 1859. Before the end of the year, a meeting of the London Emancipation Committee, chaired by the renowned George Thompson, passed a resolution declaring its sympathy with the objectives of the African Civilization Society, so far as these activities promoted the growth of Free Produce and the establishment of a line of five settlements along the west coast of Africa—a policy that was expected to secure the final extinction of the slave trade.[78] At least one agent fot the African Civilization Society was in England seeking support and had been cordially received by a committee of the British and Foreign Anti-Slavery Society.[79] Before the year had ended, Greeley had given the first of a number of lectures in behalf of the reading room which Garnet had opened to the public at large. In addition, Garnet had held a meeting in behalf of one of the Oberlin rescuers, men who had aroused much sympathy when tried for freeing a runaway. The most famous rescuer was Charles H. Langston, secretary of the Ohio Anti-

Slavery Society and the brother of John Mercer Langston,[80] who was prominent in the equals rights movement after the Civil War. Charles Langston was found guilty, but his passionate defense of liberty won him a minimum sentence of twenty days in jail and a $100 fine.

On 19 December 1859, a "Union Saving Meeting" was held in New York City at the Academy of Music. The Unionists, composed of politicians and locally prominent people, were eager to sacrifice the rights of the Negro to the goal of maintaining the federal relationship. One of them, Charles O'Conor, a lawyer of distinction and wealth, went so far as to praise the slave system as just, benign in its effects upon both white and blacks, and so ordained by nature. As expected, this position infuriated local blacks who held a large meeting at Shiloh a month later. Garnet, who chaired the meeting, and James McCune Smith delivered passionate denunciations of O'Conor's remarks. Garnet said he would "walk betimes without remorse or dread, and my first step would be on Conor's [*sic*] head." In a series of resolutions, the meeting challenged O'Conor to appear in an open forum to debate and enlarge upon his remarks. Two of them read as follows:

That this meeting do respectfully request that said Charles O'Conor, esq., to deliver a lecture or lectures, in which he shall set forth in full the views which lead him to believe that Negro Slavery is "not unjust," and that he will show when and where nature ordained Slavery.

That in the case Charles O'Conor, esq., shall consent to deliver such lecture or lectures, we pledge ourselves to procure for him a very large and attentive audience in the Academy of Music or Cooper Institute; and that in case he makes out his case, even to his own satisfaction, we will give him our recommendation to the President of the United States, as a fit candidate for the approaching vacancy in the Bench of the Supreme Court of the United States.[81]

That seemingly was the end of the episode.

Garnet further clarified his plans for the African Civilization Society in an address at Cooper Institute early in March 1860. He emphasized the need for sending out a select group and the educational and commerical alspects of the venture. His notion of helping Africans presupposed a relationship among equals. It read as follows:

> We regard the enslavement of our race to be the highest crime against God and man, and we hope, by teaching the Kings and Chiefs of Africa better things, to induce them to exterminate the slave trade and engage in lawful commerce, and in this way aid in destroying slavery in this and all other lands.

> We believed it would be preferable to sit down by their side, and not only teach the people by precept those principles which we desire them to cherish, but also to teach them by power of example those things that will elevate their manhood and exalt their nature; and to make them feel that we are a part of themselves—interested in everything which promises to promote their happiness and increase their prosperity.[82]

In evaluating his aims in terms of the treaty which was later negotiated by Delany, Garnet appeared faithful to his principles. His activities have accurately been described by one writer as "an embryonic expression of Pan-African sentiment. However, the same critic states that Garnet's aims were impractical, narrow, racist in their emphasis on Christian missionary activity, and elitist in favoring the creation of a ruling class.[83] Ultimately, the interpretation depends on whatever fact is being emphasized. Although Garnet's tone was patronizing and ethnocentric, it should be pointed that Christianity was used both to defend and to attack slavery throughout the antebellum period. Finney's contribution in altering the teachings to apply directly in the secular sphere did much to galvanize the antislavery movement in the Northwest. Also, Garnet and his teacher Wright consistently believed that a true Christian would never own slaves or be a party to the institution. So far as the notion of practicability is concerned, the answer seems irretrievably locked in history.[84] Further, any proposal which comes slightly ahead of its time is open, in retrospect, to the charge of being narrow. One might make the same criticism of Paul Cuffee who had similar views on emigration years before Garnet.

Was Garnet an elitist? While Garnet and Douglass were educated men well above the level of the black masses, it is not necessarily true that they were completely cut off from the aspirations of black Americans. Garnet's poverty, his continual, daily involvement with large numbers of working people, black and white, probably was responsible for his sympathy for the workingman in America and in Europe. That sympathy was exceedingly rare among American abolitionists, Douglass included.[85]

When Garnet announced his plan that evening in 1860 at Cooper Institute, attendance was light and opposition was smaller than usual. The quiet was deceptive. African Civilization Society sponsors in England, it was alleged, were claiming that American abolitionists and free Negroes were unanimously in favor of the society program. This news, coupled with Garnet's announced program, made it imperative that the old guard prove how weak the African movement truly was.[86]

To do this, Charles L. Reason and Downing wrote to a number of correspondents, among them Gerrit Smith, mentioning the report from Europe and stating their personal opinion that the African Civilization Society and the American Colonization Society were practically the same. This statement was followed with a question as to what the addressee thought of the new society. With responses from Smith, Nell, Franklin Turner, John F. Waugh, Oliver Johnson, William Wells Brown, Robert Purvis, Ezra Johnson, John C. Bowers, and others, the anti-emigrationists considered themselves well fortified. They were taking no chances, however. Having summoned a mass meeting with a spectacular call, Downing by prearrangement sought to have the meeting sanction a list of officers and speakers with topics selected by those who had arranged the meeting.[87]

Garnet was not cowered by such tactics. He demanded the right to be heard since it was a mass meeting. He was successful in having the election of officers separated from acceptance of the prearranged program—an arrangement that would have allowed no rebuttal from the floor. While some of the Downing letters opposing emigration were read, Garnet insisted on hearing the letter from which the responses had resulted, a letter which Downing was unprepared to produce.

Garnet's confrontation tactics paid further dividends when the convention leaders tried to condemn the African Civilization Society by resolution. At that point he managed to create enough confusion that the meeting broke up in a near riot as the caretaker, Samuel J. Howard, forced the audience out by shutting off the lights.[88] This was not Garnet's last play. Four days later, he staged a return engagement in a much smaller chamber, and perhaps by prearrangement it was filled by those favorable to emigration. No opponents materialized, and everyone was happy.[89]

In retrospect, it may be seen that each side had overplayed its hand. The fact that those who called the mass meeting included only a few of the most prominent abolitionists in the community—Pennington, Downing, and Ransom F. Wake—means, according to Bell, that many thinking men were not ready to condemn the African Civilization Society completely. Also, an examination of the list of men whose letters were read at the assembly revealed the extremes to which the planners had gone to support their position. Most of those who replied favorably enough to the anti-emigrationist view to rate a public hearing were prominent only in Garrisonian ranks. Brown, Nell, and Purvis had been dissociated from the Negro convention movement for years, except as they could appear in true Garrisonian attire. Oliver Johnson was hardly the leading editor of the period, and Franklin Turner and John Waugh played minor roles in convention circles. It is also significant that no letter from Garrison was read, though he had been honored with a second request to give his opinion of the African Civilization Society.[90]

It appears, therefore, that fear motivated the conservatives to use such extremes to quell the society's power. Garnet, on the other hand, was blameworthy for responding with a packed meeting of his own. It seems that in the spring of 1860 neither group was certain of its standing in the community.[91]

By the time of the Cooper Union meeting in March 1860, the Niger Valley party had journeyed to the Abbeokuta area and had signed a treaty with native chiefs. The terms allowed them to locate in areas not otherwise occupied by natives, though in the proximity, and to govern themselves according to their own customs. In a letter to Garnet, Robert Campbell, a Delany associate, explained that in disputes between a native and an American settler, an equal number of commissioners representing each group would have the power to decide the case. Elymas P. Rogers, a New Jersey Presbyterian minister and booster of the society, at his own expense planned to start a colony in Yoruba, but he died en route to Lagos on 20 January 1861.[92]

A few months after Campbell wrote to Garnet about his treaty, war again broke out among the chiefs, and a new phase opened in December 1860. It imperiled existing missions and made any attempt to settle colonies in war-torn Abbeokuta improbable. British traders at Lagos demanded the protection of the army; on 20 July 1861, Lagos became an appendage of the British government.[93]

While these developments set back the efforts to plant colonies, Garnet continued to raise money for worthy black charities in the city, to support the suffrage campaign regardless of its many defeats, and to serve as a city missionary among blacks.[94]

Garnet also continued to aid people who were imprisoned for aiding fugitives. A special rally was held at Shiloh Church in May 1861 to muster moral and financial support for the "Philadelphia Rescuers," individuals who had been imprisoned for aiding the fugitive Moses Horner. Two resolutions were adopted unanimously, one recognizing the heroic conduct of the unfortunate men then in jail and a second soliciting funds for their legal defense. Fifty-three dollars was collected.[95]

As the crucial election of 1860 approached and the suffrage fight for Negroes was renewed, difficult political questions would have to be faced. As early as August 1859, black New Englanders at a meeting chaired by Downing gave their endorsement to the Republican party. The delegates, however, voted to press the Republicans for support in their fight for the vote. The situation was similar in New York and Ohio.[96] Although Frederick Douglass was an elector at-large at the Radical Abolitionist convention of August, he changed his mind as the campaign progressed, and he worked for Lincoln in Michigan, Wisconsin, and Iowa.[97]

The Democrats were openly antagonistic to the full civil rights of blacks and the Republicans were against extension of slavery in the territories. Garnet probably agreed with the sentiments expressed by the New York State Suffrage Convention in May, on whose business committee he served, that neither major party was particularly helpful and that appeals should be directed to all candidates who favored the granting of equal suffrage.[98] The alternatives for Negroes, then, were narrowed in the election. The Democrats were generally repudiated as being anti-Negro; Negroes, dismissing the Radical Abolitionists as ineffectual, cast their ballots in overwhelming numbers for the less than adequate Republican party.[99]

In his antislavery efforts in 1860, Garnet was again waging a campaign on several fronts. He was fighting the old suffrage crusade in New York State and working in the city as a home missionary. He was far along in his plan to build a Negro nationality in Africa, and before the year ended, he was involved in the Haitian emigration as well.[100] Finally, he was enmeshed in a leadership struggle among black abolitionists over the acceptance of his program. By 1861, Garnet's emigrationist projects would reach their apogee among blacks and then decline for reasons largely beyond his control.

NOTES

1. Bell, *Negro Convention Movement, 1830-1861*, p. 223.
2. Ibid., p. 206.
3. Frequently, the same individuals were involved in more than one project simultaneously; the same is true for organizations.
4. Bell, pp. 209-210.
5. Ibid., pp. 210-211.
6. Ibid., pp. 226-227. See the entire chapter for a complete explanation.
7. Ibid., p. 226.
8. Ibid., p. 215.
9. *Douglass' Monthly*, January 1859, p. 2. In the same issue, p. 4, Douglass denounced the African Civilization Society as American Colonization under a different name. He also denounced any notion of a black nationality; see also Bell, p. 215.
10. Bell, pp. 215-216.
11. Ibid., pp. 216-217.
12. Richard MacMaster, "Henry Highland Garnet and the African Civilization Society," *Journal of Presbyterian Church History* 48 (Summer 1970): 96.
13. A glance through *The Liberator*, the *National Anti-Slavery Standard*, or the *New York Daily Tribune* during the Hungarian Nationalist's visit to the United States will reveal long articles set aside in his honor.
14. MacMaster, p. 96.
15. Ibid., pp. 99-103.
16. *The Colored American*, 27 February 1841, p. 1.
17. Ibid.
18. Ibid., pp. 1, 4.
19. See Chapter 1, p. 19, above.
20. See Chapter 5, pp. 101-103, above.
21. Floyd J. Miller, "The Father of Black Nationalism," *Civil War History* 17 (December 1971): 310-319.
22. Nuermberger, *The Free Produce Movement*, p. 59. The author contends that the literature in the United States reached few people besides their Quaker sponsors. This may have been true in the Northwest; her study does not deal with

the British wing of the movement. Nuermberger did not know that Garnet and Pennington were paid lecturers in Free Produce.

23. MacMaster, pp. 99-100. The author discusses the several purposes of the Free Produce movement.

24. Ibid., p. 101.

25. Ibid., pp. 102-103.

26. Benjamin Coates, *Cotton Cultivation in Africa. Suggestions on the Importance of the Cultivation of Cotton in Africa, in Reference to the Abolition of Slavery in the United States, Through the Organization of an African Civilization Society* (Philadelphia: C. Sherman and Son, 1858).

27. Ibid., pp. 4, 6, 8-12, 15, 17-18.

28. Benjamin Coates to Alexander Crummell, 14 April 1862 (Philadelphia): (Manuscript Collection, Pennsylvania Historical Society.

29. *New York Daily Tribune*, 11 August 1858, p. 7.

30. *Constitution of the African Civilization Society and etc.* (New Haven: Thomas J. Stafford, 1861), p. 1. (New York Public Library); also another copy in the Spingarn Collection, Howard University.

31. MacMaster, p. 104.

32. Floyd J. Miller, "The Search for a Black Nationality: Martin R. Delany and the Emigrationist Alternative," p. 339.

33. *New York Daily Tribune*, 4 August 1856, p. 7.

34. Bell, p. 228. Outside the Chatham community, Delany's group was unknown and dissolved as soon as Delany left Canada for New York late in 1858 or early 1859. See Miller, p. 218.

35. Bell, p. 227. Even after necessity had driven Delany to accept financial support from whites, unlike Garnet he refused to give up the appearance of acting independently, regardless of the reality. See Miller, p. 239.

36. Miller, p. 367.

37. Bell, p. 243.

38. *The Liberator*, 19 November 1858, p. 186.

39. *The National Anti-Slavery Standard*, 18 September 1858, p. 2; and 6 November 1858, p. 1.

40. The fact that *The Standard* gave space to emigrationist projects to Haiti and Jamaica as well as to Africa indicates a reluctance to give specific endorsement. See 25 September 1858, p. 1. According to Bell, (p. 214) established abolitionists did not favor emigration under any circumstances in 1858.

41. Favorable letters came from Eli Thayer, 15 November 1858, p. 6; J. Sella Martin, 19 November 1858, p. 7; and Coates, 19 November 1858, p. 3.

42. *New York Daily Tribune*, 8 December 1858, p. 7.

43. Ibid., 10 December 1858, p. 3. Downing was probably more emphatic in his opposition to emigration than Douglass. See Bell, p. 223.

44. Bell, pp. 228-229.

45. The African Civilization Society, he continued, was a doubtful and indirect means of abolition. It was based on the assumption that whites and Negroes can never live together in the same land on terms of equality. The slave trade

could be abolished by activity in America; and the savage kings would not reverse the century-old practices of enslaving captives. Douglass's fifth argument was that four million American slaves made this country the best place to effectuate emancipation. Sixth, slavery was not confined to cotton; slave labor could be employed at any task. Finally, the black person's search for his destiny would be held back by Garnet's scheme. See *Douglass' Monthly*, February 1859, pp. 19-20.

46. This was discussed in Chapter 6. The same conclusion is reached by Earl Ofari, "*Let Your Motto Be Resistance*," pp. 67-69.

47. *Douglass' Monthly*, June 1859, p. 87; *New York Daily Tribune*, 10 November 1858, p. 7. Unfortunately, there is no record of Garnet's remarks. Another activity in which Garnet may have participated in 1858 (although the evidence is conflicting) was the anniversary meeting of the American Abolition Society, a group similar, if not identical, to the Radical Abolitionists, which included Gerrit Smith, Arthur and Lewis Tappan, William Goodell, and James McCune Smith. They advocated use of the federal government to destroy slavery. Garnet may have addressed the society and participated in its work. In the *New York Daily Tribune* (13 May 1858, p. 7), there appeared a notice in which Garnet was listed as a speaker. Yet, in subsequent issues no reference was made to his speech, while the other addresses were published. In the edition of 14 May 1858, p. 4, reference was made to resolutions offered by Reverend Mr. Gardner, who was probably another individual. In the *National Anti-Slavery Standard* (17 April 1858, p. 3), Garnet was listed as one of the speakers. Ofari is more certain; see p. 103.

48. *The New York Colonization Journal*, February 1859, p. 2.

49. Ibid., April 1859, p. 3; July 1859, p. 4.

50. Ibid.

51. Miller, "The Search for a Black Nationality," p. 219.

52. Martin had already stated his approval in a letter to the *New York Daily Tribune*, 19 November 1858, p. 7.

53. Bell, p. 229.

54. Ibid., pp. 229-230.

55. *The Liberator*, 26 August 1859, p. 134.

56. Bell, p. 230.

57. *The Liberator*, 2 September 1859, as cited by Bell, p. 231; *The Weekly Anglo-American*, 17 September 1859, p. 2.

58. *The Weekly Anglo-African*, 10 September 1859, p. 2.

59. Ibid. Later in his speech, Garnet answered Brown's accusation that his organization was a begging concern by suggesting that Brown himself was guilty of the same offense. He insinuated that Downing would rather do business with whites than blacks. This brought a heated response from both Brown and Downing in which Downing threatened to club Garnet if they should meet. It is likely that Garnet's proposal was really the source of anger among them rather than the personal remarks made in the heat of argument.

60. Ibid.

61. Ibid.

62. Ibid.

63. Ibid.

64. Ibid.

65. *Douglass' Monthly*, October 1859, p. 151; also Bell, p. 251.

66. *The Weekly Anglo-African*, 15 October 1859, pp. 2-3.

67. Ibid.

68. Garnet to Joscelyn, June 1860 (New Orleans: Amistad Research Collection).

69. Ibid., 14 September 1859.

70. Ibid. 27 November 1859.

71. Ibid., 1 March 1860.

72. Louis B. Wright, et al., *The Democratic Experience*, p. 193.

73. Bell, p. 217; *The Weekly Anglo-African*, 7 April 1860.

74. *The Weekly Anglo-African*, 5 November 1859.

75. Ibid., 10 December 1859.

76. Ibid.

77. Ibid.

78. *The Weekly Anlgo-African*, 17 December 1859.

79. Ibid., 3 September 1859, p. 2.

80. Ibid., 10 September 1859, p. 2; 22 October 1859, p. 3. Quarles discusses the Oberlin rescuers briefly in *Black Abolitionists*, pp. 213-214.

81. *New York Daily Tribune*, 20 December 1859, pp. 4, 5, 8; 20 February 1860, p. 7. Resolutions are on p. 7. See also *The Weekly Anglo-African*, 28 January 1860, p. 2, which contains Garnet's quoted statement. Between January and March, Garnet dedicated a Presbyterian church in Elizabeth, New Jersey, and spoke at a rally which focused attention on the seriousness of the rights fight and urged resistance short of violence to segregated public accommodations. See *The Weekly Anglo-African*, 26 January 1860, p. 3, and 3 March 1860, p. 3.

82. *The Weekly Anglo-African*, 17 March 1860, p. 2.

83. Ofari, pp. 97-98.

84. If an investigation of Garnet's financial supporters, his political contacts, and friends here and in Britain were made and if statistical estimates were projected as to the costs involved, a case for "practicability" might be made.

85. Quarles, *Frederick Douglass*, pp. 150-151. See Chapter 5, p. 96 and Chapter 6 for Garnet's concern for working people generally.

86. *The Weekly Anglo-African*, 17 March 1860, p. 2; also Bell, pp. 231-232.

87. *The Weekly Anglo-African*, 21 April 1860, p. 2; also Bell, pp. 232-233.

88. *The Weekly Anglo-African*, 21 April 1860, p. 2; also Bell, p. 233.

89. *The Weekly Anglo-African*, 28 April 1860, p. 2; also Bell, p. 234.

90. Bell, pp. 234-235.

91. Ibid., p. 235.

92. MacMaster, pp. 109-110. Delany's and Campbell's account of the Niger explorations and agreements are given in Delany and Campbell, *Search for a Place*. An excellent account of the involvement of the British government and other institutions in Delany's plans is given by Miller, pp. 231-360. There are two biog-

raphies of Delany: Dorothy Sterling, *The Making of an Afro-American: Martin Robison Delany, 1812-1885* (New York: Doubleday & Co., Inc., 1971), and Victor Ullman, *Martin R. Delany: The Beginnings of Black Nationalism* (Boston: Beacon Press, 1971).

93. MacMaster, p. 110.

94. *The Weekly Anglo-African*, 19 May 1862, p. 2, discusses Garnet's remarks at the suffrage meeting of 10 May; also ibid., 5 May 1860, p. 3. Garnet spoke at the anniversary of the Colored Home; see 16 June 1860, p. 1. His work as a city missionary is described in a letter to Joscelyn, 1 June 1860 (New Orleans: Dillard Amistad Collection.

95. *The Weekly Anglo-African*, 26 May 1860, p. 2.

96. Quarles, *Black Abolitionists*, p. 190.

97. *Douglass' Monthly*, October 1860, p. 352; also Charles Wesley, "The Negro in Anti-Slavery Political Parties," p. 73.

98. *The Weekly Anglo-African*, 19 May 1860, p. 2.

99. Quarles, *Black Abolitionists*, p. 190.

100. *Douglass' Monthly*, January 1861, p. 399.

9

Africa, Haiti, and America: Part Two

With Lincoln's election came the secession of seven states of the lower South from the Union, and with it the president-elect was immediately faced with a grave crisis. Not only did he have to bring the seven back, but at the same time he had to placate the other states as yet still in the Union, avoid the anti-abolitionist opinion in the North, and soften abolitionist criticism. In an effort to win friends in the border states, in his inaugural address he stated that only those Southern citizens who had left the Union were to be condemned as insurrectionaries. Doubtless such a remark won him some respite in the pivotal states. Yet, no amount of caution could prevent the confrontation over Fort Sumter. Defending Sumter cost him four more slave states and plunged the country into civil war.[1]

Throughout the opening months of 1861, abolitionists found little solace from the new administration. When Negroes rushed to serve in the Union forces, they were rejected outright. Then, too, at first there was no clear governmental policy on escaped slaves who found their way to Union lines. Not until the Confiscation Act of 6 August 1861 was there anything resembling a uniform policy. The act declared that when property was used by the owner's consent to advance insurrection, it was subject to seizure. If the property consisted of slaves, they were to be free.[2]

Lincoln's willingness to place Union before abolition during 1861 further weakened the moderate elements among the Negro leadership, particularly Douglass who had campaigned vigorously for Lincoln. He became increasingly suspicious of the chief executive, and in private correspondence confessed his disappointment. Soon, he was expressing his bitterness in public.[3] Emigrationists, in the meantime, were proceeding at full steam. During the early months of the year, Garnet was actively promoting Negro emigration to Haiti as well as Africa. At the end of 1860, James McCune Smith wrote an open letter to him which criticized Garnet's acceptance of a position in James Redpath's Emigration Bureau. Smith reminded Garnet of his youthful resolve to devote his life to the elevation of free people on this soil and to the emancipation of Southern slaves. He claimed Garnet was embracing schemes of a diversionary nature. In the Garrisonian fashion, he urged Garnet to "shake yourself free of these migrating phantasms, and join us with your might and main."[4]

Garnet replied that except for menial jobs Negroes were denied economic opportunity in this country:

> Go to our hotels and private mansions of the rich, and on board of our steamboats, and you will find many skillful carpenters, masons, engineers, wheelwrights, and blacksmiths, millers, as well as female mechanics, who are wasting their talents for a mere pittance. You will see many of them borne down with discouragement, and they will tell you that the reason they do not work at their trades is, because they have been told over and over again when they have applied for work—"We don't employ niggers."[5]

Increasingly, men who shared Smith's viewpoint were finding themselves in the minority.[6] Douglass, impatient with Lincoln's inactivity, yielded to the emigrationists in January 1861. He published a long editorial on that date which reviewed the Negroes' interest in Haiti over the preceding thirty years. Douglass opined that blacks had been strongly attracted to Haiti only when it had had a reasonably stable government. He admitted that the trend toward Haiti was probably stronger in 1861 than at any previous time, but held that African enthusiasts were beginning to lose faith in their enterprise. Favorable conditions in Haiti, increasing proscription at home, and the neutral attitude of the Republican party on the slave question, were sufficient reasons for Douglass to support the Haitian venture. Finally, the Negroes' livelihood would be even further curtailed by hordes of European immigrants who were taking over the jobs which they had once monopolized. Douglass had come to believe with Garnet that the inducements offered his brethren in the United States were "few, feeble, and uncertain."[7]

Refusing to give up all hope, Douglass admitted no harm in emigration for personal reasons. He made this concession but suggested areas in the Western Hemisphere rather than Africa. A homeland was attainable in the Gulf islands; migration to Haiti would help counteract filibustering expeditions designed to increase slave territory.[8]

Douglass elaborated on his new position on emigration in an editorial in March 1861. Although he opposed emigration en masse, he contended that people could emigrate to better their moral or physical condition, but those who were well established and satisfied in America should not give up their dreams for Haiti. He did not personally intend to leave, he continued, but he was willing to visit the country where he expected to see many former Americans. He expressed full confidence in James Redpath, the general agent of the Haitian Bureau of Emigration.[9]

By May, Douglass had beyond doubt determined to cast his lot with the emigrationists. At that time he printed an editorial which was already in type when the momentous events of April plunged the nation into civil strife.[10] He had already accepted an invitation of the Haitian government to visit at its expense,[11] and he now recognized that emigration was an accepted answer to the Negro's dilemma. He wrote as follows: "We propose to act in view of the settled fact that many of them [Negro Americans] are already resolved to look for homes beyond the boundaries of the United States, and that most of their minds are turned towards Haiti."[12] With war certain, Douglass printed the editorial, adding a paragraph indicating that he would stand by and see what happened rather than go immediately to Haiti.[13]

Thereafter, Douglass refrained from active support of the Haitian scheme, although from June 1861 to well past the middle of 1862, a full-page advertisement from the Haitian government for Negro American immigrants appeared regularly in his *Monthly*. Thus, the Civil War saved Douglass from fully embracing emigration and Negro nationalism, as so many others had done in the 1850s.[14]

Another convert to emigration was William J. Watkins, a Douglass associate, who in 1860 began to make ardent emigrationist lectures.[15] So, too, was William Wells Brown who completely reversed himself on the traditional abolitionist stand of proximity to the slave. He wrote: "All objections to emigration appear to center in the feeling that we ought not to quit the land of our birth, and leave the Slave in his chains. This view of the case comes at first glance with some force, but on a closer examination, it will be found to have but little weight."[16] By using the term *little weight*, Brown was in fact easing himself into a complete reversal of his position. Even Downing could not hold out for more than another year; his capitulation may well have marked the end of an era. Bell's assessment is as follows:

> Thirty years of bondage to an artificial loyalty to the slave was at last a thing of the past. The free Negro had won his right to live his own life without incurring the accusation that he was selfishly seeking his own interests. As the nation entered four years of civil conflict, the Negro emerged into a new era of psychological freedom from a concept of self-sacrifice—a concept fostered by the Garrisonian school of abolition, and a severe detriment to progress.[17]

Garnet, meanwhile, preparing for his second trip to England in the summer of 1861 to promote his African venture, was riding the crest of the emigrationist wave. He was part of a respectable minority within the black community among whom emigration had become a fever.[18] It was to subside subsequently in the face of new realities; even so, an estimated two thousand Negroes would attempt to find homes in Haiti, Latin America, or Africa.[19] In his determination to promote his program, Garnet came into conflict not only with fellow abolitionists like Nell, who held different views, but also with some of his trustees at Shiloh Presbyterian Church.

Some of the trustees attempted to force Garnet from the pulpit. In reviewing the sporadic evidence, it is difficult to determine the exact cause of Garnet's conflict with the trustees. It was probably precipitated by his antislavery crusading, the struggle over the utilization and control of church property, a common problem in Presbyterian church affairs of the day, and the personal reprimands and expulsions which Garnet issued from the pulpit.[20] The trustees closed the Shiloh church on the evening of 7 July 1861 on the eve of his departure for Great Britain. Before he left the country, Garnet held a sessional meeting in protest condemning the temporal leadership for flagrant violations of God's authority and the laws of New York.[21]

Members of the congregation held a testimonial dinner in his honor at Garnet's residence. The trustees (who apparently paid the rent) interpreted this gesture as an invasion of their authority. Eventually, a case was brought before the Third Presbytery which recommended that Garnet remain as pastor, although it advised each party involved to harmonize their relations.[22] The matter seemingly rested there; however, Garnet wrote a fellow minister that he fully expected that he would have to defend himself in a court of law.[23] During Garnet's absence from Shiloh, the Reverend John N. Gloucester was chosen to take his place. As late as the end of April 1860, Gloucester had been a vigorous opponent of Garnet's emigrationist programs. The two had battled in the columns of *The Weekly Anglo-African.*[24] Gloucester's appointment was thus a small defeat for Garnet at the hands of his trustees. Eventually, a reconciliation social was announced on 12 December 1861 while Garnet was out of the country. Pastor Gloucester presided, and the common theme of the occasion was simple "united we stand, divided we fall,"[25] as a church group.

Before leaving to raise funds in England for this proposed expedition to Africa, Garnet had stated his motto: "Immediate, Unconditional and Universal Emancipation, African Civilization; God and Negro Nationality."[26] Such were his goals in 1861. He would live only to realize the first.

Garnet's greatest civil rights contribution that year occurred when the federal government granted him a passport. Blacks had previously been granted passports, although the practice was not widespread. Even then, the citizenship question could be skirted by stating on the passport that the recipient was "dark" in color. When Secretary of State Seward granted Garnet his passport, however, the question was forced into the open. Garnet met it head-on. While many men were dark-complexioned without being considered Negroes, Garnet was truly black, and so he insisted upon the inclusion of the word *Negro* upon his passport. "The point must be tested," he said, "so better do it at once," and color in this instance assumed its proper position.[27]

In a larger context, granting Garnet a passport suggested to many that the Republican administration was going to ignore the Dred Scott precedent.[28] In the words of *The Anti-Slavery Reporter*, Garnet became "the First Black Citizen of the Dis-United States."[29] When *The Weekly Anglo-African* went to press, its editors stated that his passport meant that the question of Negro citizenship had at last been settled favorably. They were overstating the case,[30] for the issue of federal citizenship was not settled favorably in law until the Civil Rights Act of 1866 was enacted and the Fourteenth Amendment to the Constitution became operative.[31]

When Garnet revisited England, Douglass gave the event an enthusiastic treatment in his *Monthly*. Douglass's more favorable attitude toward emigration was reflected in a more positive attitude toward Garnet. He wrote: "His color [Garnet's], as well as his high character will give him influence among the good people of that country, and enable him to battle successfully with the evident sympathy with the slaveholders which a class in that country are endeavoring to create."[32] Although Garnet was an emigrationist, Douglass continued, he still claimed America as his home and planned to return. "His presence and labors there [England] cannot fail to react in our favor here, for in these days of rapid travel, a word spoken abroad soon finds its way home, and often comes with added power."[33] Douglass had thus journeyed a great distance intellectually from Garrison. As further evidence of his reconciliation with Garnet's views, he also began to reprint Garnet's letters from England.[34]

By September, Garnet was en route to England, having left Henry M. Wilson to manage the affairs of the African Civilization Society in New York. He arrived in Liverpool on 13 September; on his voyage he had been spared the discrimination he encountered ten years before. Perhaps to maintain the enthusiasm for his African project, he wrote optimistically of his meeting with Robert Campbell, who had arrived in England from the Niger region with treaty in hand. Garnet told the readers of *The Weekly Anglo-African* that the mottoes of British philanthropists and men of good will were universal emancipation, Negro nationality, extermination of the slave trade, and the redemption of Africa. In the same letter, he expressed approval of the British annexation of Lagos and control over the area of Abbeokuta on the grounds that the British would encourage development of Central African resources, introduce Christianity, and drive out the slave traders. To find alternative sources of raw cotton, he continued, the British government's official policy was to introduce large-scale agricultural improvements. Somewhat simplistically, Garnet concluded that most Britishers would be unsympathetic with the war so long as the American government refused to make abolition the main issue.[35]

While Garnet was overseas, the African Civilization Society held its third annual meeting in New York City. Delany attended. The constitution was modified slightly, emphasizing self-reliance and self-government on the principle of African nationality.[36] Although the meeting itself was not of great significance, it revealed a continuing enthusiasm for a Negro state in Africa as late as November 1861 and marked Delany's decision to cooperate fully with the society. Later in November, Garnet was promoting African nationality before a large meeting of cotton producers from Birmingham and Manchester, England. Although the purpose was to seek alternative sources of raw cotton, the meeting passed two resolutions specifically favoring a Negro state. The first resolution began as follows: "Resolved, that this meeting recognized in the special qualities of the African race the promise of an African nationality, and anticipates in that nationality a valuable element in the commonwealth of nations."[37] The second resolution came after Garnet's speech in which he stressed the settlement of Christian families in Abbeokuta for missionary, agricultural, and mechanical purposes: "The effect would be amazing and powerful, if the natives could see among them civilized colored people, fully imbued with Christianity, who had come to live and die with them. They would be taught how to till the land, how to plant and crop, how to live and labor, how to worship the true God, how to hope and how to die." He played upon the humanitarian and commercial motives: "Give her your civilization, and she will give you her commerce and wealth." A marriage between Anglo-Saxon energy and African industry would in his view accomplish almost anything within reason. When he had finished, the second resolution was unanimously carried: "That the introduction of Christian Colored families from Canada into Africa is eminently calculated to advance the influence of Christianity and Civilization in that country."[38]

Although the speech had a missionary flavor, it was tailored to a British audience, one from which Garnet needed financial support. He was not so presumptuous as to suggest that his culture was superior to that of the African; rather he emphasized that, by establishing a permanent relationship, both Negroes and Africans would benefit.

Neither Garnet's nor Delany's African plans were to be realized. As the Civil War came and dominated the national awareness, both Garnet's scheme and the Haitian venture were relegated to the back pages of history. As the war progressed, a good chance appeared for improving conditions at home,[39] and so emigration plans were largely abandoned.

Bell gives excellent summaries of the Haitian and African projects.[40] He claims the Haitian venture failed first, because of the threat of military occupation by Spain; second, the selection of many colonists unsuited to the rigors of frontier life; third, sickness and death among the colonists was rampant and fourth, the Haitian government was unable to do as much for the emigrants as they had expected. Economic and physical factors were responsible for the failure of the Haitian and African projects, rather than the Negro's loyalty to the land on which he was born.[41]

The failure to develop settlements in Africa should not be allowed to overshadow the good that was accomplished through the education acquired. Through the emigration controversy, Negroes in Canada and the United States learned much about the land of their cultural and physical heritage.[42]

Hence, the events after 1861 necessitated further shifts in the Negro leadership's strategy. Emphasis was now placed on efforts on behalf of slaves, free Negroes, and a newly liberated group, the so-called contrabands of war. As the emigrationist movement began to wane, Garnet's African Civilization Society moved in the direction of educating the newly freed in schools run by the society. One tenet of the society schools which gained greater significance in the postbellum period was that "the black man is the better leader and teacher among his own people than the white man; that while we can do this work just as well, we can do it under fewer disadvantages, and at far less expense, than he."[43] When he returned from England in early 1862, Garnet took an immediate interest in the slaves who had escaped to Fortress Monroe.

In January 1862 a large meeting was held at Shiloh to raise money and clothing for contrabands. Garnet chaired the meeting. Reverend L. C. Lockwood, a missionary for Fortress Monroe, told the gathering that the federal government was gradually becoming a huge slaveholding operation. Lockwood's message was probably eclipsed by that by William Davis, himself a former slave, who spoke for over an hour on the day-to-day life of the contraband. In anticipation that Davis would make many speeches and thus obtain funds for others, the editors of *The Weekly Anglo-African* did not print his remarks. Meetings to aid these new-ly freed men were held in February.[44]

During the opening months of 1862, Garnet established a Religious and Literary Reading Circle at Shiloh which was to meet once a week during the year and was open to all without distinction. He also worked to build a li-brary for the Young Men's Literary Association of New York City. In these efforts, he was hampered by a continuation of his struggle with his church trustees. He won a substantial victory in April when the congregation voted by an overwhelming majority to accept the resignation of the entire board.[45] An additional cause of the struggle, discussed earlier, was Garnet's insistent, uncompromising nature and the anxieties his frequently unpopular programs created within his congregation. As emigrationist sentiment began to recede however, Garnet appeared less fearful to the more conservative elements of the Negro community.

Ironically, just as the blacks enthusiasm for emigrating began to decline, the Lincoln administration became very interested in black colonization. Lincoln himself had long held the Jeffersonian view of compensated emancipation; yet, unlike the Virginian, he favored the voluntary emigration of freedmen. By April 1862, emigrationist efforts had so far advanced that they gained official public approval. James Mitchell of Indiana was appointed to the Lincoln cabinet solely to keep Lincoln informed on the Negro's attitude toward national emi-grationist schemes. When Mitchell accepted his appointment, he told executives of the African Civilization Society that their advice on all matters touching the plans of his office would have "a proper bear-ing."[46] His efforts did not end there; to facilitate voluntary emigration, he presented the government proposal in leading black and white news-papers. He imbued the movement with a holy banner and stressed the building of a Negro nationality abroad. Wherever Negroes settled, he said, "they would be laying the foundation of a 'Christian State,' add-ing another province to the Empire of Him who claims the Kingdom of His Own." This rhetoric was much like that used by the African Civili-zation Society.[47]

Before the war had ended, the African Civilization Society was to receive some federal funds for its projects.[48] Nonetheless, the drift among Negroes away from emigration continued unabated. In April 1862, Lincoln's recommendation for the emancipation of slaves in the District of Columbia became law. The statute that was passed also contained provisions for the voluntary emigration of blacks to a permanent settlement in the Tropics. When news of the legislation reached Garnet, he was overjoyed at its emancipation aspects and he held a large meeting at Shiloh tó express his sentiments. He told the audience that forced contact between Northern men with Southern rebels would quickly make the former into abolitionists. Shortly before, he continued, regiments of men full of the most rabid pro-slavery feeling had passed through the streets of New York City to the seat of war, and their subsequent experience in combat had reversed their initial sentiments, making them ultra emancipationists.[49]

As emancipation became increasingly likely, emigration became less attractive to Garnet. He singled out for condemnation the clauses of the District of Columbia Proclamation dealing with the classification and settlement of contrabands, captured Africans, liberated slaves, and emancipated slaves of Washington. Garnet marveled at the absurdity of transporting men who had watered their native soil with the sweat of their unpaid labor to another country when freedom finally arrived.[50] Garnet had come full circle to his earlier civil rights views. Yet the government continued its emigration policies.

Until late in the Civil War, Lincoln persevered in his compensated emancipation and emigrationist efforts. He signed into law the Confiscation bill on 17 July 1862 which expropriated Confederate property including slaves. Under provisions of the act, freedom was granted to slaves in rebel lands, and the President was authorized to transplant, colonize, and settle permanently the freedmen in tropical areas. Blacks themselves had to be willing to go, and the President was to safeguard their liberties in the place of their choice. Some $600,000 was appropriated for the resettlement, most of which went unspent when the act was suspended on 2 July 1864.[51]

At the same time, Lincoln initiated the policy of emancipation beginning in June 1862 with the law abolishing slavery in the territories.[52] Just what his motives were in carrying out these different policies still remains controversial.[53] Mitchell had told the President that thousands of Southern contrabands would prefer emigration to the tropics rather than face the possibility of return to slavery.[54]

In any event, Lincoln summoned to the White House a delegation of Negro leaders on 14 August 1862, ostensibly to advance his Central American Colonization plan.[55] He told them: "Your race suffers greatly, many of them, by living among us, while ours suffer from your presence. In a word we suffer on each side. If this is admitted, it affords a reason why we should be separated."[56] It is well Garnet was not among those the President summoned; he had become wary of emigration. Most black leaders were emphatic in their opposition to colonization. Although the government made efforts for some time to settle Negroes in Panama and on the Ile a Vache, a Caribbean island, they too fell by the wayside. Without the support of black emigrationists, who had adopted a wait-and-see attitude, and without the support of the rest of the Negro community, the federally financed colonization schemes failed. Northern victories sealed the issue for the period. As of 2 July 1864, the Senate suspended further expenditures for Negro colonization.[57] President Lincoln did approve a request for $5,000 at the prompting of Mitchell on 5 November 1865,[58] but by that date the African Civilization Society was to use the money in its efforts to educate the newly freed.

It was a month from the President's meeting with Negro leaders to the Union victory at Antietam; then five days more until Lincoln issued a preliminary proclamation.[59] At the time of its issuance, the President himself considered the document a war measure, authorized by war powers and justified by military necessity.[60] The measure, which incorporated compensated emancipation and the prospect of colonization, was a moderate one which Lincoln believed to be of dubious legality. Nor did he wish by this act to turn the war into a moral crusade; yet that is precisely what was happening.

For Negroes, the immediate effects of the preliminary Proclamation proved to be a mixed blessing. While many whites could now be safely abolitionists and proclaim a kinship with the martyred Brown, other elements among the whites began to feel their initial sacrifices had been subverted by the cause of emancipation. Certainly, this was true in New York City where white reaction was perhaps the most severe. When Garnet held his meeting on 29 September 1862 to honor the occasion and to reapply pressure for full equality, frightened well-wishers cautioned him to expect violence from poorer white elements.[61] The violence did not occur immediately as anticipated. The tension was to explode in less than nine months into New York City's worst antebellum riot.

Garnet held a New Year's Eve celebration at Shiloh in honor of emancipation. He also spoke in January at an Emancipation jubilee held in Weeksville, Long Island. He told the audience that Negro poets and orators would remember Nat Turner and Denmark Vesey as forerunners of John Brown. He hoped to see them all honored, and he expressed doubts of the Union Army's success, but he had faith in the ultimate triumph of liberty. That same month he participated in another jubilee ceremony on behalf of emancipation held at Cooper Institute.[62]

At about the same time, Garnet began to recruit troops for the Union Army, a task in which he was joined by Delany, Douglass, Downing, and almost all leading black abolitionists. If willingness to serve had been the sole criterion, Negro troops would have been in Union ranks shortly after Sumter. But since color prejudice was pervasive, the government flatly refused to accept them at the outset. The stock objections were that Negroes would not fight; whites would refuse to fight with them and enlistments would slacken; and Negroes would stiffen Southern resistance.[63] Lincoln also feared that recruiting Negro troops would seriously alienate the border states and some elements in the North. Therefore, he did not seriously consider arming Negroes until the spring of 1862; by then he had little choice.[64]

The federal government's months of vacillation on the treatment of runways, Negro relief measures, and Negro military service had a disquieting effect on the black Americans status. Private citizens responded only in the usual trifling way to appeals from Douglass, Langston, Remond, and William Wells Brown to uphold the Negroes' rights. Abysmal relief measures were probably a large factor in the African Civilization Society's focus on education after 1861. In the recruitment of Negro soldiers, abolitionists had the additional task of gaining the cooperation of local authorities, some of whom were openly anti-Negro after the elections of 1862. Horatio Seymour was elected governor of New York largely on the basis of his opposition to the Emancipation Proclamation.[65] It was therefore necessary to secure Seymour's approval of a black regiment and at the same time to begin the recruitment process.

Garnet began recruiting work in January 1863 with rallies at his church. Because New York was as yet uncommitted to a Negro regiment, Garnet found himself raising troops for the 54th Massachusetts regiment, which had come into existence largely through the zeal of John A. Andrew, war governor of the Bay State.[66] Since Massachusetts did not have the requisite number of Negroes to make up a regiment, recruiters were hired for other states.

Authorized by Lincoln's secretary of war, Edwin M. Stanton, to organize a black regiment of volunteers to serve for three years, Andrew persuaded George L. Stearns to head a commission of prominent citizens to superintend the recruitment operation. Stearns raised money and hired Garnet, Douglass, Brown, Remond, and Delany, who were required to submit daily progress reports and expense accounts. Although the quota of a thousand men was soon met,[67] Garnet encountered resistance to enlistment among black New Yorkers.

After 1863, the Negroes were not as enthusiastic about fighting in the war. There were several reasons. First, the economic boom of that period had created some prosperity for blacks in parts of the North. Secondly, Confederate sources had hinted that captured Negro soldiers would not be treated as ordinary prisoners of war. Naturally, prospective Negro recruits were hesitant to join until they learned what measures the federal government would take to protect them if they were captured. Finally, in the authorization which the War Department granted to Andrew, it was stated that all commissioned officers in the Negro regiment had to be white. Andrew's protest to Lincoln and Stanton proved unavailing because they feared the possible effect of Negro officers on public opinion. Douglass, too, was somewhat disappointed, yet he hailed the opportunity of wearing the Union uniform as a significant advance for blacks. Although there were not many recruits from New York, among the first to sign up were Douglass's two sons.[68]

Having agreed to recruitment, Garnet was well aware of both white and Negro resistance to military service. As a trial balloon on the evening of 20 April 1863, he discussed the following details of what Negroes desired in exchange for participation:

Now I wish to know what have black men to fight for in this war? What encouragement has been offered to them to fight? What does a soldier fight for? He fights for three things: love of country, promotion on the field, and for honor. What has the black man to fight for? Under the present call of the President, a colored soldier cannot be promoted higher than a captain, a mere company officer. Are these encouragements for colored men to enlist? But I believe that if they will put a black Major-General in the field, there would be thousands of men of black skins flocking around him. But do not call the black man a coward. If he will not fight, it is because he has not justice done him. Do him justice, give him a chance equal that with a white soldier, and he will show you how he can fight.[69]

Evidently, the price Garnet suggested was too high for Lincoln. Having made his suggestion of a black major-general public knowledge, Garnet then chose to accept less.

At a war rally seven days later at Shiloh, he, Douglass, Pennington, and others gave the enlistment program their wholehearted support. Garnet began his address to the rally with a list of reasons why Negroes were reluctant to join. He objected to the "tardy, back-door manner" in which Negroes were being brought into Union ranks. Garnet alluded to Jefferson Davis's proclamation, which threatened the shooting of all white men found in colored regiments and the punishment of all blacks found in arms for aiding the enemy. The government, he pointed out, had taken no measures to protect them; nor were they eligible for commissions. Under such degrading conditions, it was a manly act to hesitate before enlisting. He reminded the audience that while General Andrew Jackson called the "fellow-citizens" to come to the rescue, the government in Washington remained silent. This attitude also angered Garnet.[70]

While condemning the federal policy, Garnet praised Massachusetts for recognizing the importance of Negro participation. Having focused the audience's indignation on the government, he advocated enlistment because in his view the Confederacy was seeking the enslavement of every black living in the United States. Even the federal government, while it had not offered them commissions, had emancipated Negroes in the District of Columbia, which was a noble act in itself.[71]

After his address, only one recruit stepped forward. This angered Douglass who told the audience that he was ashamed of them.[72] One man in the crowd rose to protest the lack of federal equality of treatment and demanded such reassurances before recruits would come forward.[73] Evidently, he articulated the universal sentiment of those assembled.

The recruiters agreed to try another time at a meeting held on 30 April 1863. The newest development consisted of a message from the governor of Massachusetts with belated federal guarantees that Negro troops would be treated in every way equal to whites.[74] Several resolu-

tions were passed under Downing's sponsorship in favor of Negro participation in the war. In reality, they were a compromise. Although the
meeting voted in favor of encouraging enlistments in Massachusetts, it
did so only as long as New York refused to create a Negro unit for the
state.[75] The meeting also resolved to set up a committee of thirteen,
appointed by Garnet, to draft an address to Governor Seymour urging
him to encourage Negro enlistments. The resolution subtly covered up
the blacks' hesitation by making it appear that they would be eager to
enlist when Seymour acted favorably on the request for a regiment from
New York. It read as follows: ". . . that we desire this that other states
may not draw too much upon the patriotism which we would, as New
Yorkers, have set down to the credit of our own state; but until the
State of New York shall call upon the colored people of the State to
take up arms in defence of the Union, it is the part of wisdom for them
to accept the invitation for Massachusetts to do so."[76]

Such maneuvers were not without effect. By December 1863, Negro
troops were being recruited into black fighting units. Within sixty days
of the authorization, twenty-three hundred blacks had enlisted.[77] As
will be shown, Garnet continued to press for equal treatment of blacks
troops while acting as a recruiting agent.

Inputs for Negro enlistments in New York came from other sources
as well. A petition signed by fifteen prominent New Yorkers, including
Horace Greeley and William Cullen Bryant, requested authorization of
a black unit from New York and was sent to Lincoln in June 1863.[78]
During the same period, the Union League Club, composed of over five
hundred of the "wealthiest and most respectable citizens" of New York,
was formed. The club's membership collected a large sum of money for
raising and fielding a Negro regiment from the state.[79] Black city leaders
had formed the Association for Promoting Colored Volunteering. In
spite of the riots in July, Garnet, as one of the association leaders, still
claimed that Negroes were eager to do their utmost to put down the
rebellion.[80]

Late in the year, the Union League and the association joined forces
to form the Joint Committee on Volunteering. By December, after
Secretary of War Stanton had authorized the formation of a regiment
from New York, the committee raised nearly $20,000 and proceeded
to recruit Negroes to help fill New York's draft quota.[81] Such were the
origins of the 20th Regiment United States Colored Troops.[82]

Both the process of recruitment and treatment of volunteers at Riker's Island was fraught with corruption. White recruiting agents met Negroes in the streets, offered them coachmens's jobs at high wages, ten or twenty dollars to bind the bargain, and frequently drugged them into signing enlistment papers. In such a state, they were frequently hurried off to the rendezvous.[83] Mindful of these and other violations of the rights of Negroes, Garnet temporarily assumed the duties of chaplain to the recruits. They were exposed to cruel treatment on Riker's Island, and in crossing from the city, they were not uncommonly assaulted by rowdies in the streets. On one occasion, Garnet and two friends were set upon and so maltreated that the Union League Club requested special police at the ferry crossing solely to protect recruits.[84]

New recruits were protected in several ways. First, public meetings were held in Negro churches, where, before large audiences, Garnet, Vincent Colyer, the superintendent on recruiting for the Union Club, and other knowledgeable people described the details of neglect that were discovered. They demanded an immediate end to these outrages.[85] Secondly, circulars, handbills, and other printed matter correctly stating the amount of bounties and wages paid to the recruit and the rights of his family to the Relief Fund which had been provided by the supervisors of the state counties were printed and given wide distribution.[86]

Garnet was directly employed by the Union League Club to visit Riker's Island and record statements from the men who had been swindled by bounty runners. Once presented to the commanding officer, General Dix, the information led to the prompt arrest of those who had cheated them and their exposure in the press. These three steps helped to secure the confidence of the Negro people in the recruitment enterprise.[87] Garnet was so successful as chaplain that the League Club tried to hire him as the permanent chaplain—that officer being the only one who could by existing regulations be a Negro. A physical defect (probably his missing leg), disqualified him from the position, however.[88]

Through Garnet's influence, an association of Negro women was formed whose members diligently visited the men and cared for the sick. They administered such aid as was needed and received the support of the Union League Club in their recommendations.[89] Through the combined efforts of these groups, the regiment reached one thousand men by January 1864.[90] The black auxiliary groups which were scheduled to escort the regiment through the city held a mass meeting in Garnet's church on the Monday evening following the parade. The audience adopted the following resolution:

That the State of New York owes a debt of gratitude to the Union League Club of this city for the part they have taken in the organization of colored troops in this State, and that the prompt and patriotic response of the colored men of the Empire State to their country's call to arms, is worthy of the highest commendation; and having gone forth to fight for liberty and the Union, we will remember them affectionately, and pray God to make them strong, defend them in the day of battle, and give them victory.[91]

Scarcely eight months after the most serious race riot in the history of New York City, a black regiment proudly marched off to combat. July 1863 had witnessed a bloody retribution: strewn on the farm lands about the town of Gettysburg, Pennsylvania, lay the hopes of Confederate victory in the flesh of their deceased soldiers. As Lee retreated to the banks of the Potomac, lately swollen from rains, the plantation myth began its slow death in the minds of many Southern survivors. In New York City, the black man also paid his price in blood as mad Irish mobs tried vainly to destroy him.

NOTES

1. Franklin, *From Slavery to Freedom*, p. 271.
2. Ibid., pp. 272-273.
3. Quarles, *Frederick Douglass*, pp. 190-192.
4. *The Weekly Anglo-African*, 5 and 12 January 1861, as cited in James McPherson, *The Negro's Civil War* (New York: Vintage Books, 1965), pp. 83-84.
5. *The Weekly Anglo-African*, 26 January 1861, as cited by McPherson, p. 84.
6. Bell, pp. 223-224.
7. *Douglass' Monthly*, January 1861, pp. 386-387, as cited in Bell, pp. 217-218.
8. Bell, p. 219.
9. *Douglass' Monthly*, March 1861, p. 420, as cited in Bell, pp. 219-220.

10. Bell, p. 221. As early as April, Douglass had printed a recantation of a faithful anti-emigrationist, H. O. Wagoner, from Chicago. See Bell, p. 220.

11. Bell, p. 221.

12. *Douglass' Monthly*, May 1861, p. 450, as cited in Bell, p. 221.

13. Ibid., pp. 449-450, as cited in Bell, p. 221.

14. Bell, p. 222.

15. Ibid.

16. *The Pine & Palm*, June 2, 1861, p. 2, as cited in Bell, p. 223.

17. Ibid., p. 223-224.

18. Ibid., p. 265.

19. Ibid., pp. 259-260. Bell cites the figures of John W. Cromwell, *The Negro in American History* (Washington, D.C.: The American Negro Academy, 1914), p. 44.

20. *Minutes of the Session of the Shiloh Presbyterian Church*, 2 (Philadelphia: Presbyterian Church Archives, 1857-1867), pp. 17-18.

21. Ibid., p. 57. Also *The Pine & Palm*, 13 July 1861, p. 3.

22. *Recommendations of the Third Presbytery in the Case of Shiloh Church* (Philadelphia: Presbyterian Church Archives, 1862).

23. Garnet to Reverend T. Ralston Smith (Philadelphia: Presbyterian Church Archives), 16 June 1862.

24. *The Weekly Anglo-African*, 31 March 1860, p. 2; 7 April 1860, p. 2; 28 April, 1860, p. 2.

25. Ibid., 7 December 1861, p. 3.

26. Ibid., 27 April 1861, p. 1.

27. *The Anti-Slavery Reporter*, 1 October 1861, pp. 218-219.

28. *Douglass' Monthly*, November 1861, p. 558.

29. *The Anti-Slavery Reporter*, 1 October 1861, p. 218.

30. *The Weekly Anglo-African*, 10 August 1861, p. 2. Douglass was also a little overenthusiastic; see *Douglass' Monthly*, 13 September 1861, p. 557.

31. Franklin, p. 323.

32. *Douglass' Monthly*, September 1861, p. 516.

33. Ibid.

34. Ibid., November 1861, p. 557.

35. *The Weekly Anglo-African*, 19 October 1861, p. 2.

36. Ibid., 16 November 1861, p. 2.

37. Ibid., p. 4.

38. Ibid.

39. Bell, p. 236,

40. Ibid. A discussion of Africa appears on pp. 228-238; a discussion of Haiti appears on pp. 238-254.

41. Ibid., pp. 255, 258-259.

42. Ibid., 244-245.

43. *Freedom's Torchlight*, December 1866, p. 1 (Washington, D.C.: Library of Congress, Murray Collection).

44. *The Weekly Anglo-African*, 25 January 1862, pp. 2, 3; also 15 February 1862, p. 3.

45. Ibid., 8 February 1862, p. 2, reference to the library; 19 April 1862, p. 3, discusses the church vote.

46. United States Office of Emigration, *Annual Report, 1863*, p. 3, as cited in Tinsely Spraggins, "Economic Aspects of Negro Colonization During the Civil War" (Ph.D. dissertation, American University, 1957), pp. 98-99.

47. Spraggins, p. 100.

48. George Sinkler, *The Racial Attitudes of American Presidents from Abraham Lincoln to Theodore Roosevelt* (New York: Doubleday, 1971), p. 53.

49. *The Weekly Anglo-African*, 22 February 1862, p. 3.

50. Ibid.

51. Spraggins, pp. 80-81, 102.

52. Franklin, *From Slavery to Freedom*, p. 281.

53. The question raised here is whether these moves accurately reflected a consistent attitude toward Negroes on the part of the president. As indicated in an earlier chapter, Dumond takes the view that Lincoln was a thoroughgoing abolitionist. Franklin's view is that of the political pragmatist (pp. 280-284), as is Willis Boyd, "Negro Colonization in the National Crisis," (Ph.D. dissertation, University of California, 1953), p. 113.

54. Spraggins, p. 99.

55. *Douglass' Monthly*, September 1862, p. 712.

56. As cited in Franklin, p. 281.

57. Spraggins, p. 102.

58. Sinkler, p. 53.

59. Franklin, p. 282.

60. C. Vann Woodward, *The Burden of Southern History* (New York: Vintage Books, 1960), pp. 72-73. An insightful discussion of war aims and goals appears on pp. 69-82.

61. Quarles, *The Negro in the Civil War* (Boston: Little, Brown & Co., 1953), pp. 163-164.

62. *The Weekly Anglo-African*, 14 February 1863, p. 2; also 24 January 1863, p. 3.

63. Hirsch, p. 447.

64. Franklin, p. 277.

65. Hirsch, p. 449; Franklin, p. 278.

66. Quarles, *The Negro in the Civil War*, p. 8.

67. Ibid., pp. 8-9.

68. As cited in McPherson, *The Negro's Civil War*, pp. 173-177.

69. *The Weekly Anglo-African*, as reprinted in *Douglass' Monthly*, June 1863, p. 840.

70. *Douglass' Monthly*, June 1863, p. 838.

71. Ibid.

72. As cited in McPherson, p. 177.

73. *The Liberator*, 22 May 1863, p. 84.

74. Ibid., 29 May 1863, p. 88.

75. Ibid.

76. *Douglass' Monthly*, June 1863, pp. 838-839.

77. Hirsch, p. 448.

78. Ibid., p. 447.

79. *Report of the Committee on Volunteering* (New York: Club House Printers, 1864), p. 7.

80. Quarles, *The Negro in the Civil War*, p. 189.

81. Hirsch, p. 448; Quarles, *The Negro in the Civil War*, p. 190.

82. *Report*, p. 8.

83. Ibid., p. 35.

84. Ibid., p. 36.

85. Ibid., p. 37.

86. Ibid., pp. 37-38. One such handbill contained the name and endorsement of Garnet and other eminent Negro clergymen.

87. Ibid., p. 38.

88. Ibid., p. 17.

89. Ibid., p. 17.

90. Quarles, *The Negro in the Civil War*, p. 190.

91. *Report*, p. 46.

10

Succeeding
Though
Unsuccessful

Without reviewing the numerous works here, it may be stated that the few bloody July days at Gettysburg were the highwater mark of the Southern cause. Defeat was not a certainty at that point; theoretically the South could hold out for years to come. After July 1863, however, Southern victory on the battlefield was no longer possible. Now, the black American at last had a substantial stake in the outcome. This may have been another factor facilitating recruitment for Garnet after the summer of 1863. The terror which prevailed in New York City in that same month must have militated against such efforts, however. According to Hirsch, the July draft riots were the most important single event of the antebellum period for free, black New Yorkers.[1] Quarles has called them "the bloodiest race riots in the annals of American social pathology," engendered by resentment and fear of the Negro's upward climb in socioeconomic status.[2]

   White laboring men feared that liberated slaves would overrun the North and that they would be displaced from their jobs. While the first fear was imaginary, since Southern Negroes were largely agricultural and remained in native surroundings, the fear of labor competition had some basis. Manpower shortages brought on by enlistments and the war industry boom increased employment; however, prices tended to outstrip increases in wages. Then, too, the heavy flow of immigrants to America in the late 1840s had driven blacks from their unskilled jobs, a fact that was probably unknown or ignored by whites. Under these circumstances, white laborers felt that they had to strike. Mounting strikes in turn led to the use of more blacks as strike-breakers, particularly in waterfront jobs in the port cities along the Eastern seaboard.[3]

To reduce black competition, whites resorted to all-white unions and to violence, the most direct means.[4] A bitter foreshadowing came as early as August 1862 when a mob composed mainly of Irish working people attacked a cigarette factory in Brooklyn which was employing Negroes, most of them women and children. Five hundred whites attacked five men, fifteen women, and children with stones and brickbats. For nearly an hour, the blacks held the mob off on the stairway. At that point, police using clubs freely hammered their way into the mob, and after a furious struggle in which several on both sides were seriously injured, the mob was subdued. One Negro was severely injured, and several ringleaders, including a candidate for alderman, were detained for trial.[5]

Garnet suggested that ministers, public servants, and private citizens of color say nothing that "may have a tendency to excite the murderous spirit that is cherished towards us in the minds of many persons in this community." "It is the religious duty of every man to act according to his natural instincts in the defence of his house, wife, children and his helpless ones—and by God's help we will do it."[6]

Undeterred by fears of violence, a condition with which he had learned to live almost daily, Garnet continued in his recruitment and welfare work. In September 1862, he spoke in black churches in Newport, Rhode Island, to bring recruits into the newly formed 6th Regiment of Rhode Island Volunteers; for his efforts he received the thanks of the sponsors.[7] He threw his own church open to Mrs. Elizabeth Keckley, Mrs. Lincoln's seamstress, who had organized the Contraband Relief Association in the District of Columbia to assist fugitives coming into that city. Garnet's church was merely one stop for her during her tour up the East Coast and in her solicitations overseas in search of funds.[8]

If the trouble in Brooklyn was the tryout, then the riot in Buffalo, New York, provided the dress rehearsal for New York City. The confusion in Buffalo began when Negroes were put to work as stevedores in the loading and unloading of cargo. Three blacks were killed and twelve were severely hurt. One week later came the draft riot in New York City.[9]

On 3 March 1863, Congress enacted the first comprehensive draft law in American history. It was immediately denounced as unconstitutional and despotic; any person with $500 could obtain release from the draft. "Many of the white workers," writes Quarles, "who could not raise this sum were inflamed by 'Copperhead' orators who, anxious to undermine the war effort, proclaimed that the white workingman was being made to shoulder a gun to free the slave who would soon become his rival for a job." On 12 July 1863, the names of the drafted men for New York were printed in the newspapers. On Monday morning, the mob stormed into the enrollment office where the names had been drawn. So began four days of widespread, unfocused violence, with looting which wrecked warehouses, saloons, and federal property, and the attempted murder of abolitionists and blacks.[10]

During the first day, thousands of factory and shipyard workers joined in looting stores and burning warehouses. Offices of the *New York Tribune* were damaged as mobs took control of the streets. That evening the rioters lit bonfires in the middle of the streets. The criminal elements joined in with the workers on the second day, now that the factories were shut down. With federal troops at Gettysburg, both public buildings and private residences became the targets of the mob. Businesses, homes of abolitionists, and private residences employing Negroes were marked for visits. The mayor's home was stripped of its furniture, and Negroes were pursued relentlessly.[11]

On the second day, there was fighting everywhere. Firebells rang out continually, and terror became more widespread, reaching out to the Negro population which was trying to flee. They crowded the ferry boats in every direction, but the old and the poor, unable to leave, stayed behind to meet the fury of the mob. The sight of one black person in the street would call forth a "haloo," as when a fox is seen, and half a dozen men or a whole crowd would dash after him. If overtaken, the individual was pounded to death; if he escaped into a house for shelter, it was set on fire, and all inside would share a common fate.[12]

On the corner of Twenty-seventh Street and Seventh Avenue, a collection of Irishmen danced wildly around the remains of a Negro. Two black boardinghouses were broken into; the proprietor was beaten unmercifully, and the buildings were burned. Stores were likewise fired. Joel Headley, a former law enforcement officer and an authority on riots in New York, provides the following graphic description:

> Sometimes a stalwart Negro would break away from his murderers, and run for his life. With no place of safety to which he could flee, he would be headed off in every direction, and forced toward the river. Driven at last to the end of a pier, he would leap off, preferring to take his chances in the water rather than among these bloody men. If bruised and beaten in his desperate struggle for life, he would soon sink exhausted with his efforts. Sometimes he would strike out for a ship, but more often dive under the piers, and hold on to a timber for safety, until his yelling pursuers had disappeared, when he would crawl stealthily out, and with a terrified face peer in every direction to see if they had gone;[13]

Even the police station was no haven if the force had left it vacant.[14] On 6 July 1863, a week before the outbreak, Garnet had chaired a meeting at Shiloh at which the Reverend Dr. Massie from England presented the slavery views of English ministers of different denominations. Massie said the initiative of his particular movement came from Parisian ministers; one hundred ministers in France alone signed an antislavery statement, while in England thousands of ministers signed.[15]

Massie paid a visit to Garnet during the riot. When he arrived at Shiloh, he found the church in total darkness. When he was finally admitted, he was conducted to Garnet's home where, earlier in the day, Mary Highland, his daughter, had taken the precaution of removing the name plate from the door. In a darkened parlor, Massie found Garnet surrounded by four friends, one of whom had had a narrow escape. They sat in tense and watchful silence, growing rigid at the sound of every footfall that approached the front steps.[16]

Perhaps the worst tragedy of the riot was the attack on the Negro Orphan Asylum on Fifth Avenue, a philanthropy which black leaders subscribed to and helped maintain. To raise funds for the home, Mary Highland Garnet had sponsored and participated in different jubilees and social occasions.[17] The orphanage was probably the best of its kind in the entire northeast.[18] In its strange logic, the mob turned its fury on the asylum after it had stopped the draft. Headley theorizes that the mob reasoned as follows:

There would have been no draft but for the war—there would
have been no war but for slavery. But the slaves were black,
ergo, all blacks are responsible for the war. This seemed to be
the logic of the mob, and having reached the sage conclusion to
which it conducted, they did not stop to consider how poor
helpless orphans could be held responsible, but proceeded at
once to wreak their vengeance on them.[19]

Headley also describes the firing of the four-story building, the heroism of a few firemen, and the escape of the children:

Superintendent William E. Davis hurriedly fastened the doors; but
knowing they would furnish but a momentary resistance to the
armed multitude, he, with others, collected hastily the terrified
children, and carrying some in their arms, and leading others,
hurried them in a confused crowd out of the rear of the building,
just as the ruffians effected an entrance in the front.[20]

The children had to be kept temporarily in stationhouses. Three
days later, they were transferred under police protection to Black-
well's Island for safety.[21]

It was an impressive spectacle this army of children presented, as
they drew up in line in front of the arsenal to wait for those within
to join them. The block was filled with them. The frightened
little fugitives, fleeing from they scarcely knew what, looked be-
wildered at the novel position. It seemed impossible that they
ever could have been the objects of any one's vengeance.[22]

Such were the costs of the New York draft riots for blacks. Garnet
miraculously escaped. Even a shotgun blast from a student dormitory
would have been insufficient to deter such a mob if it had come upon
him during any of those four days.[23] It is difficult to estimate the number of injuries and damages the Negro citizens suffered. There were ten
known dead; in addition, a Mohawk Indian mistaken for a Negro and
the white wife of another black person were slain.[24] After the federal
troops restored order, began the painful task of estimating the extent of
the catastrophe and of helping the injured. Garnet and a half dozen fellow ministers were called upon to play an important role.

Shortly after the riot, local businessmen met to raise money both for those who had been injured in the line of duty and for the riot victims. A special commission of merchants—the New York Commission for Colored People—was formed specifically to aid the black victims. Garnet, Ray, and others were employed by the committee as missionaries to the injured. Between the middle of July and 22 August 1863, the last day of the relief effort, they made three thousand visits, personally relieved the wants of a thousand people, examined three thousand cases, and recommended nearly all payments of the last week.[25] Garnet himself received a small grant of twenty-five dollars.[26] In addition to his relief effort, Garnet helped to draft a public statement of gratitude to the New York Relief Commission from colored ministers and laymen when their labors had terminated. A document of some one thousand words, it served as an official statement of the black community's sentiments. In its refusal to yield to despair, it also reflected Garnet's personal feelings. "When in the pursuit of our peaceful and humble occupations we had fallen among thieves, who stripped us of our raiment and had wounded us, leaving many of us half dead," Garnet wrote, "you had compassion on us."[27]

"We were hungry," he continued, "and you fed us. We were thirsty and you gave us drink. We were made as strangers in our own homes and you kindly visited us."[28] Perhaps the most appreciative sentiments were as follows:

> But as great as have been the benefit that we have received from your friendly and unlooked for charity, they yet form but the smaller portion of the ground of our gratitude and pleasure. We have now learned by your treatment of us in these days of our mental and physical affliction, that you cherished for us a kindly and humane feeling of which we had no knowledge. You obeyed the noblest dictates of the human heart, and by your generous moral courage you rolled back the tide of violence that had well-nigh swept us away.[29]

Garnet concluded with a final plea of fairness from his benefactors:

> If in your temporary labors of Christian philanthropy, you have been induced to look forward to our future destiny in this our native land, and to ask what is the best thing we can do for the

colored people? This is our answer. Protect us in our endeavors
to obtain an honest living. Suffer no one to hinder us in any
department of well directed industry, give us a fair and open
field and let us work out our own destiny, and we ask no more.[30]

Even in thanking those who had aided the Negro community, Garnet
continued to advance the cause of civil rights. His aid to the committee
was probably the last service he rendered to the people of New York
until the end of the Civil War when he was recalled to Shiloh. To be near
his daughter and to furnish assistance to the newly freed, Garnet
accepted the call to the Fifteenth Street Presbyterian Church of Washington, D.C., in February 1864. While at Shiloh, Garnet had won much
respect. Later, Crummell recalled this fact in his eulogy of Garnet:

Amid the immense population of the Metropolis [New York City]
there never was a man of our race so well known and so popular
as Dr. Garnet. The laboring classes of the whites, reporters for
newspapers, the politicians, the clergy of all names, the great merchants of the city, the grand dames on the avenues knew him and
respected him. One public journal declared at the time of his
death [1882], that he was "the best known colored clergyman in
the United States."[31]

Garnet came to Fifteenth Street in March 1864.[32] At this time he
also became one of the prime movers behind the proposed National
Convention of Colored Men which was planned in the fall at Syracuse,
New York.[33] By that date, it was clear that changes resulting from the
North's victories on the battlefield would work to the advantage of
Negro Americans. Not only had the Emancipation Proclamation gone
into effect, but also Union successes held the promise of effective enforcement. By July 1864, Congress, no longer seriously considering
colonization as a solution to the race issue, voted to freeze the unex-
pended monies appropriated for that purpose. President Lincoln continued to maintain some interest in voluntary colonization after that
date, but the failure of these experiments finally convinced him that
they were unworkable.[34]

Of the $38,329.93 spent by the chief executive, nearly two-thirds
went to Senator Pomeroy, the promoter of Chiriqui—a transisthmian
project in Panama; the remainder was spent on such miscellaneous

items as Commissioner Mitchell's salary and the rescue expedition to
Ile à Vache,[35] an island off the coast of Haiti, where blacks were
settled.

By September 1864, the African Civilization Society was appealing
for aid in sustaining schools in the South and in providing positions
for young blacks who had received a liberal education. It asked women,
especially those from large cities, to aid in the work of educating
children and providing proper situations for Negro youth, many of
whom were sponsored by the African Civilization schools in Washington.[36] Thus, by the time of the national convention, both white and
Negro Americans had generally abandoned emigration altogether and
had become concerned about relief, rehabilitation, and the future
status of the freedmen. A long-time advocate of Negro nationality,
Garnet was increasingly isolated at the convention and held up to public ridicule by some of the delegates, particularly Downing.[37] Adding to
the pain of rebuff from his peers was the assault on Garnet en route to
the meeting by rowdies in Syracuse who took his cane.[38]

Garnet gave the invocation and address at the meeting. He mentioned
that he had been asked to define his position but felt that such a request, coming so late in his career, was exceedingly humiliating.[39] The
Downing and Garnet forces were to clash during the meeting. By now,
however, the subject of a Negro nationality was virtually insignificant,
having been superseded by concerns for black troops, freedmen, and
discrimination.

Garnet began his speech with the remark that there had been a
strong disposition to throw him on the shelf because of his connection
with the African Civilization Society.[40] (Later events in the meeting
seemed to bear out the accuracy of his observation.) He then vividly
described the July days in New York City in which a demoniacal hatred
had taken hold of the mob. He told the convention of one man who
was hanged from a tree, his living flesh cut out in pieces and offered to
the bloodthirsty mob. "Who wants some nigger meat?" was the question to which was replied, "I! I! I! as if they were scrambling for pieces
of gold."[41]

Garnet, referring to the nationality of the mob, marveled how it was
that the men had changed so radically merely by crossing the ocean. In
his journeys from Belfast to Cork and from Dublin to the Giant's Cause-
way, the treatment he had received had been uniformly kind. He had

stood in public beside the great O'Connell who hated oppression. Garnet attributed the change among the Irish to the debasing influence of unprincipled American politicians.[42]

On the final convention day, the Downing-Garnet friction erupted openly over Reverend Mr. Cain's motion to endorse the African Civilization Society's efforts. Downing immediately voiced his disapproval on the grounds that the society was colonization under another name and that the convention should not appear on record as endorsing such an organization. He further stated that the society used white money and was organized by Negro nationalists who did not believe that Negroes could be elevated in America. So far as the work in schools was concerned, Downing continued, the society had not gone where it was needed.[43]

Reverend J. Sella Martin's and Garnet's rebuttal failed to convince Downing. A restrained Garnet, after thanking Cain for his remarks on the work of the society in Washington, casually mentioned that as a resident of Washington himself [Downing lived in Newport, Rhode Island], he was very familiar with the benefits resulting from those schools. Then he answered the personal accusations. His remarks were reported as follows:

> As to the personal matters referred to by Mr. Downing, he [Garnet] would say he might appeal to all present whether they believed, that now, so late in his public life, he had begun to falsify himself by putting himself under the direction, and being made the tool of white men. He had during all that life been unpopular, for the very reason that he was too independent to be used as a tool. For that independence he had sacrificed something, and today was poor because of it. Mr. Downing made the objection, that the African Civilization Society takes money from white men. "I think," said Mr. Garnet, "that when this hall was filled,—the major portion white people—the Finance Committee of the Convention passed among them, and I was not aware that they refused any means because a white man gave it."
>
> "If Jeff[erson] Davis would send an amount to educate the colored children I would gladly receive it, and I would say to

him, 'That is one good act you have done, if you have done
no other.' Mr. Downing, even, takes money from white men.
As regards the other personal remarks of Mr. Downing, I pass
them by. Those who know me, know well that I could retort
if I chose. But I will not retort. Mr. Downing and I have in days
gone by had many hard intellectual battles. He has hurled
against me all the force of his vigorous logic, and I struck him
back with all my power. If I smarted from his blows, I think I
may say he went away a little lame; and he has never forgotten
it. If Mr. Downing has intended to cripple my influence in this
Convention, to keep me out of office and off of committees,
he has successfully accomplished that purpose. But we will work
in our humble way, as we are laboring now, to lift up the race
with which we are identified, but especially to give to the
children of the people the education of which for so long they
have been deprived.[44]

Downing and Garnet were of opposite temperaments. Downing, a
wealthy, light-skinned businessman and Garnet, a poor black minister
with strong ancestral memories, had very different approaches to abolition and black advancement. Although they cooperated from time to
time on matters such as the enlistment of Negro troops, the chasm between them remained unbridgeable for the rest of Garnet's life. To the
end, they conflicted sharply on African culture and emigration as a
means of obtaining rights for black Americans. Garnet became embit-
tered as the years went by not merely because men like Downing continued to distrust him, but because he did not obtain the recognition
from the black community which he richly deserved.[45]

George B. Vashon tried to soothe the situation by a compromise
resolution which, by implication, would recognize the African Civilization Society and would give it credit as an agency of relief to freedmen.
Garnet disdainfully waved it aside. The matter was finally concluded by
equating the society with the National Freedmen's Relief Association
and the American Missionary Society as dispensers of domestic good
works to the Negro in the Southern states.[46]

Despite all the internal problems, the convention itself was one of
the most successful Negro conventions in the history of the movement.
It sent petitions to Congress asking for fair treatment in army pay,

labor, and promotion. It looked to the federal government to give the black man his full rights under the Constitution and asked for the franchise in the District of Columbia.[47] These requests were in large measure granted. Perhaps the most significant work of the convention was its creation of a new organization, the National Equal Rights League whose purposes were as follows: ". . . to encourage sound morality, education, temperance, frugality, industry, and promote everything that pertains to a well ordered and dignified life; to obtain by appeals to the minds and conscience of the American people, or by legal process when possible, a recognition of the rights of the colored people of the nation as American citizens."[48]

The election of John M. Langston, a young and energetic lawyer, to the presidency of the National Equal Rights League was a signal that a younger generation of leadership was coming into being. Neither Garnet nor Douglass was named as an officer, though they were offered other posts. Garnet was to organize blacks into an equal rights movement during the postbellum period.[49] During the Convention, he was presented with the bloodstained banner which Negro soldiers had carried at Port Hudson,[50] an affirmative proof of their heroism under fire.

During the first days of 1865, Garnet spoke in celebration of the Emancipation Proclamation in Washington at his church and in Philadelphia.[51] The Washington celebration was heavily attended, and Garnet shared the platform with Senator Pomeroy of Kansas. At a meeting of the Mutual Building Association on 5 January 1865, in Washington, the company president made Garnet a stockholder, raised the amount necessary, and had his first five installments paid in. At the congregational meeting of his church for the election of trustees, a splendid report was read, showing an expenditure of over $2,000, the pastor's salary of $800 per year, and only a debt of $28 on the church. Garnet's congregation had grown so large that the demand for pews could not be met. Garnet was quite pleased.[52]

In February 1865, Congress passed a bill ending slavery which was subsequently to become the Thirteenth Amendment. To commemorate the adoption of this historic measure, President Lincoln, with the unanimous consent of his cabinet and both the congressional chaplains, asked Garnet to deliver a memorial sermon in the House chambers. Garnet complied on 14 February in a special Sunday morning service. William J. Wilson of Washington attended and recorded the event:

I arrived at the Hall of Representatives, at 11 A.M., and found
every seat upon the floor occupied, and the galleries filled to
overflowing. The choir of the Rev. gentleman's church, which,
by the way, is one of the very best we have in the country, was
also invited to serve on this occasion, and crowned itself with
honor. It was a strange sight, in the presence of the assembled
wisdom, and, I say, to see this little band of vocalists, stand up
in places where but one year ago only white persons were allowed
to stand, and there chant up hymns of praise to God for his good-
ness and his wonderful works to the children of men; and it was
a sight stranger still to see this colored divine stand up in the
dignity of his high office as a priest of the Most High in that
Speaker's desk.

But, we are assembled; white and colored—all mingled and all
seemingly comfortable. Perhaps it is always thus when we occupy
the highest places at the *feast* [Author's italics] . It is then, that
our white friends, even the most fastidious of them, feel truly
comfortable, and it is only natural that they should. But we are
all seated, or positioned on our feet, as the case may be, and are
as still as the lake at eventide. All eyes are turned toward the
reverend gentleman, who in that quiet dignity which impresses
every one, rose and offered up a fervent prayer to the throne of
Grace. His words were unction, and I have wondered, who of
that vast assembly were not touched by their pathetic wail as
they came forth from one who wrestled with an angel. The
preacher then read the first hymn,
       All hail the power of Jesus' name.
Then followed the reading of the Scriptures. Then all eyes were
turned toward the choir as in sweet and touching melody it
warbled forth the beautiful sentiment,
       Arise, my soul, shake off thy fears.
And now the text is read; from the choir back again to the
clergyman, attention is turned as a wheatfield upon a sudden
change of wind. All the attention which that vast congregation
can give, is, unreservedly at the speaker's command, while he
proceeds to unfold the text, make plain its meaning, and apply

its divine teachings to the hearts and understanding of his hearers. For the space of an hour what a breathless house! What suppressed emotions!

Breathless house, did I say? When standing in the Speaker's place, with the full length portrait of Washington on his right and that of Lafayette on his left, the eloquent preacher appealed as authority to both "that our land was made for free men and free women," the silence was broken, and, but for the Sabbath morning the restrained applause would have been unbounded: so also when, in a sudden outburst, he exclaimed, "Should any poet have attempted to write in praise of American Slavery, the ink would have frozen upon the point of his pen!" and, too, in his tribute to Washington, Jefferson, and Adams, and the host of freedom's champions who have passed away, a thrill ran through the house which surpassed all the applause I have ever heard. When he said, "These worthies, if they looked down on the scene which transpired in this hall a few days since, when the great National Work was consummated, they must have responded with the angel choir, an hearty amen!" and uncontrollable emotion, for the moment, took entire possession of the audience.

It is needless to say more. Men who went to the house to hear a colored man, came away having heard a MAN in the highest and fullest sense. Many who went there with feelings of curiosity, came away wrapped in astonishment. Not only a man, but a great representative man had spoken, and they were amazed.[53]

Since Garnet's discourse on that occasion is well-known and has recently been reprinted, it will not be reproduced in full here.[54] The address was an intense, vivid exposition of American slavery as only a former slave could have presented it. He said:

I was born among the cherished institutions of slavery. My earliest recollections of parents, friends, and the home of my childhood are clouded with its wrongs. The first sight that met my eyes was a Christian mother enslaved by professed Christians, but, thank God, now a saint in heaven. The first sounds that startled my ear, and sent a shudder through my soul, were the cracking of the whip, and the clanking of chains. These sad memories mar the beauties of my native shores, and darken all the slave-land, which, but for the reign of despotism, had been a paradise. But those shores are fairer now. The mists have left my native valleys, and the clouds have rolled away from the hills, and Maryland, the unhonored grave of my fathers, is now the free home of their liberated and happier children.[55]

His remarks contained numerous allusions from Plato and Moses to Washington and Jefferson which universally condemned the institution. Garnet concluded with a statement that insisted upon justice and equality for every American:

It is often asked when and where will the demands of the reformers of this and coming ages end? It is a fair question, and I will answer.

When all unjust and heavy burdens shall be removed from every man in the land. When emancipation shall be followed by enfranchisement, and all men holding the allegiance to the government shall enjoy every right of American citizenship. When our brave and gallant soldiers shall have justice done unto them. When the men who endure the sufferings and perils of the battlefield in the defence of their country, and in order to keep our rulers in their places, shall enjoy the well-earned privilege of voting for them. When in the army and navy, and in every legitimate and honorable occupation, promotion shall smile upon merit without the slightest regard to the complexion of a man's face. When there shall be no more class-legislation, and no more trouble concerning the black man and his rights, than there is in regard to other American citizens. When, in every respect, he shall be equal before the law, and shall be left to make his own way in the social walks of life.[56]

He ended with an appeal to the legislators: "Favored men, and honored of God as his instruments, speedily finish the work which He has given you to do. *Emancipate, Enfranchise, Educate and give the blessings of the gospel to every American citizen* [Author's italics]."[57]

Most of the accounts of Garnet's discourse in the Washington newspapers were favorable. The writer in *The Washington Daily Intelligencer* said that all present were pleased with his message, and that many whose proclivities may have been Southern and who were attracted by the novelty of a black man preaching in the hall of the House of Representatives expressed surprise at the speaker's skill in handling the subject and at his fund of information.[58] The report in *The Washington Daily Morning Chronicle* was even more laudatory: "This is but a faint sketch of his able discourse, and several times during its delivery, the audience was so thrilled by the power of his logic that it was with difficulty that their enthusiasm was restrained, and a half-muffled applause was at times discernible."[59] The editors of *The Washington Evening Star* also gave the discourse some attention: "His [Garnet's] discourse was directed principally to the wrongs inflicted on the African race, and concluded by denouncing slavery and demanding at the hands of the white man equal rights. The discourse attracted much attention."[60] The reporter for *The Washington Daily Times* was almost alone in his denunciation of Garnet's address: "Our readers are already aware that the Hall of the House of Representatives of the United States, was polluted on last Sunday and the Sabbath was desecrated by one Rev. H. H. Garnet, Negro have been permitted to occupy the Speaker's desk and deliver a political harangue—miscalled a sermon—in the presence of a large audience, composed of Negroes, white and black."[61]

Garnet was now nationally famous. Not only was he on speaking terms with Greeley, Lincoln, Andrew Johnson, and many congressional leaders but through his oratory he was also reaching a larger audience. At Cooper Institute early in April 1865, over two thousand people heard him discuss the effects of the proposed Thirteenth Amendment on the cause of freedom. He cited slave insurrection as an expression of the Negro American's attitude toward the institution. After citing the efforts of abolitionists, he updated the topic and sought to glean from it new meaning. To Garnet, the fact that free Negroes in 1865 were on the banks of the James River, armed with rifles and bayonets, was miraculous. He saw something of the hand of God in the fact that forty-eight thousand black Yankees were marching into Richmond, some of them returning to the nation's capital as the guards of captured Confederate prisoners. Then he quoted Lincoln's well-known tribute to the Negro troops on whom the chief executive was so dependent. He had the highest personal regard for Lincoln and for Andrew Johnson with whom he had had a recent interview. He reassured the gathering that Johnson had expressed his determination to give every man, white and black, a fair chance. The next battle to be fought, he went on, would be over prejudice, and Johnson had refuted slanders made against black men, praising their conduct during the war in the highest terms, and declaring it to have been unparalleled. Then came the proposed amendment which when passed, he believed, would mean the end of slavery.[62]

On the evening of 14 April 1865, Lincoln was assassinated and thus was gone a statesman whose acts had greatly benefited black Americans. His widow, Mary Todd Lincoln, was placed under the constant attention of Elizabeth Keckley, a black woman; other Negro acquaintances offered her their services. The bereaved widow sent Douglass and Garnet canes which Lincoln had prized, as tokens of the high regard he had had for the two men. As a testament to their love for the Lincolns, Garnet and Douglass, at the suggestion of Mrs. Keckley, agreed to lecture to raise money for Mrs. Lincoln who was in difficult financial straits. Mrs. Keckley also wanted to send circulars appealing to the generosity of the American public. Garnet accompanied her to Horace Greeley who gave the plan his tentative approval.[63]

Almost immediately upon the news of Lincoln's death, Negroes in all walks of life began to seek funds for a suitable monument. The original and foundation subscription for the monument came from a former slave, Charlotte Scott. When sympathetic public officials took up the cause, sufficient monies were raised for a statue.[64] In an effort to turn the widespread sympathy for the deceased president to the advantage of the Negroes, Garnet organized the National Monument Association of the District of Columbia on 25 April 1865. The hope of the founders was to create the National Lincoln Memorial Institute in Washington which would serve as a model for the education and elevation of Negroes throughout the land. A celebration to raise funds for the project was held on Independence Day on the presidential grounds. Garnet enlarged the aims to include all people who sought admission.[65] Little came of their plans beyond the erection of the statue in Lincoln Park in Washington.

On 11 May 1865, a group of Negro pastors called on the new president, Andrew Johnson. Garnet was in the city on that date and may have been a member of the delegation. After discussing the problems which Negro Americans faced, Johnson pledged all his resources to the elevation of the Negro people.[66]

With the return of peace, Garnet was invited by Negro clergymen in Norfolk, Virginia, to help them prepare an address from local blacks to the people of the United States. The resulting document, directed at both whites and blacks, made a fervent plea for full civil rights on humanitarian, political, and constitutional grounds. It deplored the practice which planters had initiated of hiring only former slaves and threatening with violence those who refused to return to work. Specifically, it asked the whites for the suffrage and promised that peace and justice for all would result.[67]

The document also advised the Negro brethren to form state and national associations immediately whose object would be agitation, discussion, and enforcement of claims to equality before the law and equal rights of suffrage. Secondly, it advised formation of labor associations to fix and maintain the wages of Negro workers, since their former masters had already formed associations to depress wages. Third, it advocated acquisition of land through formation of land associations. Then associations provided that, by the regular payment of small installments, a fund would be established for the purchase, at all land sales, of acreage on behalf of any investing member in the name of the association. The associations would hold a mortgage on the property until the sum advanced and the interest were paid. Then the occupier would get a clear title.[68]

Early in July, Garnet informed the sessional meeting of his church that the American Home Missionary Society had asked him to become their exploring agent among freedmen. He had been commissioned to spend the next four months traveling in the South and Southwestern states and had agreed pending the consent of the church. Consent was given. On 22 July 1865, Garnet became the editor of the Southern Department of *The Anglo-African* and began his journey.[69]

His first stop was New Market, Maryland, near where he had been born into slavery. While there, he spoke with a number of former slaveholders and "was most kindly received by them." According to Garnet, they seemed proud that even a black man, a native of Kent, had received some little consideration from his fellow men. His journey took him from Kent to St. Louis, where he reported that "everywhere my friends welcome me."[70]

In many of the towns he visited, local black residents asked him to speak. During the several days he was in Richmond, he made the rounds of the Negro churches and was also requested to speak at a mass meeting that was being held to appoint delegates to the upcoming Virginia state convention.[71]

As indicated by the statement drafted at Petersburg, Garnet fully supported the freedmen's demand for land and the franchise, which would be the real basis for a just and democratic society in the South and would prevent the former planters from returning to power. The success of Reconstruction, Garnet thought, depended largely on the division and equitable distribution of the former planters' lands among the freedmen.[72]

From his travels, Garnet saw that the government was not moving fast or far enough on the land question. He told Gerrit Smith that the Reconstruction plan "may be disastrous to the cause of freedom." Garnet suspected that President Johnson was backsliding on the promises the government had made to the freedmen.[73]

Hence, when the war ended, the struggle for civil rights was raised to a new level. Having helped to bury slavery in law, Garnet was soon laboring to make emancipation meaningful in fact. His efforts entered a new phase after he returned from his tour of the former slave states. Before him lay more than a decade of toil in relief, education of freedmen, and the cause of Cuban emancipation.[74] As he looked ahead, there was an uncertain future of anticipated and prolonged struggle; as he looked behind, there was the hard evidence of worthwhile work.

NOTES

1. Hirsch, p. 448.
2. Quarles, *The Negro in the Civil War*, p. 235.
3. Ibid., p. 236.
4. Ibid., p. 237.

5. *The Weekley Anglo-African*, 9 August 1862, p. 3.

6. Ibid.

7. Ibid., 28 September 1862, p. 3.

8. Ibid., 2 December 1862, p. 2; also Quarles, *The Negro in the Civil War*, p. 129.

9. Quarles, p. 238.

10. Ibid., pp. 238-239.

11. Ibid., pp. 239-240.

12. Joel Headley, *The Great Riots of New York: 1712-1873* (Reprint; New York: Bobbs-Merrill Co., 1970), pp. 206-208.

13. Ibid., p. 208.

14. Ibid., p. 208-209.

15. *The Anglo-African*, 11 July 1863, p. 2.

16. Quarles, *The Negro in the Civil War*, p. 239. In other accounts, Garnet was actually pursued by a howling mob but escaped, hidden under a stable by a friend. See James Padget, "Ministers to Liberia and Their Diplomacy," *Journal of Negro History* 22 (January 1937): 71; and Brewer, "Henry Highland Garnet," pp. 36-52.

17. *The Weekly Anglo-African*, 24 March 1860, p. 2.

18. Headley, p. 169.

19. Ibid., pp. 169-170.

20. Ibid., p. 170.

21. Ibid., p. 250-251.

22. Ibid.

23. It is possible that some of his relatives were injured as a result of the riot. Mary Highland Garnet was sent to Washington, D.C., where she was reported as recuperating. See *The Anglo-African*, 13 February 1864, p. 2. Also, a claim was presented to the committee by Mrs. Susan Garnett, *The Anglo-African African*, 19 September 1863, p. 3.

24. Headley, pp. 271-278.

25. *Report of the New York Relief Commission for Colored People* (New York: Whitehorne, Steam Printer, 1863), pp. 9, 11.

26. Ibid., p. 31.

27. Ibid., pp. 31-34

28. Ibid.

29. Ibid.

30. Ibid., p. 34.

31. Crummell, *The Eulogy of Henry Highland Garnet*, pp. 22-24.

32. *The Records of the Session of the Fifteenth Street Presbyterian Church*, 1 (Washington, D.C.: Moorland Foundation, 1841-1868), 133.

33. *The Anglo-African*, 24 September 1864, pp. 2, 3.

34. Quarles, *Lincoln and the Negro* (New York: Oxford University Press, 1962), pp. 193-194.

35. Ibid., p. 194.

36. *The Anglo-African*, 24 September 1864, p. 4.

37. *Proceedings of the National Convention of Colored Men Held in the City of Syracuse, New York, October 4-7, 1864* (New York: Wesleyan Methodist Church, 1864), p. 19.

38. Ibid., p. 12. Also, *The Anglo-African*, 5 November 1864, p. 1. The meeting raised over $40 to replace his cane. A full account of the attack appeared in *The New York Evening Post*, 8 October 1864.

39. *Proceedings*, p. 19.

40. Ibid.

41. Ibid., p. 20.

42. Ibid., p. 21.

43. Ibid., pp. 26-27. At least two of the society's schools were operating in the Washington-Georgetown area by the end of the war. One met in the hall belonging to the Union Bethel Church of Washington. In another school, Garnet's second wife, Sarah J. Garnet, worked as a teacher. Eventually, these schools were absorbed into the public school system. See Winfield S. Montgomery, *Historical Sketch of Education for the Colored Race in the District of Columbia, 1807-1905* (Washington, D.C.: Smith Brothers., 1907), p. 17; and Record Group #105, Monthly School Reports of the District of Columbia (Washington, D.C.: The National Archives, Boxes 6-15), contain reports written by Mrs. Garnet.

44. *Proceedings*, pp. 27-28.

45. Garnet came to feel totally unappreciated during his declining years. When Crummell and other close friends begged him to reject the federal appointment to Liberia because of the health hazard, Garnet refused. "What," he answered, "would you have me linger here in an old age of neglect and want? Would you have me tarry among men who have forgotten what I have done, and what I have suffered for them? To stay here and die among those ungrateful people?" See Crummell, p. 27.

46. *Proceedings*, pp. 25-29, 35.

47. Ibid., pp. 33-34.

48. Ibid., p. 36.

49. Immediately after the war, Garnet traveled in the Southern states and helped to organize the Garnet Equal Rights League, which probably merged into the larger league. See Record Group #105, Letters to General Howard (Washington, D.C.: The National Archives).

50. *Syracuse Daily Standard*, 6 October 1864, p. 3.

51. *The Anglo-African*, 14 June 1865, pp. 1, 2.

52. Ibid., p. 2.

53. The source of the invitation extended by the administration to Garnet is Samuel A. Smith, *Letter to the Signal*, 3 December 1883, p. 2. James McCune Smith, *A Memorial Discourse*, pp. 65-67.

54. In addition to the James McCune Smith work which has been reprinted, the discourse is in the appendix of Ofari, *"Let Your Motto Be Resistance,"* pp. 187-203.

55. Smith, p. 73.

56. Ibid., pp. 85-87.

57. Ibid., p. 89.

58. *The Washington Daily Intelligencer*, 13 February 1865, as cited in Walter Dyson, *The First Negro to Speak in Our National Capitol as Reported by Eye-Witnesses* (Washington, D.C.: Moorland Foundation), p. 4. For the accounts in the Washington, Boston, and New York papers, I am indebted to Dyson.

59. Dyson, p. 6.

60. Ibid., p. 8.

61. Ibid.

62. *The Anglo-African*, 16 April 1865, p. 1.

63. Quarles, *Lincoln and the Negro*, p. 247; also Quarles, *Frederick Douglass*, p. 236.

64. Quarles, *Lincoln and the Negro*, pp. 3-14.

65. *The Anglo-African*, 22 July 1865, p. 4; also *Celebration by the Colored People's Educational Monument Association in the Memory of Abraham Lincoln* (Washington, D.C.: McGill & Withrow, 1865), pp. 14, 34.

66. *The Anglo-African*, 27 May 1865, p. 4.

67. *Address from the Colored Citizens of Norfolk, Virginia, to the People of the United States. Also an Account of the Agitation Among the Colored People of Virginia for Equal Rights, with an Appendix Concerning the Rights of Colored Witnesses Before State Courts* (New Bedford, Mass.: E. Anthony & Sons, 1865), pp. 3-5, 15.

68. Ibid., pp. 7-8.

69. *The Records of the Session of the Fifteenth Street Presbyterian Church*, 1, 151; *The Anglo-African*, 22 July 1865, p. 1.

70. Ofari, p. 117.

71. Ibid., pp. 117-118.

72. Ibid., pp. 118.

73. Ibid., p. 119.

74. Woodson, "Henry Highland Garnet," *DAB*, pp. 154-155.

11

Conclusion

In the early 1840s, when Garnet's influence among Negroes in New York State and on a national level was at its height, he and his compatriots championed the path of political abolition. They were doing for blacks what Salmon P. Chase had done for white abolitionists—making them into political as well as social activists. At nearly every state suffrage meeting held during that period, resolutions were introduced in favor of the Liberty party; the suffrage campaign went hand in hand with politicizing for that party. Over the years, as Garnet moved in and out of parties considered too radical by his followers, he made a significant contribution in the initial political organizing.

Garnet accepted an interpretation of the Constitution which saw it as an essentially antislavery document for ideological purposes. Such a view enabled a stronger attack on the Southern position than was possible with the views of Garrison and his protege, Frederick Douglass. Part of this difference in orientation is explained by differences in the abolitionist circles in which the two men traveled. Moreover, on certain issues Garnet had greater insights than Douglass. Political organization and a wise choice of ideology, then, constitute Garnet's primary and earliest major contribution.

His second contribution was in the advocacy of civil disobedience and resistance to slavery on the part of slaves themselves. In less than five years after he announced this position, the novelty and shock it occasioned wore away as increasing numbers of black and white abolitionists came to accept the inevitability of armed confrontation to end slavery. With minor fluctuation, events seemed to favor the Garnet view.

Douglass, Remond, Brown, Downing, and other opponents among Garnet's peers eventually came to accept political abolitionism and physical resistance. Garnet's strategies were probably influential in changing their position. Certainly the Mexican War, the Fugitive Slave Law, the Kansas warfare, and the Dred Scott decision played necessary parts in the process. The rivalry between the Douglass and Garnet forces throughout the 1840s and 1850s, especially in the Negro convention movements and to a much lesser extent in Douglass's publications, also helped to bring about the black leadership's change in views.

Finally, there remains the question of emigration and Negro nationality. This subject remains controversial. While Negro abolitionists were justifiably condemning colonization as a racist subterfuge, Garnet was almost alone in contemplating the effects of a black industrial state in West Central Africa on abolition and uplift in the United States. His reading of Lord Fowell Buxton's plans in *The Colored American*, his lectures abroad for the Free Produce movement, and his investigation of conditions in Jamaica were formative influences for his African Civilization scheme.

Garnet's idea of limited emigration to establish a Negro nation was initially met by total rebuke among his peers. Downing's response was most typical. Before others reversed their stand, it was necessary for Douglass, for example, to be forced from the country after Brown's raid and for the Republican party to hedge on its commitments to Negro Americans. By 1861, most of the leadership had accepted the value of limited emigration projects. This was another new development and part of the leadership crisis of the period. Garnet's view of emigration in the dark days of 1860 and 1861 was shared in part, if not fully, by a respectable minority of his peers. Only the outbreak of war saved Douglass from full endorsement.

The notion that a man might emigrate to fulfill his individual destiny was also tied up with the ideological view of emigration. When the black leadership, prodded by Garnet and his supporters and by the course of American history, abandoned the Garrisonian position of proximity to the slave—in itself a hypothetical notion—and assented to voluntary emigration, this position represented a liberating advance over the previous Garrisonian strategy. For the first time in several decades, Negroes had the right—the intellectual right—to choose for themselves their own mode of fulfillment, and would not be considered cowardly if the decision was to leave. Garnet deserves some credit for these developments.

Political abolition, militancy, and voluntary emigration, then, constitute Garnet's major contributions to Negro social and protest thought during the period under study. As important as his address of 1843 was in summoning slaves to resistance and in influencing John Brown, it was only his second major contribution. Garnet's influence on Brown was inferential, if not real. His attitude toward Brown remained consistent over some twenty years. From his pulpit in New York City, Garnet courageously called the man a heroic martyr on the eve of his demise.

Another level of contribution was made in indoctrinating Garnet's foreign audience with the goals of Free Produce. As a result of his lectures in one year alone, twenty-six Free Produce chapters were formed. Garnet's effect on English abolition was greater than simply that of one lecturer in a group, which in turn belonged to a larger movement. His jet black color enormously strengthened his rapport with this audiences, more so than the props which the abolitionists used in delivering their message.

Garnet's work among Jamaicans and freed slaves, though of a lesser order, was also valuable. His efforts on behalf of the black needy, including fugitives in Troy, Geneva, New York City, and Washington, D.C., were inspired acts, albeit not readily quantifiable.

The same may be said for his journalistic efforts as an editor of three Negro newspapers—*The Clarion, The National Watchman*, and the Southern section of *The Anglo-African*. Garnet the journalist, minister, and home and foreign missionary was essentially the abolitionist and civil rights fighter. Remarkably, Garnet never gave in to despair, as is shown by the fact that he was deeply involved in a variety of civil rights activities which went on simultaneously. He would not have been able to recruit troops, aid hundreds of riot victims in New York City and take time to thank the Merchants Committee for their help if he had given up on America as a viable place for Negroes. Clearly, Downing's argument that Garnet had done so by advocating a black state and taking money from whites was false.

The African Civilization Society, because of the anxiety it generated among black leadership, was not judged on its own merits in the antebellum period. Consequently, the value of this abolitionist approach is uncertain. Some emigration did occur, and if the war had not come, as Bell states, there would have been more. When the war broke out,

Southern cotton was not as essential to British factories as many had thought. More than Downing, it was the Emancipation Proclamation, supported and sustained by federal troops, that ended the African phase of the society, if not its educational aspect. Certainly, the latter was a contribution made by operating schools in the Washington area.

This evaluation of Garnet's role may necessitate a reevaluation of Douglass's position among black leaders. If Douglass is viewed as the leader of one faction—the moderate element—then Garnet's role becomes clearer. In that sense, Garnet was part of the vanguard of Negro abolition and thus deserves greater recognition than he has heretofore received.

Garnet's address to Congress in 1865 is another significant, if secondary, contribution. It was a testament to the regard of the white abolitionists for Garnet. It was also a reward held out for Negroes now that they had achieved some measure of political influence. Greeley, Lincoln, and Johnson considered Garnet to be as important as Douglass because these were the two most conspicuous black leaders of the times. Among Negroes the question was probably moot.

Garnet's abolition role has been examined here to vindicate black radicalism as a positive force within the Negro community. As we look back from the early 1970s, the time has come to give those to the left of Douglass their rightful place and credit. Though Garnet's task (and that of reformers in general) was incomplete, and remains so, he brought America a little closer to its revolutionary ideals.

Bibliography

Books

Andrews, Charles C. *The History of the New York African Free Schools*. Reprint; New York: Negro University Press, 1969.

Aptheker, Herbert. (ed.) *A Documentary History of the Negro People in the United States*. Vol. 1; New York: The Citadel Press, 1967.

——. *The Negro Peoples in the United States*. New York: The Citadel Press, 1951.

——. *One Continual Cry*. New York: Humanities Press, 1965.

Barnes, Gilbert H. *The Antislavery Impulse, 1830-1844*. New York: D. Appleton-Century Co., 1933.

Bell, Howard H. *The Negro Convention Movement, 1830-1861*. New York: Arno Press, 1969.

Coffin, Levi. *The Reminiscences of Levi Coffin*. Reprint; New York: Arno Press, 1968.

Cooper, Thomas V. *American Politics*. Philadelphia: Fireside Publishing Co., 1882.

Delany, M. R. and Campbell, Robert, *Search for a Place: Black Separatism and Africa, 1860*. Ann Arbor: University of Michigan Press, 1971.

Douglass, Frederick. *The Life and Times of Frederick Douglass as Written by Himself*. Reprint of 1892 rev. ed.; New York: Crowell Collier Books, 1962.

Dumond, Dwight. *The Anti-Slavery Origins of the Civil War*. London: Oxford University Press, 1939.

——. *The Letters of James G. Birney: 1837-1857*. Vol. 1. Reprint; Gloucester, Mass: Peter Smith, 1966.

Farrison, William E. *William Wells Brown*. Chicago: University of Chicago Press, 1969.

Fladeland, Betty. *Men and Brothers: Anglo-American Antislavery Cooperation*. Urbana: University of Illinois Press, 1972.

Foner, Eric. *Free Soil, Free Labor, Free Men: The Ideology of the Republican Party Before the Civil War*. New York: Oxford University Press, 1970.

Franklin, John Hope. *From Slavery to Freedom: A History of Negro Americans*. New York: Alfred A. Knopf, 1967.

Gara, Larry. *The Liberty Line*. Lexington: University Press of Kentucky, 1961.

Green, Samuel. *Berish Green*. New York: No. 18 Jacob Street, 1875.

Hart, Albert Bushnell. *Slavery and Abolition*. Reprint; New York: Negro Universities Press, 1968.

Headley, Joel. *The Great Riots of New York: 1712-1873*. Reprint; New York: Bobbs-Merrill Co., 1970.

Katz, Loren, ed. *Walker's Appeal and an Address to the Slaves of the United States of America*. Reprint; New York: Arno Press, 1969.

Lewis, Matthew G. *Ambrosio or The Monk*. Vol. 2; New York: J. A. Chessmen, 1830.

Litwack, Leon F. *North of Slavery: The Negro in the Free States, 1790-1860*. Chicago: University of Chicago Press, 1961.

McPherson, James. *The Negro's Civil War*. New York: Vintage Books, 1965.

Mabee, Carleton. *Black Freedom: The Non-Violent Abolitionists from 1830 Through the Civil War*. New York: The Macmillan Co., 1970.

Meier, August. *Negro Thought in America 1880-1915*. Ann Arbor: University of Michigan Press, 1966.

Meier, August, and Rudwick, Elliott, eds. *The Making of Black America*. Vol. 1; New York: Atheneum, 1969.

Montgomery, Winfield S. *Historical Sketch of Education for the Colored Race in the District of Columbia, 1807-1905*. Washington, D.C.: Smith Brothers, 1907.

Nuermberger, Ruth. *The Free Produce Movement*. Durham, N.C.: Duke University Press, 1942, in Vols. 23-25 of the *Trinity College Historical Papers*, pp. 4-137.

Nye, Russel B. *William Lloyd Garrison and the Humanitarian Reformers*. Boston: Little, Brown, 1955.

Oates, Stephen. *To Purge This Land with Blood: A Biography of John Brown*. New York: Harper & Row, 1970.

Ofari, Earl. *"Let Your Motto Be Resistance": The Life and Thought of Henry Highland Garnet*. Boston: Beacon Press, 1972.

Penn, Garland I. *The Afro-American Press and Its Editors*. Springfield, Mass.: Wiley & Co., 1891.

Pessen, Edward. *Jacksonian America: Society, Personality and Politics*. Homewood, Ill.: The Dorsey Press, 1969.

Quarles, Benjamin. *Allies for Freedom: Blacks and John Brown*. New York: Oxford University Press, 1974.

————. *Black Abolitionists*. New York: Oxford University Press, 1969.

————. ed. *Blacks on John Brown*. Urbana: University of Illinois Press, 1972.

————. *Frederick Douglass*. New York: Atheneum, 1970.

————. *Lincoln and the Negro*. New York: Oxford University Press, 1962.

————. *The Negro in the Civil War*. Boston: Little, Brown & Co., 1953.

Ray, F. T. *Sketch of the Life of Charles B. Ray*. New York: J. J. Little & Co., 1887.

Rezneck, Samuel. *Profiles Out of the Past of Troy, New York*. Troy, N.Y.: Chamber of Commerce, 1970.

Roberts, William H. *A Concise History of the Presbyterian Church*. Philadelphia: Presbyterian Board of Publishers, 1922.

Robinson, Wilhelmena S. *International Library of Negro Life and History*. New York: Publishers Co., Inc., 1968.

Seifman, Eli. *A History of the New York Colonization Society*. New York: Phelps-Stokes Fund, 1966.

Siebert, Wilbur H. *The Underground Railroad*. Reprint; New York: Arno Press, 1968.

Sinkler, George. *The Racial Attitudes of American Presidents from Abraham Lincoln to Theodore Roosevelt*. New York: Doubleday, 1971.

Smedley, Robert. *History of the Underground Railroad*. Reprint; New York: Arno Press, 1969.

Smith, James McCune. *A Memorial Discourse by Henry Highland Garnet*. Philadelphia: Joseph M. Wilson, 1865.

Smith, Theodore Clark. *Parties and Slavery, 1850-1859*. Vol. 18 of *The American Nation: A History,* ed. by Albert Bushnell Hart, 28 vols.; New York: Harper and Brothers, 1904-1918.

Sterling, Dorothy. *The Making of an Afro-American: Martin Robison Delany, 1812-1885*. New York: Doubleday & Co., Inc., 1971.

Still, William. *The Underground Railroad*. Reprint; New York: Arno Press, 1968.

Tappan, Lewis. *The Life of Arthur Tappan*. Reprint; New York: Arno Press, 1970.

Tyler, Alice Felt. *Freedom's Ferment*. Reprint; New York: Harper & Row, 1962.

Ullman, Victor. *Martin R. Delany: The Beginnings of Black Nationalism*. Boston: Beacon Press, 1971.

Ward, Samuel R. *Autobiography of a Fugitive Slave*. Chicago: Johnson Publishing Co., 1970.

Wesley, Charles. *Negro Labor in the United States*. New York: Vanguard Press, 1927.

Williams, George Washington. *History of the Negro Race in America: 1619-1880*. Reprint; New York: Arno Press, 1969.

Woodson, Carter G. *The History of the Negro Church*. 2d. ed.; Washington, D.C.: The Associated Publishers, 1921.

——— . *The Mind of the Negro as Reflected in Letters Written During the Crisis, 1800-1860*. Washington, D.C.: The Association for the Study of Negro Life and History, 1926.

——— . *Negro Orators and Their Orations*. Reprint; New York: Russell and Russell, 1969.

Woodward, C. Vann. *The Burden of Southern History*. New York: Vintage Books, 1960.

——— . *The Strange Career of Jim Crow*. 2d rev. ed.; New York: Oxford University Press, 1966.

Articles and Periodicals

Abzug, Robert. "The Influence of Garrisonian Abolitionists' Fears of Slave
    Violence on the Antislavery Argument, 1829-1840." *Journal of Negro
    History* 55 (January 1970): 15-26.
African Repository & Colonial Journal, 18-58, 1837-1882.
American and Foreign Anti-Slavery Reporter, 1-3, 1840-1846.
American Missionary, 2-14, 1847-1870.
Anti-Slavery Reporter.
Aptheker, Herbert. "Militant Abolitionism." *Journal of Negro History* 26
    (October 1941): 438-484.
Brewer, William. "Henry Highland Garnet." *Journal of Negro History* 13
    (January 1928): 36-52.
British and Foreign Anti-Slavery Reporter.
Edmonds, Irene C. "An Aristotelian Interpretation of Garnet's Memorial Dis-
    course." *Research Bulletin: Florida A & M College* 5 (September 1952):
    20-28.
"Fugitive Slave Act." *The Eclectic Review* 93 (May 1851): 661-669.
Gara, Larry. "The Professional Fugitive in the Abolition Movement." *The Wis-
    consin Magazine of History* 48 (Spring 1965): 196-204.
Hirsch, Leo H., Jr. "New York and the Negro, From 1783 to 1865." *Journal of
    Negro History* 16 (October 1931): 382-454.
Liberia Bulletin, February 1900.
MacMaster, Richard. "Henry Highland Garnet and the African Civilization
    Society." *Journal of Presbyterian Church History* 48 (Summer 1970): 91-112.
Miller, Floyd J. "The Father of Black Nationalism." *Civil War History* 17 (Decem-
    ber 1971): 310-319.
Missionary Record of the United Presbyterian Church, 1852-1856.
New York Colonization Journal, 1859.
Padget, James. "Ministers to Liberia and Their Diplomacy." *Journal of Negro
    History* 22 (January 1937): 36-52.
Pease, Jane, and Pease, William. "Black Power—The Debate in 1840." *Phylon* 39
    (Spring 1968): 19-26.
Pessen, Edward. "The Egalitarian Myth and the American Social Reality: Wealth,
    Mobility and Equality in the 'Era of the Common Man.'" *American Historical
    Review* 56 (October 1971): 989-1034.
Quarles, Benjamin. "Ministers Without Portfolio." *Journal of Negro History* 39
    (January 1954): 27-42.
The Slave, His Wrongs and Their Remedy, January 1851.
Wesley, Charles. "Negroes in Anti-Slavery Political Parties." *Journal of Negro
    History* 29 (January 1944): 32-74.
————. "Negroes in New York in the Emancipation Movement: Negro Aboli-
    tionists and Their Work." *Journal of Negro History* 23 (1939): 65-103.
Woodson, Carter G. "Henry Highland Garnet" *DAB*, 4, Part I (1932): 154-155.

Theses and Dissertations

Boyd, Willis. "Negro Colonization in the National Crisis." Ph.D. dissertation, University of California, 1953.

Cheagle, Roslyn V. "The Colored Temperance Movement: 1830-1860." Master's thesis, Howard University, 1969.

Harwood, Thomas. "Great Britain and American Anti-Slavery." Ph.D. dissertation, University of Michigan, 1959.

Miller, Ernest J. "The Anti-Slavery Role of Henry Highland Garnet." Master's thesis, Union Theological Seminary, 1969.

Miller, Floyd J. "The Search for a Black Nationality: Martin R. Delany and the Emigrationist Alternative." Ph.D. dissertation, University of Minnesota, 1970.

Spraggins, Tinsely. "Economic Aspects of Negro Colonization During the Civil War." Ph.D. dissertation, American University, 1957.

Newspapers

The Anglo-African. Originally entitled *The Weekly Anglo-African*, it began publication on 20 August 1859. It continued on a regular basis until 14 July 1860. (Microfilm is obtainable on this segment either from the Library of Congress or from the Moorland Foundation, Howard University). From that date until May 1861, the newspaper was purchased by James Redpath and renamed *The Pine & Palm*, the oracle for Haitian emigration. By 9 August 1861, the paper was again being published under its original name. In the same month, the word "Weekly" was dropped from the title, and the new name read *The Anglo-African*, which continued in publication throughout 1865.

Cincinnati Daily Chronicle. 7 September 1843.

Cincinnati Morning Herald. 25-26 September 1843.

The Colored American. Originally entitled *The Weekly Advocate* and edited by Samuel Cornish, it began publication on 7 January 1837. Volumes 1-3, 1837-1839, can be found in the Moorland Foundation and Library of Congress. They are virtually complete. Scattered issues after that date may be found at Morgan State College, Baltimore, Maryland.

Douglass' Monthly. As much of the *Monthly* that is in existence has been placed on microcards. The Library of Congress has a set. While Frederick Douglass was publishing the *Monthly*, 1859-1861, he also brought out an occasional issue of *Douglass' Paper*. A few issues are located in the Moorland Foundation at Howard. Douglass originally entitled his newspaper *The North Star*, which began publication on 3 December 1847 and lasted into the winter of 1850. From June 1851 until September 1859, it was called *Frederick Douglass' Paper* and was published sporadically.

The Emancipator. This newspaper went through several different titles and

changes in locale and ownership during the period 1840-1850 when it ceased.
The New York *Emancipator* (as distinct from the Boston *Emancipator*)
united with the *Free American* in May 1843 to form *The Emancipator and
Free American*. By 1845, the name and place of publication was again
changed to Boston. From that date until November 1848, it was known as
The Emancipator and Weekly Chronicle and then as *The Emancipator and
Free Soil Press*. In November 1848, the name was again changed to *The
Emancipator & Republican*. As the names imply, it was a chief organ of
political abolition.

Frederick Douglass' Paper. See *Douglass' Monthly*.

Freedman's Torchlight. December 1866. Ephemeral publication of the New York
office of the African Civilization Society. The document is located in the
Murray Collection, Library of Congress, Washington, D.C.

Herald of Freedom. Edited by Joseph H. Kimball and Nathaniel P. Rogers, this
abolitionist newspaper was published in Concord, New Hampshire, and ran
from 7 March 1835 to 1846.

The Illustrated London News Supplement, September 1850.

The Impartial Citizen. 1851-1852. This abolitionist paper was published in
Canada and edited by Samuel Ringgold Ward. Sporadic issues may be found
in the Library of Congress, Newspaper Reading Room, Washington, D.C.

The Liberator. Published in Boston and New York, this abolitionist paper ran
the entire length of time under study. Unfortunately, because of the rivalry
among abolitionists, there are relatively fewer references to Garnet than
expected.

The London Times. 10 November 1851.

The Manchester Guardian. 28 August 1850.

National Anti-Slavery Standard. A Garrisonian paper which contained an occasional reference to Garnet's activities.

The National Era. 17 August 1848.

New York Daily Times. Sporadic references to Garnet after 1858.

The New York Daily Tribune. From 1858 to 1865, Greeley gave some attention
to Garnet in his columns.

New York Herald. 13 April 1860.

The North Star. See *Douglass' Monthly*.

Palladium of Liberty. 27 December 1843, to 27 November 1844. Ephemeral
black abolitionist paper in the Library of Congress, Washington, D.C.

The Pennsylvania Freeman. 17 March 1841.

The Pine & Palm. 2 June 1861. See *The Anglo-African*.

The Republican. 18 September 1845.

Syracuse Daily Standard. 6 October 1864.

Troy Daily Standard. 15 September 1858.

Troy Daily Whig. 16 September 1858.

Voice of the Fugitive. 16 December 1852. Edited by Henry Bibb and published
in Canada; a few issues are in the Rare Book Room, Library of Congress,
Washington, D.C.

The Weekly Anglo-African. See *The Anlgo-African*.

Other Sources

Dyson, Walter. *The First Negro to Speak in Our National Capitol as Reported by Eye-Witnesses*. Washington, D.C.: Moorland Foundation, Howard University.

Letter. Garnet to Rev. T. Ralston Smith. Philadelphia: Presbyterian Church Archives.

Letters. Garnet and others to Gerrit Smith. New Haven: Gerrit Smith Miller Collection, Yale University.

Letters. Garnet to Whipple, Tappan, Joscelyn. New Orleans: Amistad Collection, Dillard University.

Letters. Somerville to Garnet. Edinburgh, Scotland: United Presbyterian Church Archives.

Minutes of the Session of the Shiloh Presbyterian Church. Vol. 2 Philadelphia: Presbyterian Church Archives.

New York State, *Legislative Journal*, 67th Session, 1844.

Recommendations of the Third Presbytery in the Case of Shiloh Church. Philadelphia: Presbyterian Church Archives, 1862.

Record Group #105. Letter. *Garnet Equal Rights League* to General Howard. Washington, D.C.: National Archives.

Record Group #105. Monthly School Reports of the District of Columbia. Washington, D.C.: National Archives.

The Records of the Session and the Church Register of the Fifteenth Street Presbyterian Church, 1841-1868. Vol. 1; Washington, D.C.: Moorland Foundation.

Session Book of the Liberty Street Presbyterian Church. Philadelphia: Presbyterian Church Archives.

Pamphlets and Reports

Address from the Colored Citizens of Norfolk, Virginia, to the People of the United States also an Account of the Agitation Among the Colored People of Virginia for Equal Rights. New Bedford, Mass.: E. Anthony and Sons, 1865.

Catalogue of the Officers and Students of Oneida Institute, 1836. Whitesborough: Oneida Institute Typographical Association, 1836.

Celebration by the Colored People's Educational Monument Association in the Memory of Abraham Lincoln on the Fourth of July, 1865, in the Presidential Grounds. Washington, D.C.: Board of Directors, McGill & Witherow, 1865.

Coates, Benjamin. *Cotton Cultivation in Africa. Suggestions on the Importance of the Cultivation of Cotton in Africa, in Reference to the Abolition of Slavery in the United States, Through the Organization of an African Civilization Society*. Philadelphia: C. Sherman and Son, 1858.

Constitution of the African Civilization Society and etc. New Haven: Thomas J. Stafford, 1861.

Crummell, Alexander. *The Eulogy on Henry Highland Garnet, D. D. Presbyterian Minister. Resident of the United States to the Republic of Liberia, Delivered Under the Auspices of the Union Bethel Literary and Historical Association in the 19th St. Baptist Church, May 4, 1882, by Alexander Crummell.* Washington, D.C.: [n. p.], 1882. It was published in Africa and America. Springfield, Mass.: Wiley & Co., 1891.

Garnet, Henry Highland. *The Past and Present Condition, and the Destiny, of the Colored Race: A Discourse.* Washington, D.C.: Moorland Foundation, 1848. Reprinted by Mnemosyne Publishing Co., Miami, Fla., 1969.

Green, Beriah. *Things for Northern Men to Do: A Discourse.* New York: Published by Request, 1836.

Johnson, J. F. *Proceedings of the General Anti-Slavery Convention, Called by the British and Foreign Anti-Slavery Society.* London: John Snow, 1843.

The Liberty Almanac for 1849. New York: American and Foreign Anti-Slavery Society, 1848.

Minutes of the Fifth Annual Convention of the Colored People of the State of New York, Held in the City of Schenectady. New York: Kneeland & Co., 1844.

Minutes of the National Convention of Colored Citizens: Held at Buffalo, on the 15, 16, 17, 18 and 19th of August, 1843, for the Purpose of Considering Their Moral and Political Condition as American Citizens. New York: Piercy and Reed, 1843.

Minutes of the Second Presbyterian and Congregational Convention, Held in the Central Presbyterian Church, Lombard Street. Philadelphia: [n. p.] October 28, 1858.

Minutes of the State Convention of Colored Citizens. New York: Piercy and Reed, 1840.

Minutes of the Third Presbyterian and Congregational Convention Together with the Organization of the Evangelical Association of Presbyterian and Congregational Clergymen of Color in the United States. Brooklyn: Brockway, Book and Job Printer, 1858.

Proceedings of the National Convention of Colored Men Held in the City of Syracuse, New York, October 4th, 5th, 6th and 7th, 1864. New York: Wesleyan Methodist Church, 1864.

Proceedings of the National Convention of Colored People, and Their Friends, Held in Troy, New York, on 6, 7, 8, and 9 October, 1847. Troy, N.Y.: J. C. Kneeland & Co., 1847.

Proceedings of the National Liberty Convention, Held at Buffalo, New York, June 14th and 15th, 1848; Including the Resolutions and Addresses Adopted by That Body, and Speeches of Beriah Green and Gerrit Smith on That Occasion. Utica: S. W. Green, 1848.

Report. American and Foreign Anti-Slavery Society, 1849-53. New York: American and Foreign Anti-Slavery Society, 1949-1953.

Report of the Committee on Volunteering, Union League Club. New York: Club

House, No. 26, East Seventeenth Street, 1864.

Report of the New York Relief Commission for Colored People. New York: Whitehorne, Steam Printer, 1863.

Sellers, Charles Grier, Jr. *Jacksonian Democracy*. Publication Number 9, prepared by the American Historical Association. Baltimore: Waverly Press, Inc., 1967.

Verhandlungen des britten allegemeinen Friedenscongresses, gehalten in der Paulskirche zu Frankfurt a/M Am 22., 23. und 25. August, 1850. Germany, Frankfurt am Main: F. D. Gauerlander's Berlag, 1851.

Index

Wright, 10; division of at annual meeting (1840), 30-34; Garnet's remarks before, 40-42

American Board of Foreign Missions: denounced as proslavery by Garnet before American audience, 99; denounced before British audiences, 119

American Colonization Society: advocated deporting of newly freed, 11; Garnet becomes a vice-president of in 1881, 14; denounced by Garnet, 101; promoted in New York by Rev. John B. Pinney, 110-111; Rev. Dr. Cox of New York City, an executive of, denounced by Garnet, 119; active in late 1850s, 151; used by black conservatives to discredit the African Civilization Society, 167

American Convention for Promoting Abolition (1828), 7

American Missionary Association, 29-30, 44-45 n. 6, 144, 211

Andrew, John A.: as war governer of Massachusetts, 186; persuades George L. Stearns to head commission on recruitment process, 187

Andrews, Charles C.: teaches Garnet in grammer school, 6; notes limited opportunity for black youths, 7; dismissed, 10

Anglo-African Reading Room, at Shiloh Church, 162-163

Antislavery forces, permanently divided, 3. See also American Anti-Slavery Society

Anti-Slavery Reporter (1861), declares Garnet the first citizen of the "dis-United States," 180

Anti-Slavery Reporter, The (England, 1858): carries Garnet's denunciation of the Fugitive Slave Law, 122

"Appeal to the Independent Democrats," antislavery attack upon the arguments of Stephen A. Douglas, 135

Association for Promoting Colored

Volunteering, led by black New Yorkers and united with Union League Club into Joint Committee on Volunteering, 189

Bailey, Dr. G. Gamelial (abolitionist newspaper editor and author of "The Blind Slave Boy"), 118-119

Baltimore, George (congregant of the Liberty Street Church), 36

Bell, Philip A.: as editor of The Colored American, 20; as editor of The Struggler, 82-83

Beman, Amos G. (black abolitionist at Negro National Convention, Troy, 1847), 81-82

Beman, Nathaniel S. S. (New School Presbyterian minister, Troy, New York), 28, 30

Bibb, Henry (black abolitionist): attends Free Soil Convention (1848), 97; visits Garnet's school in Geneva, N.Y., 102; involved in Garnet-Douglass conflict, 103-104, 106; editor of short-lived tabloid, The Voice of the Fugitive (1850, Canada), 117; prints eulogy of Stella Weims, 129

Bible and Tract Societies, denounced by Garnet as proslavery, 99

Birney, James G.: part of new antislavery group (1840), 3: Liberty Party candidate for president, 44; refrains from inciting slaves to revolt, 56; quoted by Garnet in Philadelphia Address, 99

Black abolitionists: divided in 1840, 4; emergence of new leaders, 4; choose sides after division within American Anti-Slavery Society, 32; struggle over Liberty Party endorsement at National Convention (1843), 50-51; struggle over the acceptance of violence on the part of the slave, 55-57; period of Douglass predominance among (1848-1858), 58;

London (1850), 117; obtains excellent response, 117-118; devotes entire year (1851) to lectures in Scotland, England, and Ireland on Free Produce cause, 118-125; singles out specific persons, such as Rev. Cox of New York City, as proslavery religious leaders, 119; makes greatest impact in Scotland and Wales, 120; speaks before British and Foreign Anti-Slavery Society soiree (1851, London), 120-121; denounces American Colonization Society; 120-121; denounces supporters of Society, 121; denounces the Negro pew, 122; denounces Fugitive Slave Law, 122; addresses annual meeting of British and Foreign Anti-Slavery Society (Exeter Hall), 123-124; delegate to World Peace Congress (1851), 124; has more speaking engagements, 124-125; employed by United Presbyterian Church as missionary in Jamaica, 125; duties at Grange Hill, 125-126; teaches freed Africans, 126; requests black emigrants to Jamaica, 127-128; arrives in United States in midst of leadership crisis among blacks (1856), 138; resumes lectures discussing development in Jamaica, 139; expresses sympathy for radical abolition but gives his endorsement to Republican Party, 140-141, 143; condemns Brooks' attack on Sumner, 141; praised for abolitionist speech in Philadelphia, 141-142; renews suffrage fight, 142-144; called to Shiloh Presbyterian Church in New York City (1856), 144; organizes church meeting to denounce Dred Scott Decision, 145; appeals to Gerrit Smith for financial aid, 145; becomes involved in Egan Brodie case, 145-146; installed by Third Presbytery of New York

(1858), 146; a "New School" Presbyterian, 146; organizes Negro clergymen, 146; promotes youth organization The Young Man's Christian Society (1858), 147; speaks at New York State Suffrage Convention (Troy, 1858), 147; supports Gerrit Smith for governor, 147; conceives of African Civilization Society, 153-156; goals of, 156-157; evokes generally hostile response from blacks, 157-158; tries vainly to persuade Downing, 158; alienates Douglass, 159; delivers eulogy for Rev. Samuel Cornish, 159; counters opponents with a meeting of his own, 160-161; accuses opponents of misrepresentation, 161; presents his expectations of the African Civilization Society, 161-162; participates in annual meeting of Evangelical Association of Colored Ministers (1858), 162; lines up lecturers, including Horace Greely, for his reading room, 162; holds services for John Brown, 164; chairs meeting (Shiloh) to denounce racist remarks of local politician Charles O'Conor, 165; expresses pan-African sentiments in Cooper Institute Address (March 1860), 165-166; critique of program of, 166-167; exposes correspondence scheme to discredit the Society, 167; holds his own meeting, 167-168; continues suffrage fight, 169; holds rally for "Philadelphia Rescuers," 169; promotes African and Haitian emigration (1861), 176; wins Douglass over, 177; Civil War saves Douglass from a complete endorsement of, 177; prepares for second trip to Britain (1861), 178-179; battles with Rev. Gloucester over emigration, 179; states his motto, 179; successfully asserts his right to a passport, 179-180; meets Camp-

About the Author

Joel A. Schor is an historian with the United States Department of Agriculture's Agricultural History Group. Among his other publications are *Blacks in American Agriculture, 1619-1974: An Annotated Bibliography* and *Agriculture in the Black College Land-grant System to 1930.* He has also written articles for *Potomac Review.*

Recent Titles in
CONTRIBUTIONS IN AMERICAN HISTORY

Series Editor: Jon L. Wakelyn

Efficiency and Expansion: Foreign Trade Organization in
the Wilson Administration
Burton I. Kaufman

Space, Time, Freedom: The Quest for Nationality and the
Irrepressible Conflict, 1815-1861
Major L. Wilson

The New Deal in Georgia: An Administrative History
Michael S. Holmes

Conflict on the Northwest Coast: American-Russian
Rivalry in the Pacific Northwest, 1790-1867
Howard I. Kushner

Confederate Women
Bell Irvin Wiley

Battles Lost and Won: Essays from Civil War History
John T. Hubbell, Editor

Beyond the Civil War Synthesis: Political Essays of
the Civil War Era
Robert P. Swierenga, Editor

Roosevelt and Romanism: Catholics and American Diplomacy,
1937-1945
George Q. Flynn

Roots of Tragedy: The United States and the Struggle for
Asia, 1945-1953
Lisle A. Rose

Henry A. Wallace and American Foreign Policy
J. Samuel Walker

Retreat from Reform: The Prohibition Movement in the
United States, 1890-1913
Jack S. Blocker, Jr.

A New Birth of Freedom
Herman Belz

When Farmers Voted Red: The Gospel of Socialism in the
Oklahoma Countryside, 1910-1924
Garin Burbank